The Literacy Club

Effective Instruction and Intervention for **Linguistically Diverse Learners**

Kathryn Henn-Reinke and Xee Yang

CASLON

Philadelphia

To teachers and administrators everywhere who work tirelessly to ensure that their language learners succeed both linguistically and academically—and to my favorite husband, John, always and forever. . . .

KATHY

To educators everywhere who work day and night helping their English learners succeed in the classroom, and to my husband and children who believed in me.

XEE

Caslon, Inc.
825 N. 27th St.
Philadelphia, PA 19130

caslonpublishing.com

9 8 7 6 5 4 3 2 1

Library of Congress Cataloging-in-Publication Data

Names: Henn-Reinke, Kathryn, author. | Yang, Xee, author.
Title: The literacy club : effective instruction and intervention for
    linguistically diverse learners / Kathryn Henn-Reinke and Xee Yang.
Description: Philadelphia, PA : Caslon, Inc., [2017] | Includes
    bibliographical references and index.
Identifiers: LCCN 2016043410 (print) | LCCN 2016054351 (ebook) | ISBN
    9781934000328 (pbk.) | ISBN 9781934000335 (ebook)
Subjects: LCSH: Education, Bilingual. | Language arts (Elementary)
Classification: LCC LC3725 .H46 2017 (print) | LCC LC3725 (ebook) | DDC
    370.117—dc23
LC record available at https://lccn.loc.gov/2016043410

Printed in the United States of America.

Foreword

Our understanding of English and bilingual learners in the United States has evolved significantly as a result of the research of Literacy Squared (Escamilla et al, 2014) and the work that has been done on translanguaging (Garcia, Ibarra Johnson, & Seltzer, 2017), as well as other contributions by researchers and practitioners. Instead of viewing bilinguals as two monolinguals in one, we understand that bilinguals develop language and literacy by using all they know in all their languages, and that when curriculum, instruction, and assessment build on the strengths students have in both languages, students do better in school. This understanding affects how we serve English and bilingual learners in terms of curriculum, instruction, and more. While our thinking about how to meet the needs of language learners through Response to Intervention (RtI) has also evolved, practitioners often feel limited in their choice of materials and the language of intervention. These choices highlight a mismatch between what we know about how bilinguals develop language, literacy, and content and how we support them as they develop these abilities and skills. *The Literacy Club: Effective Instruction and Intervention for Linguistically Diverse Learners* is a breath of fresh air. Using a growth-oriented, multilingual view of English and bilingual learners, Henn-Reinke and Yang propose a research-based, flexible, and practical approach for serving a wide variety of students in different types of language education programs. This book is a tremendous contribution to the fields of literacy, biliteracy, and language development.

Anchored in a student-centered approach for collecting and interpreting data in English (in the English as an additional language strand) and English/Spanish (in the advancing and emerging bilingual strands), the Literacy Club (LC) provides students with small group guidance using optimal instructional strategies that are scaffolded, differentiated, and focused on developing oracy, literacy, and metalanguage. Throughout the book, Henn-Reinke and Yang define and illustrate the difference between scaffolded learning activities (instruction that includes supports for guiding students to greater independence) and differentiated learning activities (changing the material and assessment to meet students' needs) as they take the reader through the four components of the LC (focus book, word work, rereads, and writing). They bring these components to life by describing how they can be adjusted to meet the needs of eight focal students in grades K–5. All the examples illustrate the pedagogical principles of the LC, such as integrating all four language domains (listening, speaking, reading, and writing), the importance of meaningful context for literacy development, building on what students already know and can do linguistically and culturally, and providing intensive instruction in areas identified by formative and summative assessment in either English only or Spanish and English. As we read about how to support students such as Mai, Sergio, and Evelyn Gloria we see how interventions are planned and implemented for various students at different grade levels using standards and appropriate texts. This flexible approach reflects best practices and research in the fields of language development, literacy, and biliteracy. It also embraces professional collaboration and teacher expertise as key tenets in designing appropriate interventions.

One of the important contributions of this book is the assertion that we should develop and use bilingual assessment data (in both Spanish and English) when planning bilingual instruction for students. Chapter 2, Goal-Setting and Progress Monitoring, walks us through the different formative and summative assessments we can collect in Spanish and English to plan small group support focused on language development and literacy. A balanced and bilingual approach to assessment, as illustrated by Juan Carlos and Sergio's samples, establishes a framework for planning instruction and monitoring student growth in a way that is doable, practical, and anchored in the type of instruction necessary for English and bilingual learners. Also, the discussion about language development in addition to literacy development is refreshing and important as teachers continue to teach to all the different standards that abound.

Another important contribution of this book is its focus on developmentally appropriate instruction and how to increase rigor, as articulated through the grades and presented in Chapters 3–6 through student case studies and grade-level clusters. This sociocultural approach allows Henn-Reinke and Yang to present complex content in a readable and enjoyable manner, enabling readers to connect to the material easily. Finally, the tips and structures in Chapter 7 that are recommended for a variety of constituents focus on the logistical and leadership considerations that are important for the LC to be successful.

Henn-Reinke and Yang are to be commended for tackling such a challenging and complex subject in a way that reflects research and best practice through a positive and effective approach that meets the needs of linguistically and culturally diverse students in a variety of contexts. This book is an excellent text to read and use as the field continues to define how to include and address English and bilingual learners in our educational system.

¡Enhorabuena!
Karen Beeman

Preface

This book is for educators, administrators, literacy specialists, parents, and others who work with language learners who are struggling with literacy and are interested in learning more about effective interventions to use with this student population. It is also a useful text in courses for the preparation of in-service and pre-service teachers who plan to work with language learners.

The Literacy Club (LC) has gone through a number of iterations before arriving at its current format, but its purpose—to support language learners in becoming more successful in both literacy and language development—has never wavered. It seems that in every classroom, no matter how effective the instruction, a handful of students always struggles with learning to read and write. The LC finds effective instruction and intervention that supports these students and enables them to make significant growth toward language and content standards.

Beginning with the initial implementation of the LC (then known as *Club de Lectura*; Henn-Reinke, 2004), some key components have been put into place and have remained constant through the various revisions of the LC that have made it more receptive to meeting student needs. There has been a consistent focus on evaluating baseline data and designing instruction to meet each student's needs. Students are organized into small groups of four or fewer and the pacing remains rigorous to guide students as fully and efficiently as possible toward grade-level literacy goals. Strategy development and student self-assessment of progress have been established as ways to develop critical thinking skills and guide students to take greater ownership of their learning. Providing opportunities for students to express understanding, both orally and in writing, is an integral component of the original plan as well.

Changes in the field of education over the last several years have dictated refinements in the LC that heavily influenced its current format. The most encompassing change has come with the Common Core Standards, which have been adopted by many states. The advent of language standards for language learners have helped to both standardize and revolutionize the education of this population by providing guidance in teaching and measuring language skills fully and directly. This emphasis on a developmental approach to language learning has led to providing opportunities for students to explore and analyze vocabulary, language structure, and discourse levels of language use, referred to as metalanguage.

Analysis of changes in population demographics show that more students in bilingual programs enter school already possessing varying levels of language ability in both languages. Therefore, simultaneous literacy models are more common among the various bilingual programs throughout the country and enable students to focus on literacy development in two languages at the same time. Students coming to school with some level of language fluency in both English and Spanish are encouraged to use what they know in each language to support their language development in both languages.

This changing demographic has dovetailed with the growth of dual language programs. Students serve as linguistic role models for their classmates and language learning is accessible for all students. In any program, however, there are some students who need additional support beyond the instruction that they receive in the classroom (Tier 1) to be successful. The LC is designed for this group of students and may focus on either English only or English and Spanish (or other languages), depending on the students' needs. Specific strands may be organized that focus on the needs of advancing bilinguals (students who already have a solid level of oral proficiency in the language of intervention), emerging bilinguals (students who need a strong emphasis on oracy), and English as an additional language (students who speak a language other than English but who are not enrolled in a bilingual program).

The design of the LC is flexible so districts can tailor its use to students' needs, district mandates, types of programs, and so forth. What is non-negotiable is the intensity and the depth of the language and literacy intervention. This rigor is achieved through an intensive and meaningful focus on oracy, literacy, and metacognition (strategy development and metalanguage) goals. The sociocultural foundations of linguistically and culturally responsive pedagogy, student-centered instruction, scaffolding and differentiation, continuous progress monitoring, and collaboration anchor the design, implementation, and refinement of the LC.

The LC may be classified as a mid-level Response to Instruction and Intervention (RtI^2; Gottlieb, 2013). It is designed to complement and augment the work of classroom teachers, which occurs when the LC and classroom teachers work collaboratively to meet the literacy and language needs of LC students. In an optimal situation, teachers who already hold English as a second language (ESL) and/or bilingual teaching licenses are selected to teach in the LC. These teachers are well versed in effective scaffolding and the integration of language and literacy and are, therefore, uniquely qualified to carry out LC instruction.

An intensive and ongoing professional development (PD) plan is a critical element of any successful RtI^2 program for language learners. This volume serves as a valuable resource in the PD process to establish the goals of the LC and the role of the sociocultural foundations in designing, implementing, and refining the LC in a school or district. Once an LC program has been established, additional PD might include an emphasis on continuous monitoring of student progress, the role of oracy and metalanguage, the development of reading and writing strategies, and differentiation and scaffolding of instruction.

OVERVIEW OF THE BOOK

- Chapter 1 provides an overview and rationale for the development of the LC and how it has been structured to effectively meet the needs of language learners in a variety of environments.
- Chapter 2 outlines the well-developed elements and structures of the assessment process, which is a key component of the LC in continuously monitoring student progress.
- Chapters 3–6 focus on specific grade-level examples of the implementation of an LC program. Work samples of students' written and oral participation shared in these

chapters reflect composites of work from actual LC students over the years. Readers are encouraged to read the examples for the target grade levels and note the developmental progression in language and literacy across the grade levels.

- Chapter 7 features guidelines and suggestions for the design and implementation of an LC program in a school or district.

Practitioners, administrators, and parents may wish to determine the needs of students relative to the development of language and literacy in English-medium and/or bilingual programs and set goals for an RtI^2 program of this nature. They are also encouraged to determine ways in which the LC might be adapted to best meet the needs of the particular students they serve.

SPECIAL FEATURES

- In-depth overview of an instruction and intervention program designed specifically for language learners with a focus on "same goals by different pathways"
- A well-developed focus on both literacy and language development
- A strong focus on the integration of metacognition in all LC sessions, specifically in terms of metalanguage and strategy development
- A flexible instruction and intervention plan that enables schools/districts to adapt the format to meet their students' needs
- A collaboration plan between LC and classroom teachers to ensure that the same standards, strategies, genres, and themes are addressed in both settings
- A well-developed assessment plan to provide ongoing progress monitoring, including a strong emphasis on student self-assessment and goal setting
- A rigorous instruction and intervention design that enables language learners to move along as fully and quickly as possible toward grade level language and content standards

ACKNOWLEDGEMENTS

Rebecca Field of Caslon Publishing was relentless in insisting that we rewrite, clarify, and rewrite yet again to make the LC come alive. The suggestions made us feel faint; the results made us feel proud. Charles Field made the initial publishing process manageable and led us to believe in the possibility of this book. His final reviews helped us bring the manuscript to a meaningful conclusion. Jennifer Murtoff offered insight and concise feedback and suggestions for improvement and production editor Nancy Lombardi was amazing.

An instruction and intervention plan will only be as successful as the knowledge and dedication of the people charged with developing and implementing that plan. Andrew Patterson had enough faith in the potential of the initial intervention plan to provide the support that many language learners needed. Allowing me to implement the *Club de Lectura* at two different schools that he administered set this process in motion. Providing PD opportunities, staff, and materials made the implementation a success. Gina Cornu Zacharias was the driving administrative force in another district that enabled the Reading Club (later renamed the Literacy Club) to be as well developed and expansive as it became. Arranging for the Reading Club to be implemented in several schools in the district and arranging for school year and summer sessions to continually refine the club happened under her leadership.

Hajira Buser, Colleen Post, and Teresa Tenorio all contributed a great deal to the first draft of the manuscript. Teresa Tenorio was an avid editor of the English and Spanish of the final version. Several other educators worked with students in the Reading Club and contributed to the growth of this project. Gretchen Lettau and Elizabeth LaNou facilitated access to district materials and documents in the writing of the manuscript and their assistance is acknowledged here.

Judy Hartl and Gina Cornu Zacharias conducted an informal study of the Reading Club, sponsored by the WSRA (Wisconsin State Association of Reading, 2011) that documented student progress and highlighted the role of oracy in the Reading Club sessions.

Special thanks to Claudia Orr and Karen Beeman for early feedback on the manuscript and later reviews from Karen Beeman, Mariana Castro, and Olivia Ruiz-Figueroa, which helped sharpen the focus of the work.

Contents

3 Literacy Club with Language Learners in Kindergarten

4 Literacy Club with Language Learners in Grades 1–2

5 Literacy Club with Language Learners in Grade 3

6 Content-Based Literacy Club in Grades 4–5

7   Creating a Literacy Club

1

Literacy Club Framework

KEY CONCEPTS

- The creation of a flexible literacy instruction and intervention plan is essential for meeting a wide range of language learners' needs.
- An effective Literacy Club model for language learners includes an instruction and intervention plan with learning opportunities that strengthen and integrate literacy, oracy, and metacognition.
- Content standards, language standards, and a rigorous assessment process guide student learning in the Literacy Club.
- Sociocultural foundations are the basis for the work of the Literacy Club.

Nearly every teacher or administrator in a preK–12 school district is challenged by how best to serve students who speak languages other than English at home, are learning a new language and culture at school, and struggle with developing language and literacy skills in one or both languages. This large and diverse category of language learners includes students who are officially designated as **English learners (ELs)**, students who are English speakers but speak languages other than English at home, and students from English-speaking homes who are learning an additional language (e.g., Spanish) at school. We find these students in general education, transitional bilingual education, dual language, world language, and English for speakers of other languages (ESOL) instructional settings. This book is for general and bilingual education classroom teachers; English as a second language (ESL), literacy, and world language specialists; and general education, bilingual, and ESL administrators who are responsible for ensuring that these students meet grade-level expectations in literacy and achieve at school.

We developed the **Literacy Club (LC)**, a field-tested, research-based approach to address the literacy and learning needs of diverse language learners in K–5 settings, in Wisconsin. Hartl, a reading specialist, and Grogan, an ESL/bilingual coordinator from a midwest district that implemented the LC, conducted a mini-study (Hartl & Grogan, 2011) supported by the Wisconsin State Reading Association. Its purpose was to investigate the impact of the LC on grades 1–3 ELs at the beginning levels of English language development (ELD), that is, Level 1 or 2 in speaking and listening. The study included 25 students from five schools within the district who had completed one year of **intervention** in the LC. The results, based on measures of ELD, district reading and writing assessments, and informal reading and writing assessments used in the LC, demonstrated that the students grew in all literacy domains, especially in the area of speaking. A focus on the development of critical thinking through discussion of concepts and vocabulary (oracy) was seen as a catalyst for progress in reading, where students averaged 1.0–2.6 levels of growth on measures of ELD, and 1.0–1.5 levels on measures of writing.

We have worked with many different types of students in the LC. Some of them have strong oracy (listening and speaking) in two languages but struggle with literacy (reading and writing) in one or both languages. Some students struggle to comprehend narrative or informational text or are challenged to use **language for academic purposes** in a variety of settings in one or both languages. Other students have some skills in one language and different skills in another language but have been unable to consolidate their learning across languages. Still others have been enrolled in schools for several years without making significant academic or linguistic progress. We include examples of these various students throughout this book, along with plans tailored to meet their specific needs.

WHAT IS THE LITERACY CLUB?

The LC can be understood in relation to the **Response to Intervention (RtI)** model (Response to Intervention Action Network), which refers to the general classroom as the Tier 1 level of instruction. Within the classroom, teachers use assessment data to determine and monitor the needs of each student. They differentiate instruction to meet the needs of all students and arrange a variety of supports, such as flexible grouping, partner work, use of word banks, and audio recordings of text, to reinforce their students' learning. Some students need additional supports beyond those offered in the general classroom and intensive, small instructional groups are often formed to supplement and complement the classroom work. This level of intervention is referred to as Tier 2 or intermediate intervention.

The LC is an intermediate intervention designed specifically for language learners who need additional support in literacy and **language development** but who are not formally identified as having special educational needs. The model draws on elements from the Reading Recovery (Clay, 1985, 2000, 2005, 2013), Guided Reading (Fountas & Pinnell, 2008, 2010), Literacy Squared (Escamilla et al, 2014), and SIOP (Sheltered Instruction Observation Protocol; Echevarria, Vogt, & Short, 2012) models. The LC also addresses state-mandated English language arts (e.g., Common Core) and ELD (e.g., WIDA) standards, and is informed by a sociocultural orientation that sees languages other than English as resources to be developed, not as deficits to overcome. Students' home languages are understood to be integral parts of their bilingual repertoires that teachers can draw on strategically to accelerate students' literacy development (Escamilla et al, 2014; García & Li Wei, 2014).

The purpose of the LC is to support struggling language learners as they progress toward grade-level content, literacy, and language expectations. Students' needs are carefully analyzed and appropriate instruction is implemented to meet these needs and move students as quickly and fully as possible toward grade-level expectations. To meet the challenge of providing effective instructional programs for language learners, it is necessary to provide a solid foundation in language/oracy and literacy in the early grades. Therefore, the LC begins as early as kindergarten and admits students through grade 5. The LC facilitates growth for language learners who would benefit from additional support in both language and literacy development.

At its heart, the LC is a Tier 2 intervention of a **Response to Instruction and Intervention (RtI²)** plan in that teachers determine the needs of individual students, target instruction to meet those needs, and continually monitor student progress.

Tier 2 of a Response to Instruction and Intervention (RtI²) model is referred to as a targeted or supplemental intervention. It consists of small groups of students (usually 3–5) who do not respond sufficiently to the most effective Tier 1 instruction and criteria. (Gottlieb, 2013, p. 6)

Gottlieb (2013, p. 7) highlights four key features of this intermediate intervention:

1. Supplemental resources to implement high-quality instructional strategies
2. Targeted intervention at high levels of intensity
3. Ongoing formative/classroom assessment to monitor students' response to intervention (often referred to as progress monitoring)
4. Team decision making and collaboration.

All of these features are firmly embedded in the LC design.

RtI² enables educators to place specific focus on the academic and linguistic needs, as well as the social and cultural backgrounds, of language learners in both general education and bilingual instructional settings. Student needs are analyzed, followed by the creation of academically, culturally, and linguistically appropriate instruction and intervention. Instruction is based on grade-level standards and does not focus on developing skills in isolation. Materials are selected that not only target content and language standards, but also build on students' backgrounds and foster positive attitudes and confidence toward learning.

An important theme of the LC is "same goals/different pathways." Students work with grade-level standards, but the learning they experience in the LC may be quite different from what they encounter in the general classroom. Because all of the students are language learners, it makes perfect sense to guide them in developing and practicing the language needed for literacy and content-area development in every lesson. As language learners they can draw on what they know in one language to support growth in the other. Many of the students also need support in areas of literacy so that they can progress fully toward the grade-level standards. The LC is an ideal setting in which to determine individual needs and address them in sessions, no matter how basic they are. Furthermore, a focus on metalanguage and strategy development enhances both the use of **critical thinking skills** and **metacognitive understanding**. The LC strives to strengthen student background knowledge, skills, and strategies; value language and culture as resources; and guide metacognitive thinking as pathways for students to become ever more successful in both language and literacy development.

In addition to employing a collaborative approach to teaching, the LC and classroom teachers have flexibility in making decisions based on their shared students' needs. Classroom teachers collaborate with LC teachers on language and learning goals and objectives across the two settings. ESL teachers and literacy specialists also collaborate with LC teachers and classroom teachers to ensure that learning experiences are aligned to promote student success. This flexibility is a major strength of the LC model. In many conventional intervention programs, for example, instructors are often limited by the dictates of a commercial program that may or may not address the academic needs of language learners, or that focuses exclusively on skills in isolation and provides little support for the development of critical thinking. Because the LC focuses on language and literacy development, the LC teacher can structure learning experiences that expand the vocabulary, language structure, and discourse levels of language learning in ongoing ways that generally are not provided in other intervention programs.

Teachers in bilingual and English-medium settings can use **translanguaging** strategies to purposefully leverage students' bilingualism to (1) strategically engage students with complex content and texts, (2) promote the use of oral and written language for academic purposes, (3) strengthen students' bilingualism and ways of knowing, and (4) support students' socioemotional well-being at school (García, Ibarra Johnson, & Seltzer, 2017). As we will see, students in the bilingual strands participate in **comparative analyses** of the structure and use of both languages (Beeman & Urow, 2013) as they develop biliteracy

[handwritten margin note: Restorative]

[handwritten margin note: Could SE teachers use LC?]

(Escamilla et al, 2014). Teachers in the English as an additional language (EAL) setting who speak one or more of their students' home languages use these languages as resources to clarify and support learning wherever possible. Students who speak the same home language and are entering-level learners of English might be encouraged, for example, to share with one another ideas for writing in their home language before writing in English.

In sum, the LC forms a sort of oasis for students who have not fully mastered skills and strategies that are essential for full classroom participation, giving them a secure learning venue to take risks in learning and practicing in these areas. After students gain understanding and confidence with these basic skills and strategies, which are grounded in authentic and meaningful learning experiences, their progress is often accelerated.

PARTICIPATING STUDENTS

Students and teachers are central to the LC. LC teachers begin their work by learning about their students' linguistic, cultural, and experiential backgrounds so that they can identify what students know and can do in each of their languages. Teachers then use these abilities to strengthen literacy development in English and Spanish (or other languages) as appropriate. The flexibility of the LC structure can accommodate all language learners along the language continuum, from **simultaneous bilinguals**, who have learned two or more languages from birth and have some degree of proficiency in both languages of instruction, to **sequential bilinguals**, who learned one language at birth and are adding another language (e.g., English) at a later point in time, often at the beginning of formal education. In general, simultaneous bilinguals have developed oracy in both languages and are adding literacy in one or both languages, while sequential bilinguals generally develop both oracy and literacy at the same time in the target language; they may or may not have developed literacy in their home language.

LC teachers begin with a clear understanding of what their students can do with the languages in their repertoires. Students who are officially designated as ELs are assessed annually to determine their English language proficiency (ELP) levels in listening, speaking, reading, and writing using state-mandated tests. In Wisconsin, where the LC originated, ELs are assessed using the **Assessing Comprehension and Communication in English State-to-State (ACCESS) for ELLs test** that is administered by the WIDA consortium. The participating students in this book all took the ACCESS for ELLs. To understand what students can be expected to do with listening, speaking, reading, and writing at different ELD levels, teachers can turn to the WIDA can-do descriptors. Teachers working in **bilingual programs** can use WIDA's definitions of Spanish language development (SLD) in the domains of listening, speaking, reading, and writing, and they can draw on *Los descriptores podemos* to understand what students at different SLD levels can do with language in each domain. Teachers working in states (e.g., NY, CA, TX) that use other ELP systems (e.g., ELPA21) can draw on their state-mandated ELD standards frameworks to understand the levels and student performance indicators used in their contexts.

Here we introduce eight participating students who represent composites of students we have worked with across grade levels and strands. We use these focal students to bring the LC to life throughout this book as we share instructional plans designed to meet their language and literacy needs. We also share examples of our work with other students in the different grade levels and strands so teachers might conceptualize how the flexible LC framework can be adapted to meet the needs of language learners at any grade level in any sociolinguistic context. As you read, we encourage you to think about the language learners in your classes who are struggling to meet grade-level literacy demands.

Kindergarten

Some kindergarten language learners may not be developmentally or emotionally ready to fully grasp emergent literacy expectations without additional support. At this level students are not far behind in literacy development, and early intervention in the bilingual or EAL strands of the LC may allow them to move quickly and relatively easily toward grade-level expectations. All of the students described in the following EAL strand began in the LC at Level 1 or 2 (Fountas & Pinnell, 2010) at the beginning of the second semester. In other words, they were able to apply basic elements of emergent literacy strategies (use of picture cues, context clues, and beginning word analysis skills), and knew some letters and sounds in English, but had little comprehension of text and wrote minimally.

- *Mai* speaks and understands both Hmong and English, although she speaks mostly English. She attends a 20-minute Hmong heritage class five times a week and is always excited about attending the class. She can answer in Hmong if she is given language cues that support her formulation of a response. In this class, she relies heavily on sentence frames and sentence starters to communicate in Hmong.

  Mai takes her schoolwork seriously. She is a quiet and well-behaved student who participates well in class. She enjoys reading and writing and always does her best. Mai draws on her stronger oral language in English to support her reading and writing development. According to the ACCESS for ELLs test, Mai has reached ELD Level 4 in speaking and listening and Level 2 in reading and writing.

- *Mario* speaks and understands both English and Spanish. He lives with his mom and dad and another sibling. He speaks both English and Spanish at home, but relies more heavily on Spanish. He likes to read and write and enjoys reading independently. He has a rich cultural background and is very proud of his heritage.

  Mario is growing in his listening, speaking, reading, and writing skills in English. He would benefit from more practice in speaking to enrich his productive language use in writing and to expand his receptive language skills in reading and listening. He is monitoring most of his reading; however, at times he needs to be reminded to stay on task. Mario has reached ELD Level 3 in speaking and listening, Level 1 in reading, and Level 2 in writing.

- *Pedro* speaks and understands both English and Spanish and often uses both languages fluidly in conversation. He enjoys interacting with friends and is very active. Many times, however, his behavior gets in the way of his learning. He can act out and might say inappropriate things that do not pertain to the learning environment. He receives special education services for behavior concerns. With respect to ELD, Pedro scores at Level 3 in speaking and listening and Level 1 in reading and writing.

- *Nhia* speaks and understands both Hmong and English. He has social language skills in both languages and responds orally in both languages. He is in a 20-minute Hmong heritage language class that meets five times a week. He enjoys learning academic language in Hmong. He does well in reading, writing, and math in English. In English, Nhia has reached ELD Level 4 in speaking and listening, Level 2 in reading, and Level 1 in writing.

A focus on daily oral discussions before and after reading and as oral rehearsal for writing will enhance both comprehension and oracy with this group of students. A major focus on emergent strategy development and application will be important for these students, as will an emphasis on word work. Because all of these students are adding English to their linguistic repertoires, the teacher will also draw on an understanding of what students can do with language in listening, speaking, reading, and writing in English and in their home languages to inform decisions about necessary scaffolding and differentiating.

The LC teacher is Hmong and uses that language regularly with the two Hmong-speaking students to clarify and extend learning. Students are free to use Hmong as needed to express ideas and respond to prompts, but are encouraged to use as much English as possible. The LC teacher also teaches in an after-school Hmong literacy program that several of her students participate in, which gives her opportunities to help them analyze how one language strengthens the other.

Grades 1 and 2

Grades 1 and 2 LC students have had 1–2 years of literacy instruction. They have learned many basic concepts about reading and writing, but their learning has been inconsistent overall and they have been unable to keep pace with grade-level expectations. Often at this level, the LC can guide students to consolidate and expand what they know and are able to do in terms of language and literacy development, which begins to accelerate their learning. *Juan Carlos*, the student introduced next, participates in the **advancing bilingual strand**.

Juan Carlos is a 7-year-old second grader who has lived in the United States since his parents emigrated from Mexico when he was 3 years old. He has very strong social language skills in English and Spanish. His parents speak mostly Spanish at home but Juan Carlos and his two younger brothers move easily between English and Spanish, depending on the language environment. Since kindergarten, Juan Carlos has been in a one-way bilingual program that promotes simultaneous development of literacy in two languages. In this bilingual program, the students have English literacy in the morning and Spanish literacy in the afternoon. Although he enjoys school, Juan Carlos has struggled a great deal with learning to read and write in both languages. Furthermore, acquiring and using language for academic purposes in content-area classes seems particularly challenging for him.

Juan Carlos' ELD and SLD levels are very similar. In English, he has reached Level 4 in listening and speaking, and Level 2 in reading and writing. In Spanish, he has reached Level 5 in listening and speaking and Level 2 in reading and writing. Juan Carlos is a full grade level below expectations for literacy in both languages, but he has a positive attitude toward school and is anxious to participate in the LC. A focus on comprehension and use of reading and writing strategies will be a major part of the plan for Juan Carlos. Development of academic language and critical thinking skills will also be highlighted.

Grade 3

The grade 3 LC examples reflect the broad range of students who might be included in the LC at this level. Some have been in U.S. schools for several years but have been unable to keep pace with literacy instruction in one or both languages. They may also have a wide variety of skills in each language. Others, like *Evelyn Gloria* who we introduce here, have relatively strong literacy skills in one or both languages but need support with oracy development in one of the languages. LC teachers take advantage of the literacy and language skills each child brings to support the growth of all students, which is an example of the LC process of working toward the same goals using different pathways.

Evelyn Gloria's parents placed her in a dual language program in 4-year-old kindergarten because they recognized the value of being bilingual, even though they speak only English at home. She is now in grade 3 and enjoys her friends and teachers at school. Evelyn Gloria has reached SLD Level 5 in listening, Level 4 in reading, Level 2 in speaking, and Level 3 in writing. Her reading and writing skills in both English and Spanish are strong. She is quite shy and has been especially reticent to speak during Spanish instructional time, though evidence shows that her listening skills are relatively strong in Spanish. Evelyn Gloria would benefit from extensive support in developing oracy in Spanish.

Although her writing skills are quite good in both languages, there are some areas that she will focus on to further strengthen her writing.

Equipped with a preliminary understanding of what language learners like Juan Carlos and Evelyn Gloria can do with listening, speaking, reading, and writing in Spanish, teachers are prepared to scaffold and differentiate instruction and assessment during LC sessions and monitor students' progress in the advancing and emerging bilingual strands.

Grades 4 and 5

At grades 4 and 5, students may have experienced several years of academic and linguistic frustration from being unable to achieve grade-level expectations. In addition, the grade-level content has become increasingly complex, making the burden even heavier for these students. With careful planning, instruction, and progress monitoring in the LC, students like Ai and Sergio can also reach their literacy and language goals.

- *Ai* is a shy fourth grader who is participating in the EAL strand. She was born in a refugee camp in Thailand, after her family fled Laos many years ago. When the camp closed, Ai moved with her family to the United States. She was about 6 years old at the time, though her exact birthdate is not known. Ai's family moved to a large supportive Hmong community, and she entered grade 1 speaking only Hmong. She has participated in English-medium instructional programs since that time, but has not demonstrated the type of progress of which she seems capable. Ai has relatively strong listening skills in English; however, she is reticent to speak it. Measures of literacy indicate that she is well below grade level in reading and writing in English, but she has a strong work ethic and strives to complete all of her assignments as best she can. Enrollment in the LC is designed to help her strengthen her skills in oracy, literacy, and metacognition. She will receive support in learning/using academic language and writing for a variety of purposes. Special attention will be given to helping Ai develop skill and confidence in expressing her understanding in English. According to the ACCESS for ELLs test, Ai has reached ELD Level 4 in listening and Level 2 in speaking, reading, and writing. Ai will need considerable support for her reading, writing, and speaking development in English.
- *Sergio* is a member of a large family that emigrated from Guatemala when he was 7 years old. He entered U.S. schools in grade 2 and is now in grade 6. His family moved several times during that period of time, and Sergio has struggled to adjust to a new school with each move. He is currently attending a progressive dual language program in the midwest and is enrolled in the advancing bilingual strand of the LC as an effective intervention to meet his needs. Although Sergio's home language is Spanish, he continues to fall behind his classmates in literacy development in Spanish. This may be the result of family moves, which have caused Sergio's schooling to be interrupted on several occasions.

  Sergio's parents now feel confident that they have found a good place for their family to remain for a long time, which would help Sergio in developing a solid academic base. In Spanish, Sergio has reached SLD Level 6 in listening and speaking, Level 3 in reading, and Level 2 in writing. In English, Sergio has reached ELD Level 3 in listening and speaking and Level 2 in reading and writing. Sergio needs extensive literacy support in both languages. It will be important for him to develop reading and writing strategies and recognize that they can be applied to both languages. Learning opportunities that compare and contrast languages will help him analyze how his two languages work together.

These eight students represent a cross section of students who have benefitted from the LC. Their wide range of language and literacy backgrounds highlights the challenge of the LC to differentiate instruction to meet language learners' individual needs.

LITERACY CLUB FRAMEWORK

The LC can be adapted and customized to meet the needs of language learners in any context. Five sociocultural foundations characterize the LC:

1. Linguistically and culturally responsive pedagogy
2. Student-centered instruction
3. Scaffolded and differentiated learning activities
4. Collaboration among the classroom and LC teachers
5. Continuous progress monitoring

The goals (oracy, literacy, metacognition) and the session components (focus book, word work, rereads, writing) are always the same. However, administrators and teachers working at the local level can develop strands that are appropriate for the school and community context. These strands can be understood as different pathways. We feature three strands in this book: advancing bilingual, emerging bilingual, and EAL. The LC framework is represented in Figure 1.1. The remainder of the chapter describes the parts of this framework, with attention to how they work together in practice.

Goals and Assessments

There are three goals for students participating in the LC—oracy, literacy, and metacognition. These goals are aligned with the goals of Literacy Squared (Escamilla et al, 2014), which include oracy, literacy, and metalanguage. In the LC, however, the goal of **metalanguage** is part of the larger metacognition goal, which includes strategy development in addition to metalanguage. The methods for achieving these goals are adapted to meet the needs of a wide range of language learners. The three goals are inextricably interwoven in the LC sessions, but are described separately to provide an overview of how each is conceptualized. Students enrolled in the EAL strand work toward these goals in English,

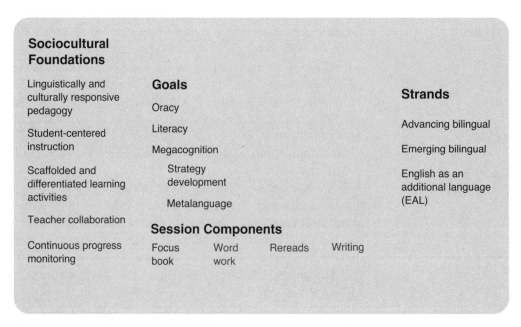

Figure 1.1 Literacy Club framework. Five sociocultural foundations characterize the LC: (1) linguistically and culturally responsive pedagogy, (2) student-centered instruction, (3) scaffolded and differentiated learning activities, (4) collaboration among the classroom and LC teachers, and (5) continuous progress monitoring. The goals (oracy, literacy, metacognition) and the session components (focus book, word work, rereads, writing) are always the same. However, administrators and teachers working at the local level can develop strands that are appropriate for the school and community context.

whereas the advancing and emerging bilingual strands develop each of these goals through a paired literacy approach, in which the instruction and assessment across the two languages are aligned to ensure that students expand their bilingual abilities while becoming biliterate.

An LC assessment plan would then, of course, need to measure students' progress toward each of these goals. This plan is touched on briefly here and expanded in Chapter 2.

Oracy

Oracy refers to language skills and structures that enable a person to understand and express him- or herself through speech (e.g., grammar, vocabulary, language structure, fluency of expression). LC sessions address specific language objectives, and progress toward these objectives is assessed through **formative assessment** measures that include anecdotal records, speech samples, and student self-assessments. Students orally rehearse what they will write about and share completed writing pieces (Echevarria, Vogt, & Short, 2012; Himmele & Himmele, 2009; Krashen, 2004). The small group format gives LC students ample opportunity to practice and receive regular feedback on their developing oracy.

Development of academic language is an important component of oracy. The development of language for the academic purposes generally associated with classroom learning experiences involves complex linguistic processes and requires extensive practice. For example, in Chapter 5 the grade 3 advancing bilingual strand is studying how animals work together to survive. The students must develop the vocabulary, sentence structure, and discourse practices necessary to orally state whether or not they agree with the notion that geese work together to survive, and then provide evidence for how they work together. Generally, students need 5 to 10 years (Thomas & Collier, 2009, 2012), depending on the type of educational program they are enrolled in, to reach grade-level expectations in their second or additional language, and development of language for academic purposes is an important element of growth toward this parity.

The strong emphasis on the development of receptive and expressive language distinguishes the work of the LC from other reading intervention models. In the LC students improve their oracy skills through multiple opportunities to use language for a variety of purposes. They share their opinions, make connections to what they have read, determine the personal or social relevance of the texts to their own lives, and listen to what others have to say. Furthermore, LC sessions encourage oral language development in both languages in the bilingual strands during discussions of readings, oral rehearsal for writing, and content-area foci.

In the example involving the study of how animals work together to survive, the students bring all their language resources to bear in determining how to state the main ideas of the Spanish text in English. This leads to discussions of irregular plurals (geese) and differences in the way ideas are stated in Spanish and English (*Cuándo el clima se pone más frío*/When the weather gets colder).

Literacy

Literacy is the ability to read and write, and includes a focus on how language works and how students use language to make meaning for themselves (Harste, 2003). State content standards (e.g., Common Core) in English language arts directly address literacy, and students explore a broad range of narrative and expository text to gain a sense of literacy for social and academic purposes. Care is taken to select texts that represent the culture and experiences of the students, as well as some that represent new cultures and experiences, to continually expand their understanding of perspective and inquiry.

Learning experiences focus on activities that guide students to read and write thoughtfully. The student-centered nature of instruction enables LC teachers to use scaffolding and differentiation to build grade-level reading and writing skills and strategies that students have not yet developed or have not developed fully. Running records, student work samples, student self-assessments, and anecdotal records are formative measures that LC teachers use to measure student progress toward goals and objectives in literacy. Quarterly LC assessments of reading and writing provide more formal summative measures of progress.

Metacognition

Metacognition is the awareness and understanding of one's own learning process. In the LC, metacognition encompasses both metalanguage and strategy development. The LC not only focuses on improving the listening, speaking, reading, and writing abilities of language learners but also provides them with tools to think about language and how they use it. To meet this third goal of metacognition, or metacognitive awareness, the LC employs two main methods: strategy development and metalanguage.

Strategy Development. Students develop and apply learning strategies and critical thinking skills (August & Shanahan, 2006; Beeman & Urow, 2013; Escamilla et al, 2014; Freeman & Freeman, 2008, 2011) throughout the LC experience. They learn, practice, and self-assess their use of reading and writing strategies, beginning at the earliest levels and proceeding through grade 5. Academic language involved with use of informational texts is addressed at all levels and progresses developmentally across the grades. Students are provided with a great deal of practice in these areas while acquiring reading and writing strategies.

As part of this development, students analyze how using a particular **strategy** enhances their learning. This metacognitive awareness of progress provides students with skills to take greater control of their own learning and to set realistic goals for growth. Teachers guide students in self-assessment of their skills and use of reading and writing strategies and regularly provide them with constructive feedback focused on both language and content goals.

Metalanguage. The structure and use of language, or "metalanguage" as referred to by Escamilla et al (2014), is the second metacognitive process that is reinforced by the LC. In every session, students explore how they use language at the vocabulary, structure, and discourse levels. Students in bilingual strands learn to apply background knowledge, new concepts, and skills across languages.

Development of metacognitive awareness in literacy and language learning provides opportunities for students to gain understanding of their own learning process. This base will enhance student learning across the curriculum, and as students experience greater success in their use of literacy and language, it affects more than their academic growth. Students generally begin to demonstrate a more positive attitude toward their work at school. This influences confidence in their ability to be successful, which in turn encourages them to participate more fully and confidently in both the LC sessions and the general classroom.

In the bilingual strands of the LC, students develop their metalinguistic skills in utilizing the knowledge base shared across their languages. Bridging, the point in a unit of study in which students are guided in transferring what they have learned from one language to the other (Beeman & Urow, 2013), is the vehicle through which students engage in comparative language analysis. Concepts from the language of study to the target language, for example, a unit of study that began in Spanish would bridge to English, are extended to provide more in-depth understanding of both language and content. This type of paired literacy learning (Escamilla et al, 2014) provides students with the tools to recognize what they know and can do in each language and how these skills and strategies are shared or distinct across their languages.

Strands

The LC is divided into three linguistic strands: advancing bilingual (Spanish/English sessions), emerging bilingual (Spanish/English sessions), and EAL (English-medium instruction). The LC may be used in conjunction with any type of instructional program, including these:

- **One-way bilingual programs:** Most students speak a language other than English and receive instruction in both languages with goals of bilingualism, biliteracy, and academic achievement in two languages.
- **Two-way bilingual/dual language programs:** About 50% of students speak English and 50% speak the target language; all receive instruction in both languages, again, with the goals of bilingualism, biliteracy, and academic achievement in two languages.
- **Transitional bilingual programs:** Students receive initial instruction in their home language while they are learning English, with English eventually becoming the exclusive language of instruction. The goals of these programs are ELD and academic achievement in English.
- **EAL programs:** Students in these programs may speak a variety of languages and receive additional instruction in English to support classroom instruction, with the goal of developing their academic and linguistic skills in English.

Schools and districts are encouraged to adapt these strands to meet the needs of their particular students. Each strand integrates oracy, literacy, and metacognition, but the use of languages for instructional purposes varies according to the instructional program.

Advancing Bilingual

The *advancing bilingual strand* targets students who have well-developed oracy in Spanish but struggle with literacy development. These students may or may not have well-developed English oracy and literacy. They do, however, need extensive support in the expansion of their language and literacy for academic purposes in Spanish. The goal for students in this strand is to develop oracy, literacy, and metacognition skills in both English and Spanish. This format could easily be adapted to focus primarily on English language and literacy development with bridging to Spanish.

Instruction begins in Spanish each week with intensive listening, speaking, reading, writing and language study. Reading and writing strategy development and student self-assessment are integral components of these Spanish literacy-based sessions. At the end of the week, students explore related concepts in English, as they use metalanguage skills in bridging activities, including comparative analyses of language structure and vocabulary between Spanish and English, along with exploration and extension of concepts in English. This design enables students to take advantage of language and literacy skills they may already have in place in both languages, and develops them further. Juan Carlos and Sergio participated in the grade 2 and grade 5 advancing Spanish bilingual strands, respectively.

Emerging Bilingual

The **emerging bilingual strand** is composed of students in bilingual programs who generally struggle with literacy development and are at beginning levels of oracy in Spanish. This strand provides opportunities for greater expansion of vocabulary, language structure, and discourse in Spanish while strengthening literacy. Some of the students in these sessions come from English-speaking homes and may not have access to Spanish outside of the classroom. Others have a range of exposure to Spanish outside of school but have greater facility with English. Like the advancing bilingual strand, the goal of this strand is to develop oracy, literacy, and metacognition through two languages. The English literacy of students in this strand ranges from entering to commanding, although most students are stronger in English than in Spanish. As we shall see, Evelyn Gloria thrived in the grade 3 emerging bilingual group.

Instruction begins in Spanish each week with oral activities designed to develop vocabulary and understanding of text. Students reread on some days and retell text to a partner on others to provide additional opportunities for oral practice. The provision of sentence frames and vocabulary prompts to guide retelling proves useful for students who need the additional support.

More opportunities for collaborative student work in listening, speaking, reading, and writing are included in the design of this strand, such as the **language experience approach**, where students and teachers participate in a shared writing activity based on a common experience. Writing is scaffolded through use of shared writing, oral rehearsal, use of sentence frames, and vocabulary supports before students write independently. Similar to the advancing bilingual strand, the week concludes with exploration of related English concepts through bridging activities that focus on rich and strategic comparative analysis of content, vocabulary, and language structures from Spanish to English, as well as writing in English to broaden the range of language practices for academic learning. This component allow students in the group to further refine literacy skills in their stronger language—English. This strand also could be adapted to place the primary emphasis on English language and literacy development with bridging to Spanish.

English as an Additional Language

The *EAL strand* is designed for ELs who are enrolled in English-medium instruction and have little, if any, classroom support in their home languages. They may also be enrolled in ESL or ESOL programs, but care should be taken to integrate the student into the experiences of the classroom as much as possible and ensure that the goals and learning experiences across all venues are aligned. In our experience, students frequently participated in the LC in lieu of ESL classes.

Instruction in the EAL strand is conducted primarily in English and groups may be composed of students from a variety of language backgrounds, depending on the linguistic diversity of the school. Students will have a range of skills in each of their languages and the LC sessions will focus on building on the language skills they already possess to enhance their English. Many of the students served in this group were born in the United States, and are in the process of developing literacy and oracy in English.

Though instruction in these sessions is conducted primarily in English, LC teachers who speak the same language as the students are encouraged to provide home language support where possible to clarify vocabulary or explain concepts they know the students will more readily grasp in their home language. This is especially helpful for groups of students who speak languages such as Arabic or Guarani, for example, but have no other access to home language instruction. The development of oracy is an integral part of these sessions, with attention to building background understanding and metacognitive awareness. Intensive reading, writing, and word work/language study further enhance student literacy development and use of language for academic purposes in this strand. The four kindergarten students (Mai, Mario, Pedro, and Nhia) and Ai all participated in EAL groups. We see examples of **continuous progress monitoring** of the four kindergarten students in the EAL strand and of Ai in the grade 4 EAL strand later in the book.

Flexibility

At the kindergarten level, students generally begin the program in semester two and the advancing/emerging bilingual strands are collapsed into a single strand because of the emergent level of literacy skills. In grades 1–3, the emerging and advancing strands operate as separate groups to more fully meet the linguistic and literacy needs of individual groups of students; the EAL sessions continue primarily in English. In grades 4–5, the emerging/advancing bilingual strands may be collapsed into a single strand once again, as it is likely that students who entered a bilingual program in the early grades with emergent literacy in one of the languages have by now acquired more advanced language skills and will be able to participate more fully in the learning experiences in both languages. Table 1.1 provides an overview of the strand configurations.

Students who participate in the bilingual strands of the LC may reflect the entire linguistic continuum in both Spanish and English oracy and literacy. For example, teachers may find students who are at early stages of development in both languages or progressing in one while struggling in the other. The LC strives to build on skills that students bring in each language and view these as resources to strengthen their level of biliteracy. It could be determined that the advancing and emerging bilingual strands should be combined at all levels to provide for greater linguistic heterogeneity. Schools without formal bilingual programs but with numbers of students with oracy/literacy skills in Spanish, for example, might also consider organizing an advancing bilingual strand to enable this population of students to expand the Spanish language skills they already have. The three strands represent examples of possible formats for emerging and advancing bilinguals, and each strand can be customized and differentiated for the actual students being served.

LC teachers already trained as ESL and/or bilingual teachers bring added expertise to the LC sessions. These teachers may readily recognize the influence of one language or the other on reading and writing and guide students to understand how well they are applying what they know from one language to the other and how they are expanding their bilingual language practices. The scaffolding and differentiation that teachers provide allow the LC model to be used to meet the needs of a variety of individuals. They are also able to assist students in refining grammar, spelling, and syntax in the target language. Cultural misunderstandings or confusion encountered in texts are also clarified because LC teachers create an environment where students feel free to take risks in asking questions to clarify language and concepts and the teachers readily provide ongoing feedback.

Students can be taught in push-in sessions within the classroom or pulled out as a small group. In either case, it is most effective when the LC and classroom teachers collaborate and work toward the same objectives and use the same supports in both settings. The placement of students in strands is subjective and depends on where teachers/administrators believe that students will benefit most. Schedules for group sessions can be adapted to match the curriculum goals of any type of language (bilingual, dual language, language immersion, ESL, etc.) or literacy program. Spanish is a popular option for the bilingual strands, but other languages could be used as well.

TABLE 1.1 Literacy Club Strands				
Grade Level	**Advancing Bilinguals**	**Emerging Bilinguals**	**Combined Bilingual**	**English as an Additional Language**
Kindergarten			X	X
Grades 1–2	X	X		X
Grade 3	X	X		X
Grades 4–5			X	X

Components

Similar to Reading Recovery, as developed by Clay (1985), each LC session consists of four components: (1) focus book, (2) word work, (3) rereads, and (4) writing. Each of the components is research-based and reflects effective practices also used in Reading Recovery (Clay, 1985, 2000, 2005, 2013) and Guided Reading (Fountas & Pinnell, 2008, 2010). These components are adapted to the language level of the student and both receptive and expressive language skills are developed. The content for reading and writing depends on the students' skills and strategies, but includes a mix of narrative and informational text. Students explore how reading and writing are interrelated and how each area informs the other. The same components are used in each of the strands and across each of the grade levels.

Focus Book

A new **focus book** that matches the group's instructional level is selected each week. It is extremely important that the selected texts reflect the standards that are being addressed and are at the appropriate level of complexity so that students progress as quickly and as fully as possible in their literacy development.

As mentioned earlier, a critical metacognitive factor of the LC is to introduce and reinforce the use of reading strategies to support students in gaining meaning from text. A strategy is introduced during the focus book portion of the session and reinforced throughout the week. Until a particular strategy is mastered, the LC teacher continues with the same strategy and selects a new text that lends itself to reinforcement of the strategy. The same strategy is emphasized when students in the bilingual strands focus on concepts in English during the bridging portion of the week. This enables students to recognize that if they know how to use a particular strategy, such as predicting or inferring, in one language they are able to transfer that understanding to English literacy. Box 1.1 includes a progression of strategies used in the LC and the approximate levels at which instruction begins with each strategy, though instruction often continues through higher grade levels until students are able to use the strategy proficiently and independently. In the districts where the LC was implemented, Level 6 was considered grade level for kindergarten, Level 16 for grade 1, Level 28 for grade 2, Level 38 for grade 3, Level 40 for grade 4, and Level 50 for grade 5.

In terms of best practices with ELs, efforts are made to provide challenging and meaningful content through materials and learning experiences that complement the academic, linguistic, and cultural experiences of the student. It is essential that students be provided with appropriately leveled, quality reading materials that include an ample selection of high-quality fiction and informational text. Some criteria the LC teachers consider in text selection include background knowledge required, connection to content-area instruction, vocabulary, language structure, and text level. Content-based topics taught through informational literature at the appropriate level of complexity and aligned with standards, themes, and genres being used in the classroom are also of critical importance. For those reading materials that are outside of the prior knowledge base of their students, teachers build or activate background understanding with their students before, during, and after reading.

LC teachers agree that it is very important that the books chosen for emergent readers be new to the students, which requires collaboration with the classroom teacher to develop a process for selecting texts for use within the LC. The district may also supply sets of books exclusively for LC use.

The LC teacher evaluates how proficiently students read the focus book by regularly completing **running records** to determine growth in fluency, accuracy, and use of cueing systems. Anecdotal records of retelling, reflection, or response questioning may be used as

BOX 1.1 Strategy Clusters Developed at Approximate Reading Levels

LEVELS 1–3

- Picture clues
- 1st letter
- Left-to-right orientation
- Concepts of print/print knowledge matching (words + print)
- Asking a question
- Rereading
- Making connections

LEVELS 4–9

- Syllables
- Chunking
- Word parts
- Does it make sense?
- Predicting

LEVELS 10–19

- Sequencing
- Prior knowledge

LEVELS 20–30

- Summarizing
- Main idea
- Supporting details
- Vocabulary: prefixes/suffixes

FLUENT+

- Foreshadowing
- Compare and contrast
- Text features
- Skimming
- Scanning
- Evaluating
- Cause and effect
- Note taking
- Establishing a clear purpose

---

ongoing measures of focus book comprehension. This evaluation is followed by discussions with the students about strategies they are using and/or to guide them in expressing their own metacognitive processes for deriving meaning from the text.

Word Work

Word study is important to help students gain facility in analyzing and producing linguistic patterns. Word work may include phonetic and meaning patterns related to key vocabulary found in the focus book for the week, high-frequency words, and functional vocabulary, but is not limited to these categories. It is also important that word work aligns with the student's reading level (Pinnell & Fountas, 2010). Independent daily practice of letters/syllables (as needed) and sight words enables students to expand their letter/syllable and sight word vocabularies.

Word work at beginning levels is designed to help students understand the concept of a word, how words are structured, and how these clues may be used to process word meaning. Patterns of onsets and rimes in English and syllables in Spanish are also emphasized. At more advanced levels, students explore the use of prefixes and suffixes to expand word-meaning skills, along with study of language structures, syntax, and semantics. Bridging activities for emerging and advancing bilingual strands provide opportunities at the end of the week for students to explore cognates and to analyze the structure and function of both languages.

Translanguaging activities that encourage students to draw on all of the languages and skills in their linguistic repertoire are an important part of the language analysis activities of the LC session. In EAL sessions, word work is conducted in English but students are encouraged to make connections to their home language. Students participate in *dictados* in the bilingual strands, and dictations in the EAL strand, which are repeated throughout the week to focus students' attention on specific areas of language. Emerging and advancing bilingual strands conduct modified *Así se dice* (That's how you say it) activities (Escamilla et al, 2014) in which they work collaboratively, making full use of their linguistic resources, to explore similarities and differences in vocabulary, language structure, and meaning across the two languages as a process for continually refining, expanding, and integrating their bilingual language practices and sense of bilingualism.

The impact of learning from the word work section is measured most fully in terms of formative assessments. Observations are made in terms of how students apply word work concepts in their reading, that is, how well they apply known word patterns and meaning to new readings. Writing samples provide clear evidence of how fully students apply word work concepts to their own writing and also inform subsequent writing instruction. Anecdotal records include observations about how students use oral and written language(s) as they engage with texts.

Rereads

Students reread texts that were previously mastered in the focus book section of the LC. Rereads are a daily component once the student has been a part of the LC long enough to have one or more books to reread. Students complete rereads independently or in pairs. Because there are no more than four students in a group, the LC teacher has the opportunity to listen to each student reread all or part of a text on a regular basis. The teacher takes this opportunity to encourage and reinforce strategy use, compiles anecdotal notes on students' reading behaviors, and provides timely feedback by sharing these observations with the students individually or collectively on the day they are recorded. The teacher files the notes to help document the progress each student is making and to use in planning future instruction. This component is critical in that students are able to solidify vocabulary, story structure, and literary concepts through rereading.

As students progress, the easiest books are removed from the set of reread texts. They maintain a list of books they have mastered, which often serves as a motivational tool as they note the number of books they can read easily and accurately.

Writing

Writing is an important component of the LC and should occur every day, especially at the beginning levels. At more advanced levels, students may write 2–3 days and read 2–3 days per week. Writing provides opportunities to reinforce the concepts, skills, and vocabulary students are learning during other LC components.

Because students who struggle with writing often do not wish to write, it is important that motivational tools be employed to build skills and enjoyment of writing. At early writing levels, students should self-select writing topics to develop independence in writing, and use of illustrations should be an integral component of the writing process. In grades 4 and 5 writing themes are developed based on content-area topics. Students are taught methods of selecting writing topics, including looking to their writing inventory, discussing ideas with a classmate, mapping interesting characters or settings, or selecting a small moment from their own lives for a personal narrative. Students also benefit from oral rehearsal and use of sentence frames as scaffolds for their writing. As their language skills progress, students generally rely less on these supports. Mini-lessons may be based on writing standards, the writing process, the current writing strategy being emphasized, or other aspects of writing as communication.

Writing strategies appropriate to the students' instructional writing level are taught directly and reinforced during the week. A developmental list of writing strategies has been created to guide teacher selection of mini-lessons and can be found in Table 1.2. Students review and edit each writing piece using rubrics appropriate to their particular level of

TABLE 1.2 Writing Strategies		
Skills and Strategy	**Mini-Lesson Date**	**Notes on Student Use of Strategy**
Text types and purposes ■ Opinion ■ Informative/ explanatory ■ Narrative		
Production and distribution of writing ■ Development and organization (gr. 3+) ■ Revising and editing ■ Technology		
Research to build and present knowledge ■ Conduct research ■ Recall relevant information ■ Use evidence (gr. 4–5)		
Range of writing ■ Extended writing timeframes (gr. 3+) ■ Presentation ■ Other		

[handwritten margin note: not very specific]

[handwritten margin note: Woe could do to mini during GR?]

[handwritten margin note: Seems long / does this take the place of other instruction?]

writing development. LC teachers generally create writing booklets that highlight characteristics of the writing strategy under study and provide space on the page for students to self-assess each day's writing. Periodic review of writing pieces enables students to note progress they are making over time. LC teachers working with bilingual strands may wish to use paired writing rubrics (Escamilla et al, 2014) to evaluate and monitor student writing.

Session Format

Session formats will vary for the different grades as dictated by the content and expectations at each grade level. The format for each grade level/strand is presented in the grade-level chapters (Chapters 3–6). Kindergarten groups often begin with 30-minute sessions during the second semester of the school year and meet four or five days per week. Students enrolled in sessions in grades 1–5 meet five times per week for 45-minute sessions. Greatest student progress is seen when these schedules are followed with minimal interruption.

In grades K–3, all students engage in reading, word work, rereading, and writing activities in the target language on a daily basis. The EAL strand completes all work in English throughout the week, though the LC teacher is encouraged to support learning in the students' home language, if possible. The advancing and emerging bilingual strands, however, use the formula Spanish–bridge–English in organizing sessions for the week (Beeman & Urow, 2013). In essence, students receive instruction in one language and then bridge to study the vocabulary and concepts in the second language, while also doing comparative analyses of the two languages. This format helps ensure high-level paired literacy development in both English and Spanish.

Sociocultural Foundations

Intervention endeavors that have a positive and lasting impact on children's academic and emotional growth are carefully planned and implemented, and continuously refined. They are based on well-defined and comprehensive sociocultural beliefs and practices. In the LC these include linguistically and culturally responsive pedagogy, student-centered instruction, scaffolding and differentiation, continuous progress monitoring, and collaboration. These practices permeate the goals, language strands, and LC session formats.

Linguistically and Culturally Responsive Pedagogy

Embedded in the LC is the importance of students' background knowledge. Connecting learning to what students already know is a critical component for language learners that must be considered in every LC session. Selecting materials that represent the cultures and experiences of the students is critical because children react positively to seeing themselves reflected in text. LC teachers must, therefore, carefully select instructional materials that authentically and positively represent specific cultures and experiences.

Opportunities should also be made available for students to build on their own experiences through speaking and writing activities. Students are able to represent their own experiences more fully than those of others and this allows them to express their thinking with greater detail and understanding. In the grade-specific chapters that follow, readers will find examples of LC teachers selecting texts related to immigration, life in the desert, and so forth because they recognize that many students have experiences in these areas and can share their knowledge orally and in writing to strengthen understanding.

Students enrolled in bilingual programs should participate in bilingual strands in the LC because it is important to continue to support them in both of their languages. As students progress in language and literacy development in their non-English language, they are able to attach greater status to that language and to participate more fully in the literacy practices of that language group. Escamilla and Hopewell (2010) and Beeman and Urow (2013) focus on positive implications when bilingual students use two languages to learn. Instructors consider and value students' home language practices in relation to their development of English for academic purposes.

Throughout the work of the emerging and advancing bilingual strands, students are given opportunities to use translanguaging strategically for learning. Teachers also implement the bridge at the end of each lesson so that students can apply what they have learned in one language to other languages of instruction. Bridging and translanguaging are pedagogical practices that teachers can use purposefully to support students as they engage with complex content and texts, and to broaden students' language practices for academic purposes. High expectations and flexible structures are put in place to create rigorous learning experiences for all students.

Student-Centered Instruction

Students come to the classroom with different backgrounds and unique skills, and their progress must be addressed by meeting their individual needs. A successful LC program is grounded in sociocultural practices and norms that recognize and work with the abilities and challenges of each individual student. In the student profiles presented earlier in this chapter, the focus on identifying the specific needs of each student or group of students is clearly evident. The four kindergarten students need to develop reading comprehension through rereading and discussion. Juan Carlos will focus on developing reading and writing strategies and critical thinking skills using Spanish for instructional purposes. Evelyn Gloria needs support in Spanish oracy and Ai in English oracy. Sergio's emphasis will be on developing reading and writing strategies across both languages, supported by opportunities for language analysis and bridging activities.

One of the distinguishing factors of the LC is its focus on dialogue. We know that students extend their oracy skills through practice using language. However, LC students are often silent in the mainstream classroom. The small group size in the LC provides them with more opportunities to express themselves and take risks with language and content in a nonthreatening environment. The specific job of the LC teacher is to provide as many guided and open-ended opportunities as possible for students to expand their oracy skills as they express ever more complex thoughts, opinions, and understanding about content and language.

The LC also encourages students to own and take responsibility for their learning. As they move through the program and advance in their understanding of skills and strategies, students are asked to self-assess their work and set their own goals for continued learning. They enhance metacognitive skills by analyzing how they use language and strategies and how this awareness affects linguistic and academic progress.

Scaffolded and Differentiated Learning Activities

LC teachers adapt activities to enable students to meet content and language objectives, as one aspect of responsive teaching. Literacy instruction is continually refined to meet students' ever-changing needs, and although the LC teacher collaborates with the classroom teacher and works with identified language and content standards, he or she organizes the LC components to best meet the students' learning levels and styles. Scaffolding and differentiation are two means of addressing those needs to ensure that students receive the type of instruction necessary for them to progress as fully as possible.

Scaffolding is the process by which supports are used in guiding students to greater understanding and independence in their learning. LC teachers use scaffolds to make instruction more accessible for students. For example, an instructor may have LC students orally discuss their writing topics prior to completing the writing assignment. Initially they may use sentence frames to support writing and speaking. As another example, after collaboratively creating a list of grade-level vocabulary that will be taught in the classroom, the LC instructor uses **total physical response** actions and visuals to introduce and apply the vocabulary before the LC students encounter the words in the classroom. The scaffolds are available for use in reading, writing, listening, and speaking. LC teachers select those that will support student learning most fully. Scaffolds are left in place as long as students need them to support learning. They have proven to be an effective tool to enable students to demonstrate maximum learning and understanding.

Differentiation—the process whereby a teacher changes the material that is being taught (content), the way the content is taught (delivery), and/or the means of assessing what has been learned (product) to better meet the needs of students—is a critical aspect of responsive teaching. Learning is often differentiated in the LC by the use of alternate reading materials. Content-area text, especially as the grade levels progress, becomes more and more challenging for students who are struggling with literacy and/or language development. The challenge is to find materials that are manageable for students but that develop concepts at a level sophisticated enough to meet grade-level content-area expectations. If students are below grade level in particular subject areas, the challenge is heightened because teachers will also need to evaluate and build prior knowledge for particular skills, strategies, and/or content.

While scaffolds may be used simultaneously with differentiation, it is important to note the difference between the two: scaffolding involves using materials and activities to enhance understanding and participation in the learning experience, whereas differentiation provides an alternate method of performing a task, alternate learning experiences, or use

TABLE 1.3 Comparison of Differentiation and Scaffolding

Subject	Classroom Activity	Differentiated Activity	Scaffolded Activity
Social studies	Read grade-level book on the Constitution	Read different book on the Constitution that is appropriate for students' reading levels but that addresses the same concepts	Watch a brief video clip highlighting the concepts the students will read about
Science	Write a description of the water cycle	Draw and label a picture of the water cycle	Ask each student to draw one picture of an event in the water cycle and, as a group, put them in order and describe the water cycle

of alternate materials. Table 1.3 gives examples of scaffolded versus differentiated activities. The LC model encourages teachers to be involved decision makers who are aware of their students' social and cultural backgrounds as they scaffold and differentiate instruction.

Teacher Collaboration

The same goals are reinforced in the LC and the classroom to ensure that learning is connected and focused between the two settings, although the learning experiences and the pace in the LC may differ from that of the classroom. It is critical that the LC and classroom teachers collaborate as a cohesive team to fully support students across both settings. In addition to language and literacy standards, LC and classroom teachers collaborate to select the same genres, strategies, and themes to reinforce concepts across the two settings. Table 1.4 reflects the work of a collaborative effort between an LC teacher and a classroom teacher.

TABLE 1.4 Collaborative Kindergarten Weekly Targets and Daily Objectives

READING TARGET

I will be able to explain the work that I do.

	Day 1	Day 2	Day 3	Day 4	Day 5
Readers' workshop objectives: I will be able to describe	all the parts of a book	the tasks I do at the listening center	the tasks I do at the name center	the tasks I do at the writing center	the tasks I do at the ABC center

WRITING TARGET

I will be able to add details to my writing.

Writers' workshop objectives: I will be able to	add details to my writing to show emotions	add details to my pictures to show emotions	go back and add words to my story	go back and add details to my story	reread my story and check my picture

The LC teacher may preteach content and language concepts prior to themes being introduced in the classroom, while at other times the teachers may choose to simultaneously teach the themes in the two settings. If LC students need additional support with specific concepts, the LC teacher may reinforce language and content after the lesson/unit has been concluded in the classroom. In any of these scenarios, students are the beneficiaries when concepts, strategies, and language skills are reinforced in both venues. Language learners then have double exposure and greater opportunity to develop understanding and application of concepts and language. According to Honigsfield and Dove (2010), "when teachers are able to consistently work together as teams" language learners participate more fully and show improved academic performance.

LC teachers can play a significant role in facilitating communication with the school team that is built around each student. LC teachers participate in the selection of students to join in the LC; analyze ongoing progress-monitoring information with the classroom teacher; and provide periodic information on student progress to administrators, ESL/bilingual coordinators, and literacy specialists. They also are an important voice in determining when students are ready to exit the LC.

Although LC teachers drive the work of the club, school administrators are instrumental in establishing the importance of the LC within the school by scheduling professional development opportunities and setting non-negotiable times for collaboration and working with students. Administrators secure materials and resources for LC sessions, support the schedule of the LC teacher, and arrange for professional workspaces within the building.

Continuous Progress Monitoring

Successful intervention programs have a specific and comprehensive progress-monitoring plan in place to gauge students' learning. Authentic and ongoing assessment is a hallmark of the LC. It determines where students are to begin when they join the LC and how they are progressing in terms of oracy, literacy, and metacognition. Both formative and summative assessment measures are used to monitor student progress and inform instruction. As we see throughout the book, collaboration between classroom and LC teachers in planning, instruction, and assessment provides a rich set of data for continuous progress monitoring of LC students.

CONCLUSION

The major goal of the LC is to provide RtI[2] for language learners who struggle with literacy and/or language development in one or both languages. The LC is flexible in nature and can be adjusted to accommodate any type of educational program for language learners or any level of language learning. Literacy (reading and writing), oracy (listening and speaking), and metacognition (strategy development and metalanguage) are the three areas that are emphasized most fully to support the academic and linguistic development of students enrolled in the LC.

Ongoing assessment is a critical component of the LC that allows teachers to monitor student growth and inform instruction to move students along as quickly as possible toward grade-level linguistic and academic expectations. Use of student self-assessment and goal-setting provides opportunities for students to take greater responsibility for their own learning. Linguistically and culturally responsive pedagogy, student-centered instruction, scaffolding and differentiation, teacher collaboration, and continuous progress monitoring are the sociocultural foundations on which the LC is based.

QUESTIONS FOR REFLECTION AND ACTION

- How do the LC components and strands work together using the same goals but different pathways to support language learners who are struggling with language and/or literacy development?
- Who are the language learners in your school/district who would benefit from LC support? What are their language and literacy needs and how might the LC address them?
- Analyze the sociocultural foundations of the LC. To what degree are they already reflected in your school/district environment? How might they be further enhanced in school/district practice?
- Prepare a critique of the effectiveness of Tier 1 classroom structures for language learners in your school/district. In what areas might they be further implemented?

2

Goal-Setting and Progress Monitoring

KEY CONCEPTS

- Literacy Club teachers use appropriate assessment measures to place students, set goals, monitor progress, and help students exit the program.
- The Literacy Club has developed a system to regularly evaluate student progress in literacy, oracy, and metacognition to inform instruction in literacy and language.
- Student self-assessment plays a critical role in monitoring growth, setting goals, and guiding students in the Literacy Club to take greater responsibility for their own learning.

Assessment is at the heart of the **Literacy Club (LC)**. Instructors use appropriate assessments to place students, set goals, continuously monitor student progress toward those goals, inform instruction, and help students exit the program. Teachers choose assessments that provide evidence of student learning relative to each LC goal—**oracy, literacy**, and **metacognition**. These goals and assessments align with state content and language development standards, reflect the LC's sociocultural foundations (i.e., linguistically and culturally responsive pedagogy, student-centered instruction, scaffolded and differentiated learning activities, teacher collaboration, and continuous progress monitoring), and correspond to the LC session components and strands.

The "same goals—different pathways" theme of the LC has strong implications for the assessment process. Because the goals of the LC are oracy, literacy, and metacognition (**strategy development** and **metalanguage**), formative assessments must be designed to continually measure growth toward these goals (in English for the English as an additional language [EAL] strand and in English and Spanish side by side for the bilingual strands). Feedback from these measures allows students to continually enhance their progress toward content and language standards, and student self-assessment and goal-setting are used strategically to motivate students to engage more fully in their own learning. Data from summative assessment measures, collected at intervals throughout the school year, provide evidence of student growth toward content and language standards. Ongoing analysis of all of the assessment data informs instruction, helps ensure that students are appropriately challenged and supported in their language and literacy development, and provides valuable information for evaluating the effectiveness of the LC.

Since 2001, states mandate that districts and schools respond to two sets of learning standards for their language learners: content standards and English language development (ELD) standards. The LC was developed in an area of the country where curriculum, instruction, and assessment are aligned with Common Core State Standards (CCSS) and WIDA ELD standards. Teachers in other contexts use assessments that correspond to their state-mandated academic achievement and ELD standards. Teachers must choose assessments that measure student growth and achievement relative to the learning goals and benchmarks for the LC in oracy, literacy, and metacognition (metalanguage and learning strategies).

ASSESSMENT PRINCIPLES AND PRACTICES

The LC follows a systematic approach to assessment and accountability to measure student progress, inform ongoing instruction, and move students along as quickly as possible toward grade-level expectations. An integration of formative and summative assessment data moves the work of LC teachers and students toward grade-level expectations in oracy, literacy, and metacognition. The student-centered nature of the LC is partially reflected in the development of student self-assessment and goal-setting.

Balance Assessments

LC teachers use a balanced system of formative and summative assessment to measure students' language and literacy skills. **Formative assessments** are used to measure student progress and provide feedback during instruction; **summative assessments** gauge student performance at the end of a unit of study or on a standardized test. Multiple measures of language development and academic achievement yield a more accurate picture of content and learning for language learners. Different sources of evidence can be triangulated and used to authentically inform instruction.

Gottlieb (2007) and Gottlieb and Nguyen (2007) provide excellent guidelines for developing authentic assessment and accountability systems in linguistically and culturally diverse contexts. Educators interested in implementing an LC in their schools/district may wish to turn to the BASIC (balanced assessment and accountability system, inclusive and comprehensive) model developed by Gottlieb and Nguyen. The BASIC model has curriculum and instruction at its core; is framed by learning standards, goals, and benchmarks; and is grounded in contextual information. LC practitioners can draw on this model to customize the LC assessment system for their particular context and integrate the work of the LC more fully into the overall school/district assessment plan for each student.

Consider Sociocultural Context

Reflecting the sociocultural perspective that characterizes LC practices, we begin with an overview of contextual information. As previously described, districts and schools can develop different LC language strands that respond to the linguistic and cultural needs of their students, while taking into consideration the available resources and constraints at the local level. Our focus is on three different strands: **advancing** (Spanish) **bilingual**, **emerging** (Spanish) **bilingual**, and **EAL** (English-medium), and teachers need to choose appropriate assessments in Spanish and/or English for students in each of these strands. The advancing and emerging Spanish bilingual strands assess student performance relative to all LC goals in Spanish and English, while the EAL strand focuses on assessment in English. Teachers who work with other languages choose assessments in the languages used for instructional purposes.

Collect Baseline Data Relative to Grade-Level Standards and Goals

The LC gives a set of assessments at the beginning of the year to establish **baseline data**; it is repeated quarterly to gauge student progress. Teachers use baseline data to target students' individual needs and develop initial instructional plans. The same process can be applied to students in any strand, at any grade level, relative to any LC goal. Here we focus on some of the baseline data on **language development** and writing that LC teachers collected for two of our focal students—*Juan Carlos* and *Sergio*.

Juan Carlos is nearly a full year below grade level in measures of English language literacy and scores only slightly higher in Spanish. He participates in the advancing bilingual strand of the LC, where he begins the week with language and literacy instruction in Spanish and bridges to English at the end of the week. Although he is clearly struggling at the beginning of grade 2, he has had two full years of biliteracy instruction and has built some background in oracy, literacy, and metacognition. Learning experiences are designed to strengthen and build on the skills he already has in both languages.

Juan Carlos' baseline data profile indicates that he has reached ELD Level 4 in listening and speaking and Level 2 in reading and writing. He has reached Spanish language development (SLD) Level 5 in listening and speaking and Level 2 in reading and writing. Teachers are using **scaffolding** and supports to help Juan Carlos move from Level 2 to Level 3 in reading and writing in Spanish and English. LC teachers organize instruction to draw on Juan Carlos' stronger oracy in both languages to support his progression to the next performance level in reading and writing in both languages. This is an example of how teachers can triangulate the different information in Spanish and English language development and literacy to get a more nuanced understanding of what students can do, and how they can draw on student strengths to inform instruction.

An analysis of Juan Carlos' writing in English and Spanish (Fig. 2.1) reflects that he has fairly comparable skills in the two languages, though he writes in Spanish with greater ease. He stays on a single topic, has control of some high-frequency words, and generally uses capital letters to begin a new idea. He controls punctuation better in Spanish than English. The LC teacher sets goals that focus on elaboration of ideas, spelling, and sentence variety as a result of this analysis, adjusting Juan Carlos' instruction to match his needs. The LC teacher helps Juan Carlos continue to expand his writing skills in both languages and ensures that he is able to apply writing strategies evenly across the two languages.

Although Sergio's profile looks somewhat similar to Juan Carlos', his needs in the emerging/advancing bilingual strand are quite different. Like Juan Carlos, Sergio struggles with literacy development in English and Spanish, reaching Level 2 in English and Level 3 in Spanish. However, Sergio has strong listening and speaking skills in Spanish (Level 6 in each domain). He has a very well-developed general vocabulary in Spanish and is able to explain his ideas in detail, though it is important to strengthen his language for academic

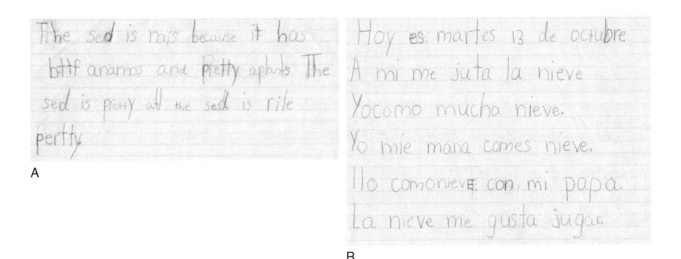

A

B

Figure 2.1 English and Spanish writing samples: Juan Carlos.

TABLE 2.1 Baseline Data Profiles: Juan Carlos and Sergio				
Name	Juan Carlos		Sergio	
Grade	2		5	
Born	Mexico		Guatemala	
Home language	Spanish		Spanish	
Age at arrival	3		7	
Type of program	One-way bilingual		Dual language	
Entered program	Kindergarten		Grade 2	
Language development	*English Level*	*Spanish Level*	*English Level*	*Spanish Level*
Listening	4	5	3	6
Speaking	4	5	3	6
Reading	2	2	2	3
Writing	2	2	2	2
Observations	■ Fairly even skills in English and Spanish ■ Stronger in listening and speaking than reading and writing in both languages		■ Comparable levels of reading and writing in English and Spanish ■ Stronger in listening and speaking in Spanish	
Recommendations	Needs more support in reading and writing: Comprehension, strategy development, content and structure of language		Strengthen listening and speaking in English to support literacy development in both languages. Focus on comprehension, strategy development, content, and structure of language for academic purposes.	

use in the content areas. The LC instructor can capitalize on these strengths to guide Sergio's progress with literacy and metacognition in both languages and oracy in English. Table 2.1 provides an overview of the two boys' profiles.

Evaluation of the baseline data for Juan Carlos and Sergio clearly reflects how an analysis of the same goals (oracy, literacy, and metacognition), with attention to language development, informs LC teachers' continuous progress monitoring along different pathways.

Identify Appropriate Summative and Formative Assessments

Summative assessment is commonly described as assessment *of* learning, in that it provides indicators of how well a student is progressing toward LC and grade-level expectations. Summative assessments in the LC may include the quarterly assessment of progress completed, to provide a more formal analysis of how students are progressing relative to grade-level literacy and language standards (i.e., product of learning). Formative assessment is generally referred to as assessment *for* learning. Measures such as writing samples and informal running records provide feedback to teachers and students about progress toward ongoing literacy and language objectives (i.e., process for learning). Data from both

TABLE 2.2 Summative and Formative Assessments Used in the Literacy Club		
SUMMATIVE		
Assessment	**Description**	**Use**
ACCESS for ELLs test	Annual standardized test to measure ELD in listening, speaking, reading, and writing	Provide data on yearly linguistic growth in English
■ Running records ■ DRA2+ (English reading) ■ EDL2 (Spanish reading) ■ District writing sample	District measures of comprehension, reading fluency, writing, and speaking	■ Provide quarterly data on student progress ■ Inform instruction regarding strengths and challenges ■ Review progress with students and set goals
FORMATIVE		
■ Student ELD performance indicators (e.g., WIDA can-do descriptors) ■ Student SLD performance indicators (e.g., *los descriptores podemos de* WIDA)	Delineate reading, writing, listening, and speaking skills of each student in English or Spanish (for students whose home language is Spanish or for students in Spanish bilingual programs)	■ Create a language profile ■ Provide information for selecting language objectives, learning experiences, and differentiating instruction ■ Inform ongoing goal-setting for language development
■ Ongoing writing work samples with rubrics ■ Student self-assessments of writing and use of writing strategies	Writing samples, reflections, word work samples	■ Measure ongoing progress in oracy, literacy, and metacognition ■ Inform instruction

ACCESS, Assessing Comprehension and Communication in English State-to-State; DRA2+, Developmental Reading Assessment; ELD, English language development; ELD2, *Evaluación del desarrollo de la lectura*; ELL, English language learners; SLD, Spanish language development.

types of assessment measures are analyzed in English and/or Spanish to determine strengths and challenges for each student. These results are used to inform instruction and provide an avenue for continual refinement and improvement in the teaching/learning/assessment process. Table 2.2 provides examples of summative and formative LC assessments and how the data from each are utilized.

Monitor Student Progress Continuously

Formative assessment data are collected on an ongoing basis during LC sessions. LC teachers analyze students' application of strategies in their reading and writing, for example, and provide immediate feedback to guide their work and strengthen their ability to expand metacognitive awareness of their learning. Classroom and LC teachers work together to select and assess language and content objectives, determine the types of assessments that best measure and promote learning in both settings, and use the assessment data to drive instruction. These teacher collaborations are an integral part of the success of the LC.

LC and classroom teachers also review available assessment data from school, district, and state-level assessments to monitor student progress. The chapters that follow highlight variations in how teachers choose and use assessments to reflect their program, school, district, and state context. In all cases, however, teachers follow the same principled approach to guide this work.

Assessment in the EAL strand is conducted in English and includes formative and summative measures of student progress in oracy, literacy, and metacognition. The assessment process for the bilingual strands includes paired analysis of skills and strategies in both languages to ensure that students are progressing as fully as possible across both languages. At times, formative or summative measures may show that students apply skills or strategies (such as using context clues or making inferences) in one language but not the other. This provides valuable information the LC teacher can use in designing instruction to ensure that students have opportunities to explore these types of learning transfers. At other times, assessments may indicate that a student is advancing very quickly in one language and could be challenged more in the target language.

Encourage Student Self-Assessment and Goal-Setting

The student-centered nature of LC instruction is reflected in the emphasis placed on student self-assessment—students assess their use of skills and strategies in reading and writing at the beginning and end of each week. Student-centered self-assessment and goal-setting are vital to achieving the metacognitive goals of the LC. Students are asked to think critically about their progress and to define their own goals. Once they have completed an assignment, students are asked to think about their work and characterize, for example, the difficulty of the task and the quality of their work. Results of the more formal summative assessments that are administered in fall, winter, and spring are reviewed with students to engage them more fully in analyzing their own learning; this generally results in students taking greater interest in and responsibility for their learning.

Use Appropriate Exit Criteria

LC team members, who generally include the LC teacher, classroom teacher, English as a second language (ESL)/bilingual coordinator, and building administrator, collaboratively review assessment data to determine if a student is ready to exit the LC. This review includes an analysis of grade-level reading proficiency (vocabulary, comprehension, fluency, and use of strategies) and evidence of the ability to write with grade-level proficiency in the target language of instruction. Students may exit from the LC once they demonstrate oracy, literacy, and metacognition skills that are at proficient or advanced levels for their particular grade. For a few students who enter the LC at the beginning of the year, this may occur as soon as the end of one semester and many others exit by the end of one academic year.

Because rapid student progress is seen in many instances, it may be tempting for educators to let students exit the LC as soon as they make substantial progress toward proficiency and replace them with other lower-performing students. However, this tendency should be avoided to ensure that student progress is solidified. Students may begin to improve quickly in the LC, but they do so because they are provided with high levels of targeted and individualized support in this setting. Students should not be allowed to exit until they have had time to practice and internalize grade-level literacy, oracy, learning strategies, and metalanguage skills and have found the inner confidence to meet grade-level classroom expectations.

COMMONLY USED ASSESSMENTS

The LC uses different assessments to focus instruction and continuously monitor student progress. Districts with similar goals and assessments in place for oracy, literacy, and metacognition should use the data they already collect from these measures as part of their assessment system. This approach avoids subjecting students to additional and unnecessary testing procedures and results in less instructional time being used for testing.

Language Development

Teachers often find it challenging to apply data from measures of language assessment in English for the EAL strand and in both English and Spanish for the bilingual strands to scaffold and differentiate instruction. The following summative measures have well-developed indicators of what students might be expected to do at each performance level, which provides LC teachers with invaluable information about how to structure instruction. The following formative measures also provide language expectation indicators at each level in each of the domains.

Standardized English Language Proficiency Tests

All students who are officially designated as **English learners (ELs)** must take standardized English language proficiency (ELP) tests annually. Wisconsin, where the LC originated, is a member of the WIDA Consortium. In states where WIDA standards have been adopted, all students identified as ELs take the **Assessing Comprehension and Communication in English State-to State (ACCESS) for ELLs test**. The test measures annual growth in English language skills in listening, speaking, reading, and writing relative to five standards: (1) social and instructional language, (2) the language of language arts, (3) the language of mathematics, (4) the language of science, and (5) the language of social studies. Educators working in states (e.g., NY, CA, TX) that have adopted a different set of ELD standards (e.g., ELPA21) would use the results of their state's language testing measures. Composite and subtest scores are analyzed to determine baseline areas of strength and areas that need specific instruction in LC sessions. WIDA also makes the *Prueba óptima del desarrollo del Español realizado* (PODER) test for Spanish language learners in kindergarten,[1] which provides comparable data to the ACCESS for ELLs and Spanish language learners.

Student Performance Indicators of Language Development

The results of standardized ELP tests (e.g., ACCESS) provide a good starting point for summative assessment of ELD levels in the four domains of reading, writing, listening, and speaking. However, these standardized test results do not provide the information that teachers need to continuously monitor students' ELD as they perform the range of academic tasks demanded at school. LC teachers therefore use student performance indicators (e.g., WIDA can-do descriptors) to identify what each student can do independently with English in each of the four domains, and what they can do at the next level (i.e., their instructional level) with appropriate scaffolding and support. LC teachers working in the Spanish bilingual strands can use the comparable *los descriptores podemos* that WIDA produces to identify what students can do in Spanish independently and with scaffolding and support in the four domains. Educators in other states and consortia can consult their state's language development standards and assessment frameworks for more on the specific performance indicators used in their districts.

Literacy Development

Assessments of literacy development indicate how students are progressing in reading and writing. Students in the EAL strand complete reading and writing assessments in English, and teachers use student performance data in English to guide instruction and monitor progress. Students in the bilingual strands complete literacy assessments in both languages. Teachers use data from paired literacy assessments in Spanish and English to accelerate literacy development and to measure students' trajectories toward biliteracy.

---

1. At the time of this writing, PODER is only available at the kindergarten level.

Reading: Developmental Reading Assessment 2+ and *Evaluación del desarrollo de la lectura* 2 Tests

Progress in literacy development is measured by the **Developmental Reading Assessment 2+ (DRA2+) test** in English and the comparable *Evaluación del desarrollo de la lectura 2* (EDL2) **test** in Spanish. The district administers these tests and information is readily available in the students' files and accessible to LC teachers. Subtest scores provide information that indicates levels of accuracy, fluency, and comprehension in each of the languages tested. Districts may have alternate measures that could be substituted to analyze student progress in literacy development. For students in the emerging/advancing bilingual strands, scores indicating strengths in one language but not the other are particularly valuable because they may indicate areas for more focused instruction in LC sessions to build language skills and/or to guide students in transferring understanding from one language to another.

Writing Rubrics

Throughout the year, writing samples can be compared to an initial baseline sample to analyze student writing proficiency in one or both languages. To bolster student interest and investment, all strands use student-selected topics for the writing assessment.

A well-designed rubric is an essential part of a writing assignment because it provides specific and directed criteria during and after writing against which student work will be measured. The EAL and bilingual strands use an LC-designed writing rubric that is aligned with the CCSS for writing with writing objectives. Students use these criteria for self-assessing their writing efforts and setting goals for continued progress. Teachers provide regular feedback to students about their writing progress and discuss writing strategies with them. A sample writing assessment sheet designed by LC teachers that has criteria and assessment included is shown in Box 2.1.

The Literacy Squared paired writing rubric (Escamilla et al, 2014) is very useful in scoring content, punctuation, spelling, and **translanguaging** for the English and Spanish strands (Box 2.2). This rubric is weighted more heavily toward content than spelling and grammar to highlight the role of written communication ability and is used to analyze writing in terms of discourse and language structure and use. Teachers examine the writing profiles across both languages to determine the bilingual writing skill of each student. Juan Carlos, for example, has reached Level 2 in English and Spanish writing, and even though he is at early stages of writing development in both languages, his work indicates that he is transferring what he knows from one language to the other in writing.

Bilingual writing analysis provides an overall evaluation of which elements of writing students have under control in each language and how they are using what they know in one language to inform their writing in the other language. Juan Carlos and Sergio have very similar writing profiles in both English and Spanish writing; however, they each have different profiles of listening and speaking skills in Spanish. Juan Carlos is fairly even in both languages and will most likely continue to expand his writing at a similar pace in both of them. Sergio's listening and speaking skills in Spanish are much stronger than in English and he probably needs more support in applying what he can do in writing in Spanish to his writing in English.

Running Records

The LC teacher frequently assesses each student's reading ability through the use of **running records** or similar measures performed approximately every 1–2 weeks using the **focus book**. These assessments provide information about student fluency, accuracy, and comprehension in reading text. Running records also indicate the types of miscues students

BOX 2.1 Student Writing and Self-Assessment Sheet

Name _____   Date _____

ORGANIZATION

_____ *Good attention getter*

_____ *Write a clear beginning, middle, and ending*

_____ *Group same ideas together*

_____ *Good closing*

_____

_____

_____

_____

_____

_____

_____

_____

_____

_____

_____

_____ *I read my writing to myself*

_____ *I revised &/or edited*

_____ *I got feedback on my writing*

How I feel about this piece:

BOX 2.2 Paired Literacy Writing Rubric

Rater ID:
_____

Student ID:
_____

Not to prompt
(Circle)

Span | Eng

Grades: K, 1, 2, 3, 4, and 5 (Circle grade)

SPANISH SCORE	CONTENT	ENGLISH SCORE
10	Focused composition, conveys emotion or uses figurative language, is engaging to the reader; clearly addresses the prompt; book language	10
9	Organization of composition includes effective transitions & vivid examples	9
8	Writing includes complex *sentence* structures and has a discernable, consistent structure	8
7	Sense of completeness—Clear introduction and clear conclusion	7
6	Includes descriptive language (use of adjectives, adverbs at the word level) or varied sentence structures	6
5	Main idea discernable with supporting details, or main idea can be inferred or stated explicitly, or repetitive vocabulary: may include unrelated ideas	5
4	Two ideas—*I like my bike **and/because** it is blue*	4
3	One idea expressed through a subject and predicate, subject may be implied (*I like my bike, amo,* or *run*)	3
2	Label(s), list of words; may communicate an idea without subject and predicate	2
1	Prewriting: Picture only, not readable, or written in a language other than the prompt	1
0	The student did not prepare a sample	0
	STRUCTURAL ELEMENTS	
5	Multiparagraph composition with accurate punctuation and capitalization	5
4	Controls most structural elements and includes paragraphing	4
3	Controls beginning and ending punctuation in ways that make sense and is attempting additional structural elements (commas, question marks, guiones, apostrophes, ellipses, parentheses, hyphens, and indentation)	3
2	Uses one or more of the structural elements *correctly*	2
1	Uses one or more of the structural elements *incorrectly*	1
0	Structural elements not evident	0
	SPELLING	
6	Accurate spelling	6
5	Most words are spelled conventionally	5
4	Majority of high-frequency words are correct and child is approximating standardization in errors	4
3	Most words are not spelled conventionally but demonstrates an emerging knowledge of common spelling patterns	3
2	Represents most sounds in words and most high-frequency words are spelled incorrectly	2
1	Represents some sounds in words	1
0	Message is not discernable	0

BOX 2.2 Paired Literacy Writing Rubric *(continued)*

QUALITATIVE ANALYSIS OF STUDENT WRITING

	Bilingual Strategies		
	(Spanish → English)	(English → Spanish)	Spanish ⟷ English (bidirectional)
DISCOURSE ■ *Rhetorical structures* (first, next, last) ■ *Punctuation* (signals awareness of code-switches—*me gusta* "basketball," or Run fast!)			
SENTENCE/PHRASE ■ *Syntax* (subject omission, word order—the bike of my sister) ■ *Literal Translations* (*agarré todas bien*/I got them all right) ■ *Code-switching* (*no puedo hablar in just one language*)			
WORD LEVEL ■ *Code-switching* ■ *Loan words* (soccer, mall) ■ *Nativized words* (*spláchate*/splashed)			
PHONICS Spanish → English (japi/happy) English → Spanish (awua/*agua*) Spanish ⟷ English (bihave/behave, lecktura/*lectura*)			

Developmental Language-Specific Approximations	
SPANISH	**ENGLISH**
Structural elements, syntax, spelling, hypo/hypersegmentation	Structural elements, syntax, spelling, hypo/hypersegmentation

make in reading and their ability to use self-correcting strategies. Figure 2.2 provides a sample running record form adapted for use in the LC. The report indicates that kindergarten student **Mario** used most of the emergent literacy strategies for the Level 1 book with which he was tested. Emphasis is placed on using the first letter of unknown words as a word analysis strategy. Other assessments indicate that support with comprehension, oracy, and strategy development supports Mario's LC progress.

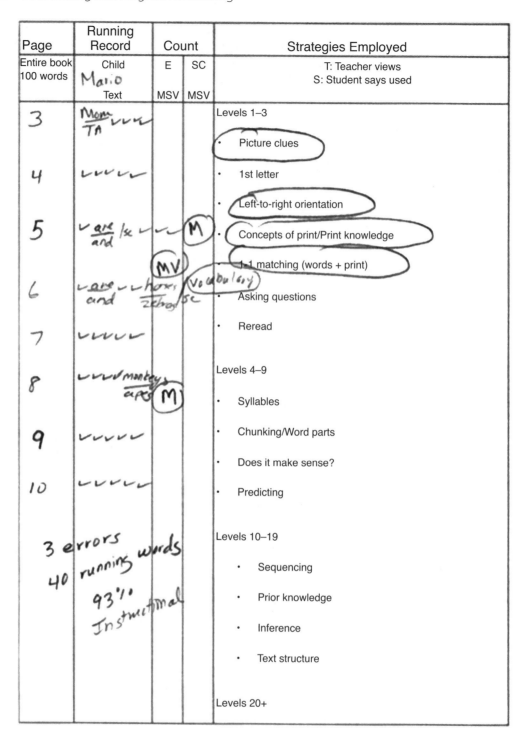

Figure 2.2 Running record: Mario.

Metacognition

In addition to the formative assessment measures mentioned previously, the small group format of the LC allows LC teachers to provide ongoing and specific feedback. Students share their writing with the teacher and/or members of the group and receive immediate feedback. LC teachers also regularly confer with each student during the LC writing section regarding his or her use of writing strategies. They review the results of assessments with students and work with them to analyze growth and challenges and set appropriate metacognition goals.

LC teachers take note of the metacognitive progress students are making in terms of the reading and writing strategies they observe students employing, and elicit explanations from them about how they perceive themselves using the strategies and how the strategies support comprehension and critical thinking. LC teachers also discuss with the students how they are using language as a way to support development of metacognitive thought processes. Students themselves are encouraged to make observations about each other's use of strategies and reasoning skills.

Attitude Surveys

Students who experience difficulty with literacy development may also suffer from a negative attitude toward reading and writing, especially at the upper grade levels. For this reason, an attitude survey is an integral part of the LC assessment plan. Attitude surveys determine how students feel about their work, and learning in general, and they are conducted at each of the summative assessment periods beginning in grade 3 (Table 2.3). More favorable responses on the survey generally accompany improvements in literacy development. The results of this survey, as well as the other assessments used four times per year, are shared with the students after each data collection period. Students are often delighted with the levels of progress they have made and this further enhances positive attitudes toward reading and writing and increases student motivation. Attitude surveys are another reflection of the sociocultural foundation of the student-centered nature of LC instruction and assessment.

DEVELOPING AN ASSESSMENT SCHEDULE

One of the sociocultural foundations of the LC is ongoing progress monitoring; an assessment schedule is one way to ensure that authentic and meaningful progress monitoring is taking place. The LC teacher may draft a plan for the groups that he or she works with and then refine it in collaboration with the classroom teachers. Table 2.4 provides an example of a K–5 assessment schedule for working with ELs in the EAL strand.

RECURSIVE PROCESS

The formative and summative assessments used in the LC are intended as much to support further learning as they are to evaluate learning at specific points in time. The assessments form an ongoing cycle of teaching, learning, and progress monitoring to continually move students forward in oracy, literacy, and metacognition. Prior to initiating the LC, the organizers will need to create an assessment plan and select baseline, formative, and summative measures to continuously monitor progress.

Collect Baseline Data and Place Students in Strands

It is recommended that a leadership or steering committee, including the LC teachers, be formed to design the process for the collection and analysis of baseline data. Data can be gathered using both summative and formative assessments, including the DRA2+ in English or EDL2 in Spanish, as well as assessments of ELD and other relevant languages. Many LC teachers print the can-do descriptors for each grade level they are working with and place student names under the appropriate reading, writing, listening, and speaking levels. This provides teachers with a clear picture of where each student is currently performing and progress can be recorded on the same form throughout the year.

Individual screening assessments also may be part of district- or classroom-level data collection. Additional formative measures might include speech samples, anecdotal records

TABLE 2.3 Attitude Survey

Name _____   Grade _____

Reading Habits and Enjoyment Survey	Fall	Winter	Spring
1. I know how to read.			
2. I am a good reader.			
3. I am good at using strategies when I read.			
4. I read a lot.			
5. I like reading.			
6. When I think of reading, I feel _____ .			
7. I read in my free time.			

Writing Habits and Enjoyment Survey	Fall	Winter	Spring
1. I know how to write.			
2. I am a good writer.			
3. I am good at using strategies when I write.			
4. I write a lot.			
5. I like writing.			
6. When I think of writing, I feel _____ .			
7. I write in my free time.			

Encuesta de actitud

Nombre _____   Grado _____

Encuesta de los hábitos y el placer de la lectura	Otoño	Invierno	Primavera
1. Sé cómo leer.			
2. Soy un buen lector. Soy una buena lectora.			
3. Sé usar las estrategias de lectura.			
4. Leo mucho.			
5. Me gusta leer.			
6. Cuando me imagino leyendo me siento _____ .			
7. Leo en mi tiempo libre.			

Encuesta de los hábitos y el placer de la escritura	Otoño	Invierno	Primavera
1. Sé cómo escribir.			
2. Soy un buen escritor. Soy una buena escritura.			
3. Se usar las estrategias de escritura.			
4. Escribo mucho.			
5. Me gusta escribir.			
6. Cuando me imagino escribiendo me siento _____ .			
7. Escribo en mi tiempo libre.			

of listening skills, writing samples, and records of reading performance to provide an indication of skills and strategies the student is currently applying independently. When a student has been recommended for LC enrollment, both the LC and classroom instructors analyze baseline data and review student strengths and challenges.

Criteria for placement of students in the LC, and the data needed to make this determination, should be clearly outlined. Rather than subjecting students to additional testing, existing district data that clearly reflect these criteria should be used. Instructors use these data to determine which language strand a student should be placed in and as a basis of progress monitoring to determine if LC instruction is meeting its oracy, literacy, and metacognition goals.

Collaboratively Determine Goals

Once a student has been selected to participate in the LC, discussions among LC and classroom teachers and ESL/bilingual coordinators are conducted to determine where instruction should begin and the goals that will be used to measure student progress. Oracy, literacy, and metacognition goals are addressed through the creation of content and language objectives. For example, **Evelyn Gloria** demonstrates that she understands concepts through her writing and in brief but accurate oral responses (Box 2.3), but is still at the early stages of developing Spanish oracy. **Ai** would also benefit from a focus on oracy, but in different ways. Ai needs much more support with metacognition and development of language for academic purposes because she struggles with both language and content. Although their goals are the same, the types and level of support differ for each of these students.

Specify Content and Language Objectives

To create lessons that are tied to state-content standards and align instruction to grade-level expectations, the LC and classroom teachers work collaboratively to determine how content objectives are developed in each setting. They strive to connect these standards to content themes from the classroom. The content objectives are posted in the learning area of the LC and are reviewed before the lesson is taught to ensure that students understand what they are expected to learn from each lesson. They are addressed again at the conclusion of the lesson so students can reflect on their learning and determine the degree to which they have met the content objectives, which enables them to develop metacognitive awareness.

TABLE 2.4 Assessment Schedules for English as an Additional Language Strand

KINDERGARTEN

	September	October	November	December	January	February	March	April	May	June
Writing	As needed	As needed	As needed	As needed	Formal	As needed	As needed	As needed	As needed	Formal
Reading (running record)					Formal (every two weeks or as needed)	Formal (every two weeks or as needed)	Formal (every two weeks or as needed)	Formal (every two weeks or as needed)	Formal (every two weeks or as needed)	Formal (every two weeks or as needed)
WIDA can-do descriptors	Formal			Formal	As needed		Formal			Formal
High-frequency words					Formal					Formal
ACCESS	Baseline for WIDA can-dos									

GRADES 1–5

	September	October	November	December	January	February	March	April	May	June
Writing	Formal	As needed	As needed	As needed	Formal	As needed	As needed	As needed	As needed	Formal
Reading (running record)	Formal (every two weeks or as needed)	Formal (every two weeks or as needed)	Formal (every two weeks or as needed)	Formal (every two weeks or as needed)	Formal (every two weeks or as needed)	Formal (every two weeks or as needed)	Formal (every two weeks or as needed)	Formal (every two weeks or as needed)	Formal (every two weeks or as needed)	Formal (every two weeks or as needed)
WIDA can-do descriptors	Formal			Formal			Formal			Formal
High-frequency words	Formal				Formal					Formal
ACCESS	Baseline for WIDA can-dos									

ACCESS, Assessing Comprehension and Communication in English State-to-State.

Selection of students for the Literacy Club begins in January when students have had exposure to letters, letter sounds, and concepts of print. This assessment schedule shows what else can be done to assess English learners before January.

	BOX 2.3 Spanish Oral Language Sample: Evelyn Gloria		
Maestro	Hemos estudiado los hábitats de los animales. Evelyn Gloria, ¿qué animal estudiaste?	**Teacher**	*We have studied animal habitats. Evelyn Gloria, which animal did you study?*
Evelyn Gloria	la jirafa		*the giraffe*
Maestro	Y, ¿qué aprendiste sobre su hábitat?		*And, what did you learn about its habitat?*
Evelyn Gloria	need arboles; necks largos [También enseña un dibujo de una jirafa en su habitat.]		*need trees; long necks [She also shows a picture of a giraffe in its habitat.]*
Maestro	¿En qué parte del mundo se encuentran las jirafas?		*In what part of the world do we find giraffes?*
Evelyn Gloria	aquí [indicando África en un mapa]		*here [pointing to Africa on a map]*

Evelyn Gloria understands the content of her science course. Her responses in Spanish are very brief and hesitant. When asked about speaking in Spanish, Evelyn Gloria says she gets nervous and then can't think of what she wants to say in Spanish. Regular, scaffolded opportunities to speak will greatly enhance her speaking ability.

Language objectives are essential for language learners. They address the academic language inherent in the content objective and suggest language supports that students and teachers can use in each lesson to reach that objective. This support is especially important for language learners who may not yet have the academic language needed to be successful in a particular lesson. For example, if the content objective requires students to compare and contrast ideas they have read about, the language objective might focus on words and phrases used to make comparisons: "I will be able to use words and phrases to tell how ideas are the same or different." Sentence frames and examples would be practiced during the week to prepare students for making these comparisons.

The language objective also serves as a reference that students can utilize as they expand their oracy skills in small groups, with partners, or with the whole group. As students become more comfortable with using language for a variety of purposes, they are better able to build on their knowledge of **language for academic purposes** and experience academic success. As with content objectives, language objectives should be made visible and accessible to students. The LC teacher must select language objectives based on students' language strengths and needs that will assist them in working toward content objectives.

Guide Students in Self-Assessing Their Learning

LC students are given opportunities to regularly self-assess and reflect on their performance and perceptions of themselves as learners. LC teachers support students in learning how to accurately self-assess their work through demonstrations and as they collect evidence of student performance and growth. Students self-assess their reading, writing, and strategy development on the first day of the week. Students practice new concepts, skills, and strategies throughout the week, and then repeat the same self-assessment at the end of the week. The self-assessment in Box 2.4 is an example of a form that might be used at both the beginning and the end of the week.

As students become more adept at self-assessing, they generally take greater ownership of their learning because they have developed a clearer sense of how they are progressing

BOX 2.4 Student Self-Assessment of Strategy Usage

Name _____   Date _____

Focus book _____

New words _____

Circle strategy used:

1. Summarizing
2. Making connections
3. Asking questions
4. Rereads
5. Predicting

Write two or three sentences about how the strategy helped you with your reading:

La auto evaluación del uso de estrategias

Nombre _____   Fecha _____

Libro de enfoque _____

Palabras nuevas _____

Rodee la estrategía utilizada:

1. Resumir
2. Hacer conexiones
3. Hacer preguntas
4. Volver a leer
5. Predecir

Escribe dos o tres oraciones acerca de cómo te ayudo esta estrategia mientras leías:

and what goals they need to set for themselves. For example, a student may set the following goal for herself: "I want to learn to read with greater fluency" or "I want to be able to summarize what I've read better."

Occasionally, it is evident from the student self-assessments that they are not yet confident with the new materials/concepts. These self-assessments provide useful data to inform instruction for the following week. For example, if a student indicated that she had met all of the criteria for "word choice" in Box 2.5 but there was little indication of this in the actual writing sample, it would provide a great opportunity for the LC teacher to work with the student on how to actually apply word choice in writing and how to find evidence of good word choice in subsequent writing pieces. As this example indicates, learning to self-assess is a complex process for students and they need a great deal of scaffolding. Self-assessments are collected in individual student folders and present a record of progress in literacy, language, and metacognition over time for review by both the student and the LC teacher.

Differentiate Instruction and Assessment

While planning lessons, LC teachers take the differing needs of students into account and adapt instruction so that students can work toward content and language objectives in meaningful ways. Teachers can use student performance indicators to scaffold, guide, and differentiate instruction for their language learners. For example, a grade 1–2 WIDA can-do writing descriptor at Level 3 states that students will: "(e)ngage in prewriting strategies (e.g., use of graphic organizers)." If it is observed that a particular group of students struggles with this concept, the LC and classroom teachers may design a simplified graphic organizer to be used in both settings. Once students are able to use that form independently, teachers can continually upgrade the graphic organizer until it matches the one used by most students in the classroom. Teachers can also use the can-do descriptors to document student performances and provide evidence of student language development in English and Spanish.

Continuously Monitor Progress

LC teachers carefully monitor student growth to determine if students are progressing at an appropriate rate. Some students progress very quickly to meet goals, while others may need additional support. If students are progressing more quickly than anticipated, learning experiences, expectations, and possibly reading levels in one or both languages are accelerated to make them appropriately challenging for the students. Conversely, when students do not seem to be making adequate progress, the LC and classroom teachers examine the work of the students, evaluate the effectiveness of the learning opportunities, and implement changes in both settings to support enhanced learning for these students. Often groups of students begin at fairly homogeneous levels but become more diverse over time. In these situations, LC teachers may consult with the ESL/bilingual coordinator to reorganize groups or they may opt to further individualize the work of students within the group.

After creating lessons plans, teachers use formative assessment data to monitor and measure student progress on an ongoing basis. At regular intervals during the academic year, the progress of LC students is formally assessed and data compiled using a common set of assessments, as described in the section on assessment as a recursive process. The analysis of the data is used to note individual student progress and to inform instruction.

Each week LC and classroom teachers collaborate on the selection of content and language objectives that reflect grade-level standards and students' linguistic needs. Objectives that students struggle with during the week are included in the following week's objectives statements. Objectives over which students show some degree of mastery but need additional practice (e.g., predicting with evidence or using beginning and ending punctuation)

BOX 2.5 Practicing and Self-Assessing Use of Word Choice

Name _____ Date _____

WORD CHOICE

_____ *Used powerful action words, such as:* _____ _____ _____

_____ *Chose words that create pictures in reader's head*

    1.

    2.

_____ *Used a variety of different words*

_____

_____

_____

_____

_____

_____

_____

_____

_____

_____

_____

_____

_____

_____ *I chose my own topic*

_____ *I worked on the target trait*

_____ *I reread my writing and made changes*

This is how I did with my writing: *3 (very well)*   *2 (average)*   *1 (not very well)* become "review objectives" in subsequent weeks to ensure that students have ample opportunities to fully master them.

PROGRAM ASSESSMENT

Data from LC student performances are analyzed regularly, first and foremost to assess the progress students are making in oracy, literacy, and metacognition. The data can also be used to assess the effectiveness of the program itself. These analyses may lead to changes that improve the efficiency of LC sessions and/or enhance student performance. The results of the data may highlight areas where LC teachers may wish to focus professional development (PD). For example, if students are not making adequate progress with writing, LC teachers may request in-service PD sessions on the effective teaching of writing with language learners, or they may arrange for times to meet as a group and analyze how they might improve student writing on their own. Analysis of students' ability to transfer and apply knowledge gained in the LC to classroom performance, as well as changes in district reading and writing assessment results over time, are other ways that districts may use data to evaluate LC effectiveness.

CONCLUSION

Assessments and goal-setting are integral components of the **continuous progress monitoring** process that underpin the work of the LC and serve as a meaningful guide for designing instruction to meet students' needs. Baseline data determine where students are performing on entry and whether they are likely to benefit from LC participation. They also determine where teachers begin instruction to meet oracy, literacy, and metacognition goals. Content and language objectives are identified in collaboration with classroom teachers. Summative and formative LC assessments, along with district assessment data, are used to monitor student progress on an ongoing and regular basis. Instruction is continually refined and advanced to keep students moving as fully and quickly as possible toward grade-level expectations. Ongoing feedback and student self-assessment characterize daily student–teacher interaction.

QUESTIONS FOR REFLECTION AND ACTION

- Familiarize yourself with formative measures of English and/or Spanish literacy development currently being used in your school/district and discuss the type of information that is provided by each measure. Which measures provide sufficient information about the LC goals of oracy, literacy, and metacognitive development?
- Familiarize yourself with summative measures of English and/or Spanish language assessments, as well as the associated student performance indicators. How can LC teachers use data obtained from these measures?
- What is the most effective information to collect in monitoring student growth over time in oracy, literacy, and metacognition?
- What are effective ways to guide students in enhancing their self-assessment skills?

3

Literacy Club with Language Learners in Kindergarten

KEY CONCEPTS

- A solid base of literacy and oracy skills enhances the opportunities for language learners to reach grade-level literacy and language standards in either bilingual or English-medium settings.
- Metacognitive development related to use of emergent learning strategies and analysis of the structure and use of language are important components of an effective response to instruction and intervention plan at the kindergarten level.
- Assessment measures at this level focus on monitoring emergent literacy skills while emphasizing text comprehension and oracy development.

The kindergarten Literacy Club (LC) is designed for students who are struggling with emergent literacy skills including letter/syllable recognition, letter sounds, concepts of print, and comprehension. **Concepts of print** refer to emergent literacy skills for young children that reflect basic knowledge about how print functions in text. These skills are reinforced through a variety of LC activities. The kindergarten LC begins in the second semester of the school year, after students have had some exposure to emergent literacy skills. They meet, in groups of four or fewer, at least four times per week.

The LC approach stands in contrast to the deficit model we so often see in relation to language learners and struggling readers. It is designed specifically for language learners in either bilingual or English-medium settings, and it views student languages as valuable resources to strengthen literacy and learning through scaffolding and differentiated instruction. Students have the same goals as their classmates but the pathways are differentiated to facilitate learning for each group of students. LC and classroom teachers create a collaborative plan that includes content and language objectives aligned with state standards, as well as **continuous progress monitoring** to support and expand student learning in both the classroom and LC setting.

This chapter first shows a combined **advancing/emerging bilingual strand**, which includes Robe, Ava, Ivan, and Nico. It then discusses an **English as an additional language (EAL) strand** that features our four kindergarten focal students from Chapters 1 and 2 (*Mai, Mario, Pedro*, and *Nhia*). As you read, consider your kindergartners, and how you could develop the kindergarten LC to best match your context. The chapter ends with progress monitoring of the focal students in the EAL strand.

LANGUAGE AND LITERACY DEMANDS

At the kindergarten level, the English language arts (ELA) standards emphasize emergent literacy expectations that include recognition of initial letters and sounds; syllables are emphasized in Spanish language arts. Kindergarten level vocabulary in reading, writing, and speaking is developed. Students learn to identify different types of texts and retell text to compare characters, settings, events, and main topics. They use illustrations in reading and writing to clarify meaning and represent ideas; they are asked to identify what their writing is about in opinion, informational, and narrative genres.

These language and literacy skills will begin to prepare students for grade 1–2 standards that move beyond the kindergarten expectations and include identification and expanded use of details and illustrations in speaking, reading, and writing. Grades 1–2 students are expected to use evidence from text and illustrations to identify and analyze the text narrator and character feelings. In writing, grade 1–2 standards highlight content development with the inclusion of an introduction, supporting evidence, and conclusion for writing in a variety of genres.

Selection of students for the LC is especially critical at this age level because some students excel in the initial development of literacy skills and others would benefit from additional early support in the LC to build the background necessary for successful literacy and **language development**. It is also effective to begin the LC in the second semester of the school year because many kindergartners do not start Guided Reading until then, and the LC follows a similar format.

TEACHER COLLABORATION

One of the many components to the successful implementation of the kindergarten LC is collaboration between the LC and classroom teachers. The kindergarten LC is designed to support and bolster student learning in the classroom. The LC teacher plans along with the classroom teacher to further support the skills and strategies being taught in the classroom. Planning together and mapping students' strengths and challenges before starting the kindergarten LC provides valuable information about each student that helps both the LC and the classroom teacher target individual needs. This collaboration also provides opportunities for the teachers to ensure that the learning experiences are linguistically appropriate and reflect the students' cultures wherever possible.

Reviewing Baseline Data

In addition to other forms of assessment required by each district, and to better understand their language learners as a whole, the classroom and LC teachers use the **Developmental Reading Assessment 2+** (DRA2+; English) and/or the *Evaluación del desarrollo de la lectura 2* (Spanish) tests to gather comparable reading data about each student's accuracy, fluency, and comprehension skills in one or both languages. Because LC students are all language learners, teachers also turn to their state English language development (ELD) frameworks for guidance about what **English learners (ELs)** can be expected to do in English in reading, writing, listening, and speaking at their independent and instructional ELD levels (e.g., the WIDA can-do descriptors). Teachers can complement these data with **formative assessments** of students' reading, writing, listening, and speaking in the other instructional (e.g., Spanish) or home (e.g., Hmong) languages. These multiple data sources give teachers valuable information about how they might scaffold, guide, and differentiate instructional pathways for their language learners to progress to the next level of language development, while also reaching their academic goals.

Co-Planning Content and Language Objectives

Another important aspect of the planning process is making certain that all lesson plans are tied to the Common Core State Standards (CCSS; or other standards endorsed by a particular state or entity) and that all instruction is aligned to grade-level expectations. One way of reaching this goal is for the classroom and LC teachers to collaboratively create content objectives based on the content standards. The content objectives are selected jointly by the LC and classroom teachers, reflecting content themes, concepts, and procedures being targeted in the classroom. Content objectives are about the big ideas of a lesson, and should be more or less the same for all students, including those in the LC. These objectives are posted in the learning area and made easily accessible to students so they understand what they are expected to learn from each lesson. Content objectives are reviewed with the students before the lesson is taught to ensure that they are prepared for what they will be expected to accomplish. They are addressed again at the conclusion of the lesson to enable them to reflect on their learning and determine to what degree they have met the content objectives.

In addition to creating content objectives, language objectives are essential for language learners and are derived from the content objectives to help guide instruction in developing appropriate academic language. Language objectives serve as a foundation for formative assessment for teachers throughout each lesson and provide a clear path for students to demonstrate what they have learned. For example, if students are to predict with evidence, they need to know what the terms "predict" and "evidence" mean and how they are used in relation to text. They also need to be able to express their predictions and supply supporting evidence; hence the following sentence frame would be useful: "I predict _____ because in the book it says _____."

The language objectives are also posted in the learning area, and they address the academic language in the content objectives and suggest language supports that students and teachers can use in each lesson to reach the content objective/standard. This support is especially important for language learners who may not yet have developed the academic language needed to be successful in a particular lesson. Teachers differentiate language objectives according to students' language development levels and the languages they use for instructional purposes. The language objective serves as a reference that students can use as they share in small groups, with a partner, or with the whole group. As students become more comfortable with using language for a variety of purposes, they are better able to build on their knowledge of **language for academic purposes** and experience academic success.

Careful selection of language objectives that match students' linguistic levels enables LC teachers to differentiate instruction in meaningful ways. Use of Spanish or other home languages serves as a resource for reaching the same high content objectives, which are aligned with the standards. Examples of content and language objectives, and how they are connected to the CCSS, are available in sample kindergarten lessons that follow. Each week, new content and language objectives are identified for students. Also, in keeping with the recursive nature of the LC, review objectives (objectives that were introduced in earlier lessons but that students have not yet fully mastered) are also listed. The additional practice helps ensure that students begin to use these skills and strategies with confidence.

CONTINUOUS PROGRESS MONITORING

At the kindergarten level it is often tempting to focus primarily on emergent word/syllable analysis skills with students. However, care is taken in the LC also to monitor student progress in reading comprehension for a variety of purposes and the application of reading and writing strategies. Formative assessment plans continuously monitor student growth in

oracy, **literacy**, and **metacognition** (metalanguage and strategy development). Student self-assessment is introduced in kindergarten so students learn how to monitor their own growth and verbalize how use of strategies and analysis of language support their learning. Continuous progress monitoring is used in every strand, and is illustrated in this chapter with Mai, Mario, Pedro, and Nhia in the EAL strand.

TEXT SELECTION

Book selection is a critical component in preparation for LC sessions. Texts must provide opportunities for students to build background knowledge, make meaningful connections to the content being studied in the classroom, and acquire vocabulary and language structure to meet the content and language objectives. While less challenging at this emergent level of literacy, LC teachers must select materials that meet required objectives but are within students' literacy development levels to help ensure student confidence and success. They also search for texts that can expand background knowledge and reflect the students' cultures and experiences as often as possible. Generally, LC texts are not the same as those used in the classroom.

EMERGING/ADVANCING BILINGUAL STRAND

At the kindergarten level, the emerging and advancing Spanish bilingual learners are integrated into a single group. Generally, the emerging bilinguals need support in Spanish not only for reading and writing activities, but also for developing initial vocabulary and oracy to understand and express understanding of content. These bilingual students may come from homes where English is spoken and be enrolled in a **dual language program**, or they may be students who speak varying degrees of English and Spanish who need support with oral language and literacy development in one or both languages. The advancing bilingual learners generally have well-developed oral language skills for social purposes but struggle with literacy development and using language for academic purposes. Because all of the students are emergent readers, there is not a wide range of literacy skills with LC students at this level. As a result, the emerging Spanish bilingual learners will likely benefit from regular and focused exposure to the language of the more experienced Spanish speakers in the group. Furthermore, during the bridging to English portion of the lesson, emergent English bilingual learners will benefit from the language skills of the more experienced English speakers in the group. (Recall that the bridge is the instructional moment when teachers help students strategically connect what they have learned in one language [e.g., Spanish] to the other language [e.g., English]. The bridge is also the time that teachers engage students in **comparative analysis** of the two languages, which not only strengthens students' oracy and literacy, but also supports their development of **metalinguistic awareness**.) All are likely to benefit from structured support for literacy development.

In the example for Spanish literacy instruction in this chapter, kindergarten students participate in LC sessions 4 days per week (Table 3.1), though the schedule could certainly be extended to 5 days per week. Also, in this example, students are immersed in Spanish instruction for 3 days; on day 4, teachers implement the bridge from Spanish to English. Depending on the students' needs, this schedule could be reversed to focus on English instruction on days 1–3 and bridging to Spanish on day 4, for students who need more support in English literacy and oracy.

Students' experiences with language outside of school are clearly reflected in their initial language skills as they begin work in the LC. Each of them brings language resources that enhance the work of the group. Of the students in this advancing/emerging bilingual

	Day 1	Day 2	Day 3	Day 4

Focus book	Introduction
	Echo read
	Self-assess
		Choral read
		Discuss
		    strategy
			Choral read
			Discuss
			    strategy
				Independent read
				Bridge general ideas

Word work	Spanish concepts *Dictado*	Spanish concepts *Dictado*	Spanish concepts *Dictado*	Cognates
Rereads	Pairs	Pairs	Independent	Independent
Writing	Spanish: LEA	Spanish: LEA	Spanish: Self- selected	Modified: *Así se dice*

TABLE 3.1 Format for Kindergarten Emerging/Advancing Spanish Bilingual Strand

LEA, language experience approach.

strand, Robe speaks only Spanish at home and relies on scaffolding and interactions with classmates when using English at school. Ava's family speaks only English and she relies on scaffolding and help from classmates when using Spanish at school. Ivan and Nico respond in both English and Spanish and often use **translanguaging** (drawing on their language resources creatively in both Spanish and English when expressing themselves orally and in writing). During the LC, students build off the array of linguistic and literacy strengths represented by the group.

Sessions generally last about 30 minutes each day, though they may be shorter initially and increase to 30 minutes or more as students build stamina. Content and language objectives are prepared for the week and reviewed with the students. A small number of objectives (1–2) are new for the week and taught intensively, while 1–2 objectives introduced in previous weeks but not yet completely mastered constitute the review objectives, as seen in Box 3.1. Objectives are posted along with picture cues to ensure student understanding.

Students complete self-assessments of the new objectives at the beginning and end of the week (Fig. 3.1). The review objectives are practiced and assessed more informally throughout the week(s).

The following plan provides an example of how the various components of a text might be developed at the kindergarten level for emerging/advancing bilinguals in the LC. This sample features development of a book in a one-week timeframe, though initially it often takes longer than a single week for students to master the first texts.

The LC teacher has written and illustrated a brief text to extend the theme "How can we be healthy and take care of ourselves?" being studied in the classroom. The classroom and LC teachers have noted that the students in the LC group continue to struggle with the strategy of using illustrations to inform text; therefore, this strategy is the focus in both settings for these students. The text reinforces the topic of "How does clothing help protect us from the weather?" which is a component of the overall classroom theme. The plan represents an integration of social studies and literacy. In social studies, the students focus on how clothing protects us from the weather and in literacy they practice using illustrations to support comprehension and writing on a single topic.

Focus Book

The **focus book** for this week is titled *Mi ropa*, and it reinforces the theme "clothing protects us from the weather" that organizes learning in the mainstream classroom at this time. The LC teacher introduces the focus book on day 1 by reviewing parts of the book

BOX 3.1 Content and Language Objectives for the Week

Tema	La ropa nos protege del tiempo.	Theme	*Clothing protects us from the weather.*

OBJETIVOS NUEVOS/NEW OBJECTIVES

Contenido	Yo podré usar las ilustraciones para ayudarme a leer.	Content	*I will be able to use illustration to help me read.*
	Yo podré escribir oraciones sobre como la ropa nos protege del tiempo.		*I will be able to write sentences about how clothing protects us from the weather.*
Lenguaje	Yo podré escribir oraciones para describir la ropa.	Language	*I will be able to write sentences to describe clothing.*

REVISAMOS/REVIEW OBJECTIVES*

	Yo podré formar y leer sílabas.		*I will be able to make and read syllables.*
	Yo podré nombrar y describir las partes de un libro.		*I will be able to name/describe parts of a book.*
	Yo podré usar letras mayúsculas y puntos.		*I will be able to use capital letters and periods.*

*Objectives introduced in previous lessons that need additional practice.

Nombre _____   Fecha _____

Yo puedo usar las ilustraciones para ayudarme a leer.   *I can use illustrations to help me read.*

Me pongo mi sombrero.   *I put on my hat.*

3	2	1
Fácil	Más o menos	Difícil
(Easy)	(Average)	(Difficult)

Yo puedo escribir oraciones sobre la ropa.   *I can write sentences about clothing.*

Me pongo mis pantalones.   *I put on my pants.*

3	2	1
Fácil	Más o menos	Dificil
(Easy)	(Average)	(Difficult)

Figure 3.1 Student beginning- and end-of-week self-assessment of objectives. Note that this is an emergent-level student self-assessment. Students self-assess their level of comfort with the content and language objectives at the beginning of the week and again at the end of the week.

and conducting a picture walk to name the items on each page. Here is the written text in Spanish with an English translation.

Mi ropa	**My Clothes**
Me pongo mi camisa.	*I put on my shirt.*
Me pongo mis pantalones.	*I put on my pants.*
Me pongo mis botas.	*I put on my boots.*
Me pongo mi sombrero.	*I put on my hat.*
Me pongo mis zapatos.	*I put on my shoes.*
Me pongo mi abrigo.	*I put on my jacket.*
Me pongo me ropa.	*I put on my clothes.*

The teacher also works with the children to develop the accompanying total physical response (TPR) activity. Recall that **TPR** is a language teaching method that links speech and actions to help students remember key vocabulary and concepts. Students then echo and/or choral read with the LC teacher, depending on their needs, and use the TPR actions.

Using Illustrations to Comprehend Text

The following vignette of classroom interaction shows how the LC teacher introduces the content objective strategy of using picture cues to gain meaning from text. The students in this group often struggle with comprehending the content of text. Focusing on metacognitive strategies such as using illustrations to support meaning and using support activities like TPR strengthens their use of the strategy and their comprehension of text. The LC teacher is careful to highlight what the strategy is and how it supports them in their reading and provides multiple opportunities for students to reflect on these two points.

Teacher	Mira la portada. ¿Qué tenemos aquí?	*Look at the cover. What do we have here?*
Ivan	Tenemos la ropa.	*We have clothes.*
Teacher	¿Qué tenemos aquí?	*What do we have here?*
Nico	a shirt	
Teacher	Sí hay una camisa. ¿Qué acción podemos usar para --mi camisa--? [indicando a sí misma] Me pongo mi camisa.	*Yes, there is a shirt. What action could we use for "my shirt"? [pointing to herself] I put on my shirt.*

The teacher continues the activity in the same way—having students use the illustrations to comprehend the new words and choosing a TPR action for each of the new words (pants, boots, hat, shoes, coat, clothes) and phrases (I put on my _____). Next, the LC teacher explicitly relates the new vocabulary to the theme (clothing protects us from the weather) by showing the students pictures of clothing worn in various climates and encouraging them to discuss how clothing protects us from inclement weather. The teacher concludes this activity by explicitly teaching the metacognitive strategy of using illustrations to comprehend text.

This example clearly shows the pathways and types of supports that may be used to develop a solid base of oracy for literacy development. Scaffolding oral language comprehension through use of visuals and TPR movements helps ensure that the language used in the reading is comprehensible and meaningful for all of the students. Note that Ivan responded completely in Spanish and served as a language model for the other students, who had less proficiency in Spanish. Nico understood the context, but was able to respond only in English. The LC teacher accepted his responses and repeated them using the appropriate terms in Spanish, thereby acknowledging what he did know and modeling the vocabulary in Spanish. Each child's language abilities are viewed as resources to be continually expanded through these activities.

On day 2, the LC teacher and the students choral read the text using the TPR actions they devised on day 1. The LC teacher reinforces use of picture clues with each reading and highlights when one or more of the children use the strategy independently. On day 3, students read the book with a partner. On day 4, students read the focus book independently in Spanish and orally share the bridging activity described in the writing portion of the session. Each day the teacher and the students continue their discussion of the theme, discussing how wearing the appropriate clothing protects us and keeps us healthy. Sentence frames such as, "*Me pongo_____ para protegerme del _____.*" ("I put on _____ to protect me from _____."), help all students, especially emerging bilinguals, to participate more fully in the conversation.

Word Work

A small number of new words from the current story are printed on word cards and placed on word rings for the students. As a student transitions to the *formando palabras*/word work component of the session each day, he or she quickly reviews the new words independently. The LC teacher observes which words students are able to recognize as sight words or sound out by syllables, and which words they find most difficult. Words from the word rings may be incorporated into word work activities for the week.

Words that students struggle with at the end of the week remain on the word rings for the next week, or until they become automatic sight words. The number of words on the ring should be manageable for the student and should not exceed about 4–6 words at this level. If students struggle each week to learn the new words, it may indicate that the reading material being used is beyond their instructional level at the moment and should be adjusted or further scaffolded.

Forming and Reading Syllables

The LC teacher begins by introducing syllables, found in one or more key vocabulary words for the week, in this case, for the sound /b/ in *ba, be, bi, bo, bu.* Students put the letter cards or magnetic letters b, a, e, i, o, u in front of them. (LC teachers generally prepare packets of the letter cards in advance to save time during the lesson and have students sort the vowels from the consonants before beginning.) The ability to form and read syllables is a critical word analysis skill in emergent Spanish literacy. Here we see that Ava and Robe are just beginning to form some syllables independently, but need a great deal of practice to become proficient with this skill. The LC teacher highlights syllable formation in the word work section in every session because this has a positive impact on the students' literacy development.

Teacher	Tenemos una palabra nueva que empieza con /bo/, botas. ¿Qué acción usamos para --las botas--?	*One of our new words begins with /bo/, (botas) boots. What action do we use for "boots?"*
	(Students perform TPR action for boots.)	
Teacher	Muy bien. La palabra tiene 2 sílabas. ¿Podemos formar las sílabas para --botas-- juntos?	*Very good. The word has two syllables. Can we form the syllables for --botas-- together?*
Robe	Sí, /bo/ /tas/.	*Yes, /bo/ /tas/.*

These syllables and the word *"botas"* would be practiced on days 1–3. On day 4, the LC teacher and the students explore English cognates—words that mean the same thing and are similar in spelling in both English and Spanish—in the text together. In this sample text, they would most likely note similarities between "pants" and *"pantalones."* The cognate pairs are put on a chart, displayed in the LC area, and reviewed regularly.

Rereads

Students use TPR actions as they read each day. On days 1–2 students reread previously mastered texts in pairs; on day 3 they reread independently. If students need more support, they may continue reading in pairs for a longer period of time. The LC teacher listens to individual children read during this time and notes when they are using picture cues as a strategy. At the end of the reread session, ways in which individual children have used picture cues or other strategies are shared with the group to help them internalize use of the strategy. On day 4 students reread one of the Spanish texts independently along with the English translation completed during the writing segment of a previous week.

Writing

On days 1 and 2 the LC teacher conducts a modified **language experience approach (LEA)** with the students. LEA activities evolve from a shared experience the students have had. In this case, the students have read the same text and explored ideas about how clothing protects us from the weather. Students are invited to provide sentences that describe, analyze, or evaluate the experience and the teacher writes exactly what the students dictate on a chart. The LC teacher and students may then revise and edit the piece, and it becomes a shared reading and writing activity for the group.

The text highlighted for this example requires readers to use either a singular (*mi*) or a plural (*mis*) possessive pronoun, depending on the picture on each page. On day 3, the LC teacher would use these pictures but not show the written text. Together they would say the word syllable by syllable for the first picture (*camisa*) as the teacher writes it on a dry erase board. The students determine whether the pronoun should be "*mi*" or "*mis*," depending on whether the word is singular or plural.

Analyzing Language Structure: Singular and Plural

The following vignette highlights how the LC teacher weaves the study of singular and plural formation of words with a discussion of the theme under study. Ivan and Robe actively participate in this activity, and they seem to have a good sense of the singular and plural pronouns. Although Ava and Nico don't orally contribute because of their earlier stages of Spanish development, the LC teacher watches to see that they are nonverbally participating using their fingers or silently moving their lips. The LC teacher then proceeds with a discussion of how the various articles of clothing protect us from the weather. This integration provides students with the tools to expand their understanding of both language structure and discourse.

Teacher	¿Hay una camisa o más de una camisa en el dibujo?	*Is there one shirt or more than one shirt in the picture?*
Robe	una camisa	*one shirt*
Teacher	Si hay solamente un objeto, vamos a usar --mi--. Si tenemos más de un objeto, vamos a usar --mis--. Entonces, ¿vamos a usar --mi-- o --mis-- con --camisa--	*If there is only one object, we are going to use --mi-- [my]. If we have more than one object we will use --mis-- [my, plural]. So, are we going to use --mi-- or --mis-- with --camisa--?*

Robe	mi camisa	*(my) --mi-- shirt*
Teacher	Muy bien. Ahora van a ayudarme a escribir la palabra --zapatos--.	*Very good. Now you can help me write the word "shoes."*
	¿Hay un zapato o más de un zapato?	*Is there one shoe or more than one shoe?*
Ivan	Hay dos zapatos.	*There are two shoes.*
Teacher	Vamos a decir --mi-- o --mis-- zapatos?	*Are we going to say --mi-- or --mis-- zapatos [shoes]?*
Ivan	mis zapatos	*my [--mis--] shoes*
Teacher	¿Por qué?	*Why?*
Robe	Porque hay más de un zapato.	*Because there is more than one shoe.*

The LC teacher continues with additional singular and plural pronouns in the same manner. She will help them apply the formation of singulars and plurals in subsequent structured and independent writing activities. Immediate feedback helps them internalize this concept over time.

The students write the phrases (*mi camisa, mis zapatos,* etc.) in their booklets and draw a picture for each on day 1. On day 2, they add the phrase "*Me pongo _____*" ("I put on _____") to each phrase to form sentences, as shown in the next section, and practice reading the new sentences, first to themselves and then to a partner. The teacher guides the students in using the pictures to review how the various articles of clothing protect us from the weather.

Writing Expanded Sentences

The following guided writing activity illustrates how the LC teacher provides scaffolding for emergent writers to guide them in expanding their ideas. The language objective developed in this activity focuses on guiding students to formulate written responses from oral language. The content objectives ask students to use capital letters and periods while writing sentences about clothing. The LC teacher completes an example with the students, reviews the concept, and then asks them to self-assess their use of this strategy in their writing.

Teacher	Vamos a añadir las palabras --Me pongo-- al principio de cada frase que escribimos ayer para formar unas oraciones. [señalando el ejemplo en la pizarra] Empezamos con --mi camisa-- y yo voy a escribir --Me pongo-- enfrente. Ahora ¿podemos leer la oración?	*Let's add the words "I put on" to the beginning of each phrase that we wrote yesterday to form sentences. [pointing at the example on the board] We started with "my shirt" and I am going to write "I put on" in front of that. Can we read the sentence now?*
All	Me pongo mi camisa.	*I put on my shirt.*
Teacher	¿Qué tipo de letra usamos con la primera letra de una palabra en una oración?	*What kind of letter do we use to start the first word of a sentence?*
All	mayúscula	*capital*
Teacher	Sí. [subraya la --M-- mayúscula] Y, ¿como terminamos la oración?	*Yes. [underlining the capital "M"] And how do we end a sentence?*
All	con un punto	*with a period*
Teacher	muy bien [subraya el punto]	*very good [underlines the period]*

As the students tried the lesson on their own, they were unclear about what they were being asked to do, so the LC teacher continued to complete each sentence with them. The next day, the concept is reviewed and students have the opportunity to practice again. Having students read and reread their sentences is an important part of the writing process. It gives them the opportunity to focus on writing for communication and also expands their repertoire of sight words recognized in their own writing.

Students use the writing sheet in Box 3.2 to write their sentences and draw pictures of what they have written. They then self-assess that they have used capital letters at the beginning of each sentence, a period at the end, and the correct form of "*mi/mis.*" The student has the rubric at the top of the page to use as a guide while writing and to self-assess when work is completed. They complete this self-assessment before sharing their sentences with a classmate, assigning a rating of 1 to 3 to their writing. The LC teacher works with individual students to complete the self-assessment. Prior to writing, students tell a partner what they plan to write, providing oral rehearsal of content, sentence structure, and vocabulary.

On day 3 students can continue with this activity if they have not finished, or they can write and draw independently in Spanish, sharing what they plan to write with a partner prior to beginning the actual writing. Independent writing provides students with the

---

BOX 3.2 Student Writing and Self-Assessment Sheet

Nombre _____   Fecha _____

Rúbrica: Dibujo:

_____ Me pongo (letra mayúscula)
        (*capital letter*)

_____ . (punto) (*period*)

_____ mi/mis ("*my*" *singular and plural*)

_____

_____

_____

_____

_____

_____ Yo puedo escribir oraciones sobre la ropa.   *I can write sentences about clothing.*

                    1   2   3

          Fácil (*Easy*)   Más o menos (*Average*)   Difícil (*Difficult*)

opportunity to use their emerging skills to develop their own topics. As their skills become stronger, they generally chose to do more independent writing at this point in the week.

On day 4 students participate in a modified ***Así se dice*** (That's how you say it), which is a metalinguistic strategy that allows students to consciously explore meaning and language structure between the two languages (Escamilla et al, 2014). Prior to this comparative analysis activity, the LC teacher determines what aspects of language are to be reinforced.

Comparing Plural and Possessive in Spanish and English

In this vignette of classroom interaction, students explore plurals and differences in formation of pronouns in Spanish and English, which is aligned with the word work activities for the week. The students are given the following phrases one at a time. They collaboratively review each phrase in Spanish and share their ideas for how each could be said in English. With the help of the LC teacher, they decipher and write each English phrase on a card, which they clip to the appropriate page of the Spanish text and use as part of their day 4 focus book bridging activity.

mis pantalones _____

mis botas _____

mis zapatos _____

mi sombrero _____

Teacher	¿Pueden leer esta frase? [enseña la frase --mis pantalones--]	*Can you read this phrase? [pointing to the phrase "my pants"]*
All	mis pantalones	*my pants*
Teacher	¿Cómo podemos decir --mis pantalones-- en inglés?	*How do we say --mis pantalones-- in English?*
Robe	my pantses	
Teacher	Casi. Decimos "my pants." Repitan, "my pants." ¿Cómo decimos "my" en español? Sí, decimos --mis-- en español y "my" en inglés. [Escribe las 2 palabras en la pizarra].	*Almost. We say "my pants." Repeat, "my pants." How do we say "my" in Spanish? Yes, We say --mis-- in Spanish and "my" in English. [She writes the two words on the board.]*
Teacher	¿Pueden leer esta frase? --mis botas-- ¿Cómo podemos decir --mis botas-- en inglés?	*Can you read this phrase, "my boots"? How do we say --mis botas-- in English?*
Nico	my boats	
Teacher	--Botas-- sueña como "boats" en inglés, pero mira el dibujo [enseña el dibujo de las botas]. Ahora, ¿qué piensas?	*--Botas-- sounds like "boats" in English, but look at the picture [points to the picture of the boots]. Now, what do you think?*
Nico	my boots	
Teacher	¿Cómo decimos "my boot" en español?	*How do we say "my boot" in Spanish?*
Ava	mi bota	*my boot*
Teacher	Sí, en inglés decimos, "my boot" y "my boots." Pero en español decimos, --mi bota-- y --mis botas--. [Escribe las frases en un gráfico.]	*Yes, in English we say, "my boot" and "my boots." But in Spanish we say --mi bota-- and --mis botas--. [She writes the words on a chart.]*

As the teacher continues with additional examples, the students have the opportunity to refine their understanding of content and language structure in *Así se dice* activities. For example, Robe used what he knew of vocabulary and formation of plurals to suggest that "pantses" was the equivalent of "*pantalones*" in Spanish. and Nico learned about the difference between "boats" and "boots" in English. These are valuable learning experiences because students explore how each language is structured and functions and refine their sense of bilingual language practices.

This example also highlights the linguistically and culturally relevant foundations of the LC. Unlike traditional bilingual pedagogy, in which the languages are strictly separated, the LC recognizes the benefit of **scaffolding** instruction and providing opportunities for students to delve into the structure and meaning of their languages to more fully embrace their bilingualism.

After this portion of the lesson is completed, the LC teacher reviews singular and plural formation of the preceding nouns in English and Spanish. They read each page of the text in Spanish and then in English, discussing what the students have learned about how the languages are similar or different and how they learn about their languages to use them as learning resources, The students are given time to practice the Spanish/English text with a partner. On day 4, this becomes the reading material for the *libro nuevo*/focus book portion of the LC session.

ENGLISH AS AN ADDITIONAL LANGUAGE STRAND

The literacy-based EAL strand sessions are conducted in English and are intended for ELs who are in English-medium classrooms with little, if any, access to first language instruction. The students in this strand may represent a wide variety of home languages, cultures, and background knowledge. This heterogeneity may be used to great advantage in expanding the prior knowledge and creative thinking for the students. Table 3.2 provides an overview of the organization of the LC for the literacy-based EAL strand.

The kindergarten EAL strand example that follows is based on the use of Readers' and Writers' Workshop, which is generally structured as a brief mini-lesson, followed by a block of independent work time, and concluded with a sharing session. Each component of the workshop sessions revolves around language and literacy objectives (expressed as "learning targets" in this example). Table 3.3 provides an overview of the collaborative efforts among the classroom and LC teachers to design the content and language objectives based on CCSS ELA and WIDA ELD standards for LC students. Focusing on the same objectives,

TABLE 3.2 Format for Kindergarten English as an Additional Language Strand

	Day 1	Day 2	Day 3	Day 4	Day 5
Focus book	Introduction Choral read Strategy Self-assess	Partner read Discuss strategy	Independent read Discuss strategy	Independent read Discuss strategy	Independent read Self-assess
Word work	Onset and rime Word patterns	Onset and rime Word patterns	Onset and rime Word patterns	Onset and rime Word patterns	Onset and rime Word patterns
Rereads	Pairs and discuss	Pairs and discuss	Independent	Independent	Independent
Writing	Self-selected	Self-selected	Self-selected	Self-selected	Share writing

TABLE 3.3 Sample of Collaborative Kindergarten Content and Language Objectives

READER'S WORKSHOP

	Monday	Tuesday	Wednesday	Thursday	Friday
Content objectives	I can find and review all the parts of a book.	I can name the tasks I can do at the listening and library centers.	I can name the tasks I can do at the name center.	I can name the tasks I can do at the poem and writing centers.	I can name the tasks I can do at the ABC center.
Language objectives	With turn-and-talk partners, students can orally describe the parts of a book using the sentence frame "This is the _____ because _____." They need to include vocabulary such as front, back, title, author, title page, and illustrator.	Using picture clues and/or anchor charts, students can orally describe the jobs at the listening center using sequential vocabulary such as first, second, next, then, last. Sentence frame: "First (second, next, then, last), I _____."	Using pictures clues and/or anchor charts, students can orally describe the jobs at the name center using sequential vocabulary such as first, second, next, then, last. Sentence frame: "First (second, next, then, last), I _____."	Using picture clues and or anchor charts, students can orally describe the jobs at the poem and writing center using sequential vocabulary such as first, second, next, then, last. Sentence frame: "First (second, next, then, last), I _____."	Using picture clues and/or anchor charts, students can orally describe the jobs at the ABC center using sequential vocabulary such as first, second, next, then, last. Sentence frame: "First (second, next, then, last), I _____."

WRITER'S WORKSHOP

	Monday	Tuesday	Wednesday	Thursday	Friday
Content objectives	I can add details (emotions) to my pictures.	I can add details (emotions) to my pictures.	I can go back and add to my words (label) when I think I am done writing.	I can go back and add details to my pictures when I think I am done writing.	I can reread my story, checking my words and pictures and then start a new story.
Language objectives	Students can visually point to their details and orally describe the details they added to their pictures using the sentence frame "I added _____ to my picture." They should include vocabulary words appropriate to their pictures.	Students can visually point to their details and orally describe the details they added to their pictures using the sentence frame "I added _____ to my picture." They should include vocabulary words appropriate to their pictures.	Students can visually point to the labels in their writing and use the sentence frame "I added _____ to my writing." They should include vocabulary words appropriate to their pictures.	Students can visually point to their details and orally describe the details they added to their pictures using the sentence frame "I added _____ to my picture." They should include vocabulary words appropriate to their pictures.	Students can identify what rereading is by correctly using concepts of print (one to one, starting at the beginning of the book, etc.).

strategies, and use of language for academic purposes in both settings provides a more comprehensive approach to oracy and literacy development for students who are learning EAL and struggling with literacy development.

The content and language objectives are embedded in the LC design and the LC teacher uses them to help guide instruction and align/reinforce skills and strategies being taught in the general classroom. Usually, the LC teacher teaches the same language objective as the classroom teacher; however, in the event that a specific skill or **strategy** needs to be added or retaught to meet individual student needs, the LC teacher would differentiate the language objective(s). At times, the LC teacher might preteach the next week's language objective that will be used in the classroom so that the EL students can participate more fully in classroom activities. Therefore, the LC teacher selects language objectives that support the development of the content objectives and match her students' language strengths and needs, while paralleling classroom learning objectives as closely as possible. This is a good example of how LC teachers use the same goals, but scaffold learning through different pathways.

The kindergarten EAL LC strand example highlights work with our four focal students, Mai, Mario, Pedro, and Nhia. Each of these students has been struggling with comprehension, as reflected by DRA2+ assessments of accuracy, fluency, and comprehension, though all have a relatively firm grasp of emergent reading strategies. Two of the four students are also struggling with transferring oral ideas to writing. The teachers also consider students' ELD levels, with attention to what students can be expected to do in reading, writing, listening, and speaking in English, independently and with appropriate scaffolding and support. After reviewing the data, the LC and classroom teachers chose to collaboratively supplement comprehension through interactive picture walks, reinforcement of new vocabulary, and retelling activities. LEA charts for shared writing and oral rehearsal for independent writing can provide support in this area. To support the classroom theme of "What makes a family?", students focus on oral rehearsal for writing and writing 2–3 sentences on a single topic. They assess progress through additional **running records** of fluency and comprehension and use of district-level writing rubrics to measure writing progress.

Letters and Sounds

The LC sessions for kindergartners begin with a quick read of the letters and sounds on an alphabet chart placed in the learning area. After this, students are given whiteboards for a quick check of about five letters and sounds. For example, the teacher might say, "T, /t/, /t/, turtle," and the students are expected to write the letter "t" on their whiteboards. This is a quick activity and should last no longer than 2–3 minutes, but it provides needed reinforcement of basic skills that students have not yet mastered. Once the students are able to readily recognize and write all of the letters of the alphabet, this activity can be discontinued.

Focus Book

At the beginning of the week, the teacher introduces a new focus book and a reading strategy. Two important reading strategies at this level are using picture clues and using beginning sounds to analyze unknown words. These two strategies go hand in hand and leveled books at this stage of reading provide ample opportunities for students to learn how to use picture clues and beginning sounds while reading.

On day 1, the teacher introduces the focus book and points out its title and author. This helps build common language and understanding of concepts of print because they also focus on these terms in the general classroom. In addition to stating the title and author of the book, the teacher does a picture walk and introduces the strategy they will be working on for the next week or longer. For example, if there is a picture of a tiger in the book, the teacher points to the word "tiger" and questions, "Why can't this word be 'bear'?" The teacher waits for students' response and then asks, "What is the first sound you hear in the word 'bear'?" Again, after waiting for students' response, the teacher points to the word "tiger" and asks, "Does this word begin with the /b/ sound?" The LC teacher can help scaffold the activity as to why the word cannot be "bear" using picture clues or the beginning sound of the word. Once the picture walk is finished, the teacher and students choral read the text. This is helpful for students because they hear and see certain words they might not have known if they were reading independently.

During the book walk, in addition to visiting the vocabulary and content objectives mutually agreed on with the classroom teacher, the LC teacher focuses on the language from the book/text and the language that the students need to use to understand the text and reach the content objective. For example, if a book has the language pattern of "Come here____," the LC teacher can do TPR movements with students. The language in the book should not come as a surprise to the students; therefore, the language needs to be front-loaded or pretaught so students are successful as they read the book.

Using Total Physical Response to Reinforce the Language of the Text

This vignette of classroom interaction illustrates what TPR might sound like. The LC teacher repeats the new phrase several times and has students use movement to reinforce meaning before they encounter the language in the text. In addition to the repetition, the students enjoy moving about and acting out the phrase.

Teacher	In this book, we will see the language pattern "come here" a lot. [Teacher shows the students the language on several pages.] We are going to act out those words. I would like Mai to go over by the door. When I say, "Come here, Mai," what do you think Mai should do? [Mai goes over to the door.]
Pedro and Nhia	She should come here.

(Mai goes over to the door.)

Teacher	"Come here, Mai." [LC teacher uses her hand to gesture Mai to come back, while using the language "come here." Mai responds by coming back to the table.]

On day 2, the LC teacher reinforces the reading strategy the students are working on. For example, the teacher might say, "Yesterday, we talked about how we can use picture clues to help us in our reading. Can someone tell me what this means?" After the students explain and show what they understand about picture clues, the teacher demonstrates the use of picture clues in the text they are reading, as was done on day 1. After the strategy has been reviewed, students partner-read. As the pairs of students find a comfortable spot in the room to read, the teacher circulates and listens to each pair read and takes anecdotal notes about their reading behaviors.

Teachers' anecdotal notes might include comments regarding the word analysis strategies used, fluency, or partner scaffolding (students helping each other). Once students have finished reading the book they may read the book again if other pairs are still reading/ conferencing with the teacher. When the students and LC teacher reconvene, the teacher reviews the anecdotal notes about the students' work, making sure to share positive comments about the children's reading behaviors.

For example, the teacher could say, "On page 11, I saw Pedro pause, look at the picture, and make a connection to the first letter sound of this word." The teacher points to the word on page 11 and asks Pedro what the word is. He reads the word and explains how he figured it out using the picture and the first letter sound. This commenting is critical because it reinforces the importance of using strategies, provides opportunities for students to articulate how they apply strategies, and helps them realize how they are internalizing use of the strategies, all of which strengthens **metacognitive awareness** and supports efforts to use oral language to explain how strategies support learning. This practice helps students feel confident about their emerging reading skills. Anecdotal notes are kept with the students' reading materials so that the teacher can evaluate and analyze their progress in the use of strategies on a regular basis. Box 3.3 shows examples of anecdotal notes for a single student.

BOX 3.3 Anecdotal Notes

Student name: <u>Pedro</u> **Date:** <u>2-21</u>	**Student name:** <u>Pedro</u> **Date:** <u>3-22</u>

Student name: <u>Pedro</u>   **Date:** <u>2-21</u>

Book: *Come Here*

Rereading the book

Strategies/Reading behaviors

- *come*—substituted *can*. Teacher assistance to reread, paying attention to the beginning sound and meaning
- *here*—new vocabulary, teacher assistance

Student name: <u>Pedro</u>   **Date:** <u>3-22</u>

Book: *Where Is My Dog?*

Rereading the book

Strategies/Reading behaviors

- Uses picture clues
- Stops after making a miscue

Student name: <u>Pedro</u>   **Date:** <u>4-18</u>

Book: *My Party*

Rereading the book

Strategies/Reading behaviors

- Picture + first letter
- Shared using picture and first letter
- Sound for new word, "party"
- Uses meaning
- Beginning to reread

Student name: <u>Pedro</u>   **Date:** <u>5-10</u>

Book: *Time to Play*

Rereading the book

Strategies/Reading behaviors

- Rereads *play*—substituted with *party*, reread and self-corrected
- Uses picture cues + first letter
- Uses context clues

On days 3–5, students read independently. As the students do so, the teacher listens to each student, notes the strategies being used, and again points out the strategies used by each student, especially if they use the new strategy being developed. The LC teacher may also elect to conduct running records during this time. On day 5, LC students self-assess their reading behaviors. LC teachers record responses as needed for those students who are as yet unable to complete them independently.

The goal is to have all students reading the book fluently. Progressing from choral to independent reading, the teacher lessens the degree of scaffolding throughout the week so students become increasingly independent in their reading. After spending at least one week on a book, students should be able to read the book with complete accuracy, which means they can read and understand the book in its entirety. Once students gain this level of mastery with the focus book, it becomes a reread book the following week.

Word Work

New words from the current story are printed on small word cards and placed on word rings for each student to practice, as described earlier in this chapter. Next, students are given a set of preselected magnetic letters for word work. The level of difficulty of the word work should mirror their instructional reading level. Word work focuses on words within the focus book or that are currently being studied in the classroom. The purpose of word work is to guide students in recognizing the letter sounds and spelling patterns they find in the books they read and to apply these skills in their writing.

Applying Onset and Rime

Word work can include building word families using onset and rime, for example, taking "an" and adding initial letters to form "man," "can," or "tan." The following is an example of what a word work session might be like:

Teacher	Let's break this word. [Teacher separates the word by sliding the "a" to the left and the "n" to the right.] We have /a/ [pause briefly] /n/ [while pushing the letters back together]. When we put the /a/ /n/ sounds together, we make the word "an."
	[Optional: teacher can direct students to make and break words themselves.]
	Now, make the word "can." What letter do you need to pull down and add to "an" to make "can"? [Teacher observes and listens to students' responses. Teacher models and checks each student's board for accuracy, scaffolding if necessary by referring back to the letter sounds and assisting the child in selecting the correct letters.]
	Let's read the word "can."
Teacher and Students	can [Everyone is running a finger from left to right while reading "can."]
Teacher	Let's break this word. [Teacher separates the word by sliding the "c" to the left and the "an" to the right.] We have /c/ [pause briefly] "an." [while pushing the letters back together]. When we put the sound /c/, and the chunk "an" together, we make the word "can."
	[Optional: Teacher can direct students to make and break words themselves. Teacher repeats the same pattern for the words "tan" and "man."]

For more advanced students, the teacher may introduce diagraphs and blends. Teacher and students can explore making and breaking words using these chunks. For example, students make the words "the" and "at" with their magnetic letters. The teacher can direct them to take the beginning chunk of "the," /th/, and add it to "at" to make the word "that."

Rereads

The next part of the kindergarten LC is rereading. This is a simple task; however, rereading helps students build fluency and become more familiar with words they encounter over and over in other texts they will be reading. In addition, rereading provides an opportunity for repetitious and meaningful use of the book to reinforce comprehension. While students are rereading, the teacher circulates and listens to each student to make certain he or she is reading the books fluently and accurately. This means the students do not make any errors, or if errors occur, that they are self-corrected. Remember, these are books students have already spent at least one week reading. Once the students have mastered a book and it has been designated as a reread, they may add the title of the book to the chart (a list of books they can read well) in their folders. If the students experience difficulty with a reread book, this book should be revisited as the focus book. Revisiting the book can take on many forms, such as choral, partner, or independent reads. If a student repeatedly struggles with the reread books or if the books are too easy, perhaps he or she would be better served in a different group where the reading materials are at his or her instructional level. Or, if it is a heterogeneous group, the materials should be evaluated and adjusted to meet the needs of the individuals in the group.

Writing

The last part of the kindergarten session is writing. Each group of LC students creates a writing inventory. That is, students create a list of topics they would like to write about, such as things they like or things they know a lot about, and keep it in their writing folders. The writing inventory is meant to give students quick access to a list of topics if they cannot think of one during writing time. This practice helps students select writing topics independently, which is one of the goals in the writing portion of the LC. Kindergarten students are encouraged to begin with drawings as a way of organizing their ideas for writing.

As in the reading section, during writing there is always a focus on a specific strategy. The focus on one strategy may last from one to several weeks, depending on students' needs. On day 1, the teacher presents a mini-lesson on a strategy or skill, whether it be periods, capital letters, or writing two or three sentences about a single topic. For example the teacher might say, "Today, we are going to work on writing two sentences about our drawings." The LC teacher draws a picture on the board and asks students what they could write about the picture. After the students share orally, two of the ideas are selected and written on the board and, as a review, the students indicate where the teacher should start writing and what to do at the beginning and end of each sentence. The LC teacher reviews and refers back to the writing strategy before students begin writing each day. During sharing sessions, the teacher and students highlight the use of the strategy in the writing samples shared. Each day, students may begin a new piece of writing or continue writing the piece from the day(s) before.

Students write for the remainder of the session. As they are writing, the teacher has individual conferences with students, asking them to read what they have written and reminding them to use the strategies that have been introduced. As the teacher talks with each student, he or she puts a checkmark on each aspect of writing that is correct, including but not limited to, appropriate capital letters, spacing, punctuation marks, spelling, and content (Fig. 3.2). These individual conferences and positive feedback checks help students feel successful about their writing and note all the things they have done correctly in their work. Students use the writing form to complete a self-assessment of their work. In the example in Figure 3.2, the student self-assessed her use of capital letters and indicated how well she thought she did by putting a sticker on one of the faces on the bottom of the form.

Sharing writing pieces contributes to student growth in literacy. Some teachers ask students to pick a writing piece from the week to share with the group and others ask students to share as they complete each piece. Sharing completed writing pieces is another opportunity for students to develop metacognitive awareness of their learning and to see themselves as writers.

Monitoring the Progress of Mai, Mario, Pedro, and Nhia

The four students featured in the EAL literacy-based sessions began participating in the LC during the second semester of the academic year. Their LC teacher's anecdotal notes describing their progress by the end of the semester are shown in the next sections.

Mai

After completing one semester in the LC, Mai progressed from Level 2 in reading to Level 8 on the DRA2+, well above the expectation at the end of kindergarten. She is now generally able to accurately retell both fiction and informational text with some detail, though occasionally she needs to use the text as a support. Her writing continues to improve, as measured by district assessments, and she is expanding her writing through the use of strategies she's learned, especially prewriting organizers. She continues to write ever more complex sentences with a clear topic and is well on her way to reaching her writing goals. Mai will exit the LC because she is performing above grade level in the LC and the classroom.

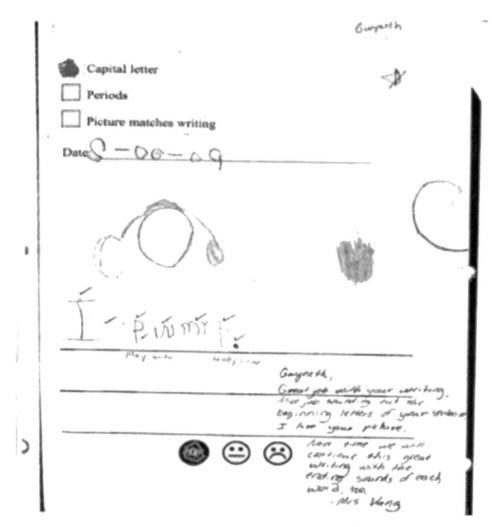

Figure 3.2 Examples of conferencing notes and checkmarks.

Mario

After beginning the LC at a DRA2+ Level 1, Mario reached a proficiency score of Level 4 in reading on the DRA2+, which is the expected level for a kindergarten student at the end of the year. His comprehension on DRA2+ measures has improved and he is able to retell many of the main ideas about what he has read when he has the text available. He generally uses emergent literacy strategies, such as picture and context cues. Mario is writing longer text (3–4 sentences) as measured by district assessments, on which he progressed from Level 2 to Level 3. He needs occasional reminders in the LC to edit his work for capital letters and punctuation. With the opportunity to practice and use his speaking and listening strengths to analyze text and orally rehearse for writing, Mario has made tremendous growth in the LC.

Mario will continue in the LC at the beginning of the next academic year. Although he has reached grade-level expectations in the LC, he has not performed at the same level in the classroom. Once he is able to transfer what he can do in the LC to the classroom, he will exit the program.

Pedro

At the end of kindergarten, Pedro reached a DRA2+ score of Level 4, after beginning at Level 1 in reading. He has begun reading with greater confidence and fluency and has greatly improved his comprehension of what he reads. With verbal and visual support, he is able to retell text he has read and provide some detail. His writing on district assessment rubrics improved from Level 2 to Level 3. He now writes 2–3 sentences on a single topic and his writing is often very creative. He is a very capable student but his behavior often gets in the way of his learning. Even with a behavior concern in the LC, Pedro made progress and reached the benchmark.

Pedro will exit the LC because he is able to work at grade level in the LC and the classroom. His behavior issues also improved a great deal while receiving additional support and attention in the LC.

Nhia

In January, when he began the LC, Nhia was at a DRA2+ Level 2 in reading. With the opportunity to use all four language domains (reading, writing, listening, speaking) in the LC, Nhia ended the year at Level 8 in reading, which exceeded grade-level expectation. He applies several emergent strategies while reading and can describe how he uses them (metacognition) to enhance comprehension. He generally retells what he has read but occasionally needs support. District writing assessments reflect that he has progressed from the random letter stage to using first and last letters on many words. He consistently uses capital letters and periods.

Nhia will exit the LC because he has exceeded grade-level expectations in the LC and the classroom. He now also demonstrates a great deal of confidence in his work.

The progress of the four focus students across the semester as measured by the DRA2+ is reflected in Figure 3.3.

End-of-year benchmark					K							1st			2nd			3rd	4th	5th
DRA2+ Levels	A	1	2	3	4	6	8	10	12	14	16	18	20	24	28	30	34	38	40	50
January		Mario Pedro	Mai Nhia																	
February			Mario Pedro	Mai Nhia																
March			Mario Pedro		Mai Nhia															
April				Mario Pedro		Mai Nhia														
May					Mario Pedro		Mai Nhia													

Figure 3.3 Student progress: English as an additional language literacy-based strand. DRA2+, Developmental Reading Assessment 2+.

CONCLUSION

The LC intervention at the kindergarten level assists students in developing a solid base for future literacy development. It provides early and intensive support for students who are struggling with emergent literacy. Emerging (English and Spanish) bilingual students in the bilingual strands also benefit from regular exposure to and interaction with experienced Spanish and English speakers. The small group setting and individualized and focused attention to oracy, literacy, and metacognition in each of the strands reflect how the same goals are developed through different pathways to ensure that students get the support necessary to be successful and make progress toward grade-level expectations.

The format of the bilingual strand, which focused heavily on Spanish literacy at the beginning of each week and bridged to English at the end of the week, can easily be adapted for students who require greater support in English literacy and oracy. For example, by beginning the week with English and bridging to Spanish at the end of the week, students who have grade-level Spanish literacy and oracy skills would receive support in developing their English literacy skills. This may be helpful in 50/50 dual language classrooms where one half of the day focuses on instruction in English and the other half focuses on instruction in Spanish.

QUESTIONS FOR REFLECTION AND ACTION

- What specific areas of metacognitive development (strategy development/ language analysis) would you focus on at the kindergarten level?
- Create a plan for a second week that would continue the work with kindergarten students. How would you include content and language standards; a text; literacy, oracy, and metacognition activities; and an assessment process in the plan?
- What are the specific literacy and language needs of the students in your school/district at this level? Map out pathways that would further support their learning.
- Create plans for collaborating effectively with classroom teachers. How would you align the work of the LC and the classroom?

Literacy Club with Language Learners in Grades 1–2

KEY CONCEPTS

- The focus in grades 1–2 is to highlight and build on skills and strategies students already have to support their development of solid literacy and oracy skills.
- Metacognitive development related to the use of learning strategies and analysis of the structure and use of language are important components of an effective grade 1–2 instruction and intervention plan.
- Assessment measures in grades 1–2 focus on solidifying emergent literacy and build on text comprehension and oracy development.

[Handwritten margin note: So different than ESL → purpose of ESL is not intervention. Kind of like LCI for bilingual?]

The grades 1–2 **Literacy Club (LC)** sessions are designed for students who are struggling with literacy skill acquisition and use of grade-level texts in English and/or Spanish. They have had literacy instruction for 1–2 years but have not been developmentally and/or emotionally ready for the challenges involved in grade-level literacy learning. As a result, they often have a very uneven profile of literacy skills and strategies that does not provide them with a solid enough base to move toward grade-level independence in literacy development. Differentiated learning experiences are especially important at this level because students may need to learn and practice very basic skills and strategies that other students have already mastered. However, once they have the opportunity to address their specific needs, they often progress quite rapidly, especially at the grade 2 level. Therefore, it is important that LC teachers have the freedom and flexibility to design challenging, developmentally appropriate learning experiences for these groups of students. It is generally effective to organize 45-minute sessions that meet 5 times per week at these grade levels.

This chapter includes all three of the LC strands: advancing bilingual, emerging bilingual, and English as an additional language (EAL). As the LC teacher uses the language resources that each group brings to the learning environment, we see how the same goals are accomplished through different pathways in these strands. The **advancing bilingual strand** is for students who have strong Spanish (or other language) **oracy**, and the LC teacher draws on that Spanish oracy as a resource to move students in this strand along the bilingual pathway. The **emerging bilingual strand** is for students with strong English oracy who are learning Spanish (or another language), and the LC teacher draws on this English oracy first to build Spanish oracy and then **literacy** in two languages. The **EAL strand** is for students who have strong oracy in languages other than English but for whom there is no bilingual strand available. The LC teacher can draw on their home languages as a resource, along with their prior experience in linguistically and culturally diverse contexts, to move them along an EAL pathway. As you read about the students in this chapter, we encourage you to bring your grades 1 and 2 students to mind.

LANGUAGE AND LITERACY DEMANDS

At the grade 1–2 levels, the English language arts (ELA) standards move beyond emergent literacy expectations by requiring students to use textual evidence, details, and illustrations more fully in speaking, reading, and writing. Students are asked to determine who text narrators are and analyze character perspectives based on evidence from text and illustrations. Grade 1–2 writing standards highlight the development of content with the inclusion of an introduction, supporting evidence, and conclusion in writing for a variety of genres.

During grade 2, the LC teacher starts preparing students for grade 3 standards, which place greater attention on analyzing how each section of text builds on earlier sections. Grade 3 standards also require students to distinguish their own points of view from those in the text and to describe relationships among concepts and texts. In addition to introducing, developing, and concluding topics, students focus attention on using linking words/phrases and dialogue in their writing. LC lessons are structured to be student-centered and flexible, in that all of the learning experiences build on what students can do and guide them to the next steps in literacy and language.

TEACHER COLLABORATION

As in the kindergarten LC, collaboration is a major factor in the success of grade 1 and 2 students in this program. The LC and classroom teachers work together to review student performance and work samples, select content and language objectives, plan instruction, and monitor progress. As the classroom and LC teachers collaborate to focus on students' needs, they use their understanding of what students can do with English and their home languages to scaffold and differentiate instruction for the group. Wherever possible the LC teacher focuses on the same skills and strategies as the classroom teacher, making certain to align with the classroom content themes.

CONTINUOUS PROGRESS MONITORING

Individualized instruction is supported by authentic and ongoing progress monitoring. A balanced plan of **formative** and **summative assessments** lets LC teachers ensure that students are gaining a solid background across all of the language domains. Ongoing use of running records, student feedback, anecdotal records, and student self-assessments create the formative LC assessment plan. Quarterly summative assessments, along with data from district and state assessments, allow teachers to clearly analyze how students are progressing and how instruction might be structured to enhance further growth. A paired literacy assessment plan in the bilingual strands allows LC teachers to continually and simultaneously monitor students' progress in both languages.

TEXT SELECTION

Careful text selection, with regard to background knowledge and experiences, content, language complexity, and reading level, can make a significant difference in the successful development of reading skills. Students read and explore both narrative and informational text linked to language and literacy standards for a variety of purposes. Because **strategy development** is a critical component of the metacognition goal in the LC, texts must be selected that facilitate strategy instruction, practice, and assessment. The language of texts must also be considered carefully and texts selected that lend themselves to growth in oracy as students explore the form and content of what they read.

ADVANCING BILINGUAL STRAND

The advancing Spanish bilingual strand in grades 1–2 is suggested for students who have well-developed listening and speaking skills in Spanish. As we can see in Table 4.1, attention is given to all language domains in Spanish but the focus is more fully on literacy development, expanded oracy, and metacognition with this group.

Box 4.1 provides an overview of content and language objectives for the grades 1–2 advancing bilingual strand related to the sample lessons that follow.

Juan Carlos, one of our focal students who we met in earlier chapters, is featured in the advancing bilingual strand, along with Ezequiel, Antonio, and Eduardo. Juan Carlos has been placed in the grade 2 advancing bilingual strand because he struggles with grade-level reading and writing in both languages. LC teachers can take advantage of his listening and speaking strengths in Spanish as he builds literacy skills in both languages. According to assessments of his English and Spanish language development, Juan Carlos is at Level 2 in reading and writing in both languages. His struggles with comprehension, strategy development, and content/structure of writing are also reflected in the results of **Developmental Reading Assessment 2+** and *Evaluación del desarrollo de la lectura 2* testing and in evaluations of his classroom writing samples.

The LC and classroom teachers collaboratively chose to address these issues by frontloading reading activities with picture walks, predictions, and strategy instruction. During reading, Juan Carlos has opportunities to evaluate his predictions, discuss content, and apply learning strategies. Retelling, making connections, and oral rehearsal for writing also target Juan Carlos' specific needs. All of these areas are reinforced during the bridging activities in English to ensure that he develops at a consistent rate in both languages. Ongoing running records, anecdotal records of predicting with evidence, use of writing rubrics, and student self-assessments of progress provide indications of growth. This section concludes with an overview of Juan Carlos' progress after LC participation.

TABLE 4.1 Format for Grades 1–2 Advancing Spanish Bilingual Strand

	Day 1	Day 2	Day 3	Day 4	Day 5
Focus book	Introduction Choral read Self-assess	Choral read Discuss strategy	Choral read Discuss strategy	Independent read Bridge general ideas	Read Spanish/ English Self-assess
Word work	Spanish concepts *Dictado*	Spanish concepts *Dictado*	Spanish concepts *Dictado*	Cognates English	Cognates English
Rereads	Pairs	Pairs	Independent	Independent	Spanish/English
Writing	Spanish*	Spanish*	Spanish*	Modified *Así se dice*	English

*Self-selected topics.

BOX 4.1 Content and Language Objectives for the Week			
Tema	Los libros pueden enseñarnos lecciones importantes.	**Theme**	*Books can teach us important lessons.*
OBJETIVOS NUEVOS/NEW OBJECTIVES			
Contenido	Yo podré emparejar el texto y las ilustraciones para hacer predicciones y recontar el cuento.	**Content**	*I will be able to match text and illustrations to make predictions and retell the story.*
Lenguaje	Yo podré describir el mensaje del autor.	**Language**	*I will be able to discuss the author's message.*
	Yo podré escribir oraciones sobre un sólo tema.		*I will be able to write sentences on one subject.*
REVISAMOS/REVIEWING			
	Yo podré formar y leer las sílabas de los verbos.		*I will be able to make and read syllables using verbs.*
	Yo podré nombrar las partes de un libro (título, autor, ilustrador).		*I will be able to name the parts of a book (title, author, illustrator).*
	Yo podré usar letras mayúsculas, y puntuación correcta.		*I will be able to use capital letters and punctuation correctly.*

Focus Book

The LC teacher introduces the text, *Los brazos son para abrazar* (Badía, 2011), by reviewing the title, author, and illustrator and doing a picture walk. The classroom and LC teachers have decided that determining the author's message is the focus in the classroom and the LC sessions with the theme "Books can teach us lessons." The group works on prediction as the strategy to be developed and uses prior knowledge and first syllable recognition to determine new words. **Total physical response (TPR)** actions are added for a page toward the end of the text because it contains the lesson from the story and will be used in a **comparative analysis** activity between Spanish and English later in the week. The teacher works with the students to select TPR actions for each of the key vocabulary words.

Discussing the Author's Message

The following vignette provides a good example of how an LC teacher might introduce students to a more in-depth analysis of their reading as they work to deduce the theme of the week's **focus book**, *Los brazos son para abrazar,* and use text and illustrations to make predictions. The LC teacher begins by reading the passage that contains the message and provides students with the opportunity to share and refine their responses. Text analysis is an area that Juan Carlos finds challenging. The LC teacher did not simply accept or reject his response in this example but instead worked with him to join his idea with Ezequiel's to more fully explain the author's message. With continued practice, Juan Carlos and the other students in the group can develop **critical thinking skills** related to text analysis.

Teacher	¿Qué están haciendo los niños en la última ilustración?	*What are the children doing in the last picture?*

Juan Carlos	Están sonriendo.	*They are smiling.*
Teacher	Voy a leer la última página y ustedes pueden seguir en sus libros. Es un poco más difícil, pero nos enseña el mensaje del libro: --Vivimos en armonía. Nos queremos y nos respetamos. El amor que compartimos.--	*I am going to read the last page and you can follow along in your books. This is a little difficult, but it shows us the message of the book: "We live in harmony. We love and respect one another. We share our love."*
	¿Cuál es el mensaje de este libro? ¿Qué quiere enseñarnos la autora?	*What is the message of this book? What is the author trying to teach us?*
Juan Carlos	Que debemos jugar.	*That we should play.*
Ezequiel	Nos enseña de la amistad.	*She teaches us about friendship.*
Teacher	Juan Carlos, ¿tú puedes juntar las dos ideas con la ilustración?	*Juan Carlos, can you join those two ideas with the picture?*
Juan Carlos	No estoy segura. ¿Somos amigos cuando jugamos juntos?	*I'm not sure. We are friends when we play together?*
Teacher	Sí, la amistad crece cuando jugamos juntos.	*Yes, friendship grows when we play together.*

The LC teacher and the students read the book chorally, stopping briefly to point out how they used the picture and their background knowledge, plus the first syllable, to figure out new words. They also stop periodically to discuss the illustrations and to share ideas about the author's message. After a brief discussion on completing the reading of the text, the teacher conducts a second choral reading of the book. Students are then asked to share a new word they learned using this week's strategy and how the strategy helped them figure out the word or its meaning. This method is a good way to enhance the use of **language for academic purposes**. The children then complete a self-assessment of how well they could read the new book and how well they used the strategy (Box 4.2). This self-assessment focuses on student evaluation of the use of strategies in reading and writing; strategy development is a key component of **metacognition** in the LC. The LC teacher might read the prompts for the self-assessment to the students, and in the beginning may also wish to have the students dictate responses.

BOX 4.2 Beginning-/End-of-Week Student Self-Assessment

Nombre _____   Fecha _____

El libro es   Fácil   Más o menos   Difícil   de leer.   *This book is   Easy   Average   Difficult   to read.*

Estrategia de lectura: Usar la predicción y lo que ya sabía   *Reading strategy: Use prediction and what you know*

es   Fácil   Más o menos   Difícil.   *is   Easy   Average   Difficult.*

Ejemplo: Palabra nueva que aprendí usando la estrategia   *Example: A new word I learned using this strategy is*

es _____   _____

Estrategia de escritura: Escribir sobre un sólo tema   *Writing strategy: Write on one topic*

es   Fácil   Más o menos   Difícil.   *is   Easy   Average   Difficult.*

On days 2 and 3, students read the focus book chorally at the beginning of the session, discussing anything new they noticed and reviewing how they are using the strategy to help them read the text. They use TPR actions when they read the page they will use for a comparative analysis activity later in the week. Students also partner-read or read independently, depending on how much support they need. This particular text has a recommended song and actions that may be used as the students read the book each day, which would also enhance comprehension and enjoyment of the text.

On day 4, the order of the writing and focus book components of the session are reversed and students read the general ideas from the Spanish texts, which they have analyzed and translated to English during the writing section that day (see the Writing section of this chapter). Day 5 is reserved for reading the Spanish text independently and then reading the bridged portion of the text in English. Also on day 5, students repeat the self-assessment they completed at the beginning of the week and compare the results to analyze how much they have improved. Students add the title of the book to their individual lists of mastered books, once they are able to read the text with complete accuracy and comprehension.

Word Work

For the *dictado* connected with the making words segment, the students listen to three sentences from the text read one at a time. They write them using a colored pencil. The teacher displays the correct spelling and the students make corrections on their papers using a different colored pencil but do not erase their original writing. They also work together to circle the syllables in each word to reinforce this concept. Students practice and analyze the same word work and *dictado* concepts on days 1–3 to help ensure that they have internalized the language and spelling structures.

The *dictado* sentences for this text were selected to review specific spelling, grammar, and semantic concepts, that is, accents (*oídos* [ears], *oír* [to hear]), spelling (*lengua* [tongue], *saborear* [to taste]), and the use of *y* (and) to join two ideas.

Los ojos son para ver.	*Eyes are for seeing.*
Los oídos son para oír.	*Ears are for hearing.*
La nariz es para oler,	*The nose is for smelling,*
y la lengua es para saborear.	*and the tongue is for tasting.*

Days 4 and 5 of *formando palabras*/making words with advancing Spanish bilingual students support their work in completing comparative analyses between English and Spanish text, which enables them to better understand similarities and differences between the two languages. Vocabulary to be used in the activities is selected and a chart of four key terms is made as each pair of words is addressed:

la boca	*the mouth*
las piernas	*the legs*
las manos	*the hands*
los brazos	*the arms*

The fact that articles in Spanish have gender (*las manos, los brazos*) but do not in English (the hands, the legs) is reviewed, as well as the fact that sometimes the articles aren't used at all in English. Students are encouraged to continually share what they notice about reading and writing across the two languages, especially during bridging activities such as *dictados* and comparative analyses, to hone their sense of their own bilingualism.

Rereads

Students reread texts in pairs on days 1 and 2; on days 3 and 4 they reread independently. During these last two days, the LC teacher may ask students to read brief sections of the story aloud to monitor comprehension, fluency, and strategy use and/or to conduct **running records**. Students can also practice rereading their previous English translations at least once per week.

As in all strands at every grade level, students must have mastered the book, that is, the LC teacher confirms that they are able to read with complete fluency and comprehension, before it becomes a reread. If an LC teacher notes that students are unable to read a text fluently, it becomes a focus book once again and additional work is done with the text until the group is able to read it at the independent level.

Writing

On days 1–3, students in this strand self-select their writing topics. This is important because it helps students develop greater independence in writing and ensures a selection of writing topics that are meaningful to them. LC students orally discuss topics they plan to write about as a way to rehearse ideas, language structure, and vocabulary. The LC teacher may ask questions to guide students in further elaborating on the topics and to generate enthusiasm for creating writing ideas.

Writing on a Single Topic

In the following vignette, students focus on the strategy of writing on a single topic (*escribir sobre un sólo tema*). Students can use this strategy to organize and expand their writing. The teacher introduces the strategy by sharing examples of cohesive and noncohesive writing and asking students to analyze which example reflects better writing.

Teacher	Yo voy a leer dos ejemplos de escritura y ustedes deben decirme cuál suena mejor.	*I am going to read two samples of writing and I want you to tell me which sounds better.*
	1. Mi mamá es muy bonita. Fui ayer al parque con mi primo. Quiero una bicicleta nueva para mi cumpleaños.	*1. My mother is very beautiful. Yesterday I went to the park with my cousin. I want a new bike for my birthday.*
	2. Fui al mercado con mi mamá. Vino también mi primo. Compramos mucha comida y algunos juguetes para mi y mi primo.	*2. I went to the store with my mommy. My cousin came along also. We bought a lot of food and some toys for my cousin and me.*
Eduardo	A mi me gusta el segundo porque es más como un cuento.	*I like the second one because it is more like a story.*
Teacher	Exacto. El segundo habla de una sóla cosa. Tiene un sólo tema. Cuando escriban esta semana vamos a practicar a escribir así. En la parte de arriba de sus papeles escriban el tema y unas ideas sobre el tema que quieren escribir.	*Exactly. The second one talks only about one thing. It has only one topic. When we write this week, we are going to practice writing like that. On the top of your paper write the topic and some ideas about the topic that you plan to write about.*

Students prepare an outline of their ideas and share them with the teacher before beginning to write. Juan Carlos needs additional support in planning to write on a single topic and the LC teacher talks with him about selecting a topic and supporting details.

As we see in this vignette, when the teacher scaffolds students' comparison of texts she guides students in seeing the difference between cohesive and noncohesive writing samples.

The LC teacher follows up by supporting Juan Carlos in selecting a theme and supporting details. Often students understand the concept but find it difficult to apply on their own. This is a good illustration of the zone of proximal development (Vygotsky, 1987, 2012), meaning Juan Carlos has some level of understanding of the concept and with support can apply the strategy more fully in his own writing.

Box 4.3 provides an example of a sheet that students might use to plan, write, and self-assess their writing. Discussions about the author's message may influence students to write about this topic or they might choose to share the author's message from other books they've read. Sentence frames such as "*Este libro nos enseña _____.*" ("This book teaches us _____.") can serve as useful **scaffolding** for students. Note that the student self-assessment includes a space for prewriting the main idea and details, which assists students in organizing their writing. After self-assessing their work, students share the completed piece with a partner, the LC teacher, or the whole group. Listeners provide feedback on whether or not the writer wrote on a single topic, that is, achieved his or her objective.

Days 4–5 provide an opportunity for students to bridge from Spanish to English using their focus book, which they are generally now reading fluently, as a resource. They begin this activity by reading a selected page of the text together in Spanish using the TPR actions

---

BOX 4.3 Student Writing and Self-Assessment Sheet

Nombre _____   Fecha _____

Tema (*Topic*) _____

Ideas _____

_____

_____

_____

_____

_____

_____

_____

Autoevaluación (*Self-assessment*):*

_____ un sólo tema (*one topic*)

_____ letras mayúsculas (*capital letters*)

_____ puntuación correcta (*correct punctuation*)

*Score: 1, fácil (*easy*); 2, más o menos (*average*); 3, difícil (*difficult*).

they have chosen. After they chorally read the entire page, the LC teacher asks students to read each line in Spanish. Together they analyze how to say each line in English, which provides them with opportunities to develop cognitive flexibility in analyzing complex text from one language to the other. The teacher records their responses on a dry erase board and guides them in making any edits. The students copy the final version and use it for reading on day 5, along with the original Spanish version.

Exploring Differences between Spanish and English

The following classroom interaction reflects a portion of the bridging activity. Initially the teacher takes a greater role in guiding the students to explore the use of language structures, vocabulary, and meaning from one language to the other. All students make contributions as they bring their understanding of each of their languages to bear in this activity.

Teacher	Vamos a leer la primera oración juntos en español, usando las acciones.	*We are going to read the first sentence together in Spanish, using our actions.*
	-- La boca es para cantar. --	*"The mouth is for singing."*
	¿Cómo podemos escribir esta oración en inglés?	*How do we write that sentence in English?*
Antonio	*The mouth is to sing.*	
Teacher	Esta es la idea en inglés. ¿Recuerden lo que estudiamos acerca de cómo traducimos --la boca-- en este cuento?	*This is the idea in English. Do you remember what we studied about how to translate --la boca-- in this story?*
Juan Carlos	Sí, decimos "mouths."	*Yes, we say "mouths."*
Teacher	Exacto. Antonio, ¿podemos decir "mouths is" en inglés?	*Exactly. Antonio, can we say "mouths is" in English?*
Antonio	Decimos "mouths are."	*We say "mouths are."*
Teacher	Sí. ¿Decimos "Mouths are **to** sing" en inglés? [Los estudiantes no están seguros.] Decimos "Mouths are **for** singing."	*Yes. Can we say "Mouths are **to** sing" in English? [The students are not sure.] We say "Mouths are **for** singing."*

As students become more familiar with this type of activity, they play a greater role in negotiating language and meaning across Spanish and English and the LC teacher steps back as much as possible. Eventually, students may work in pairs and compare and discuss their responses with a second pair of students. The objective is for students to continually expand the repertoire of language practices that they bring to each learning experience.

The LC teacher writes the sentence on the dry erase board and the students copy the sentence they formulated into their LC booklets or on an index card. They continue in this manner with the four lines, rereading all translated lines as each new line is added. During the *libro Nuevo*/focus book portion of the session on day 5, the students read the complete text in Spanish and then place the text from their **Así se dice** (That's how you say it) activity over the Spanish text and read the English text. The illustration remains visible so students can access it as an aid in reading the English text.

The remaining three lines continue with the use of gerunds and the students soon realize the pattern (though the LC teacher focuses on the /ing/ pattern and not the term "gerund" at this grade level). The translation the teacher selects simplifies the text slightly from the original English version, *Arms are for hugging* (Feldman & Karapetkova, 2010), to highlight the pattern for students. For example, the original text reads "Legs are made for dancing." but the teacher guides the students' translation as "Legs are for dancing."

On day 5, students write in English. The LC teacher provides sentence frames from the text that the students can choose to use in their writing or they can select their own topic and try independent writing in English. Sentence frames such as "_____ are for _____." can be used to support student writing in English.

Monitoring Juan Carlos' Progress

Running records for Juan Carlos indicate steady progress in both language and literacy development. As a result of carefully scaffolded instruction and practice, he is adept at using several reading strategies, especially context clues and prediction. Anecdotal records of retelling indicate that Juan Carlos has improved a great deal in comprehension of text. This evidence is supported by his improved ability to answer comprehension questions on formative assessment measures. Juan Carlos has indicated that discussions before, during, and after reading are particularly helpful for gaining meaning from text. This comment is also a good example of his progress in evaluating his metacognitive processes to identify what specific strategies support his learning.

Beginning- and end-of-year writing samples for Juan Carlos are shown in Figure 4.1. Side-by-side analysis of his writing in English and Spanish using a paired literacy rubric (Escamilla et al, 2014) highlights his progress by the end of the school year. From an evaluation of subsequent writing samples, it is clear that his writing skills in both languages have improved significantly across that time span. Oral and graphic rehearsal for writing provides the support he needs to organize and sequence his ideas for writing. Additional opportunities to create elaborated text for both narrative and informational topics would further assist Juan Carlos with his writing.

As a result of the growth he has demonstrated with oracy, literacy, and metacognition, Juan Carlos exited the LC and has continued to progress in the general classroom. His progress reflects how the advancing bilingual strand has been an appropriate pathway for him to reach LC goals. His individual needs have been assessed and addressed through use of targeted scaffolds and strategy development in Spanish and English. A focus on oracy and critical thinking assist Juan Carlos in expanding his use of language for academic purposes. Use of bridging and metalanguage help him manipulate language and concepts in both languages.

EMERGING BILINGUAL STRAND

The emerging Spanish bilingual strand for grades 1–2 is designed for students in **bilingual** or **dual language programs** who would benefit from a strong emphasis on oracy in Spanish, along with literacy support in both Spanish and English (Table 4.2). LC sessions are designed to guide students in reading, understanding, and interpreting text. Andrew, Mildred, Cyndy, and Jesse are featured in this emerging bilingual strand.

In the following example, students are studying the theme of interdependence ("We help one another.") in their classroom's integrated literacy/social studies unit about communities. There is an emphasis on analyzing how this theme is portrayed in the texts they are reading. The LC and classroom teachers have collaborated and determined that a focus on preteaching vocabulary and plot in both settings supports comprehension and writing development in Spanish for this group of students. Activities using the vocabulary and plot provide opportunities for the development of oracy, which is also a major goal for this group. Teaching these skills through an emphasis on a particular theme provides greater opportunities for the development of language for academic purposes in oracy and literacy.

The text used in the LC sessions I Want My Bone!/¡Quiero mi hueso! is an innovation on a text I Want My Banana/¡Quiero mi plátano! (Risk, 1996) that has already been used

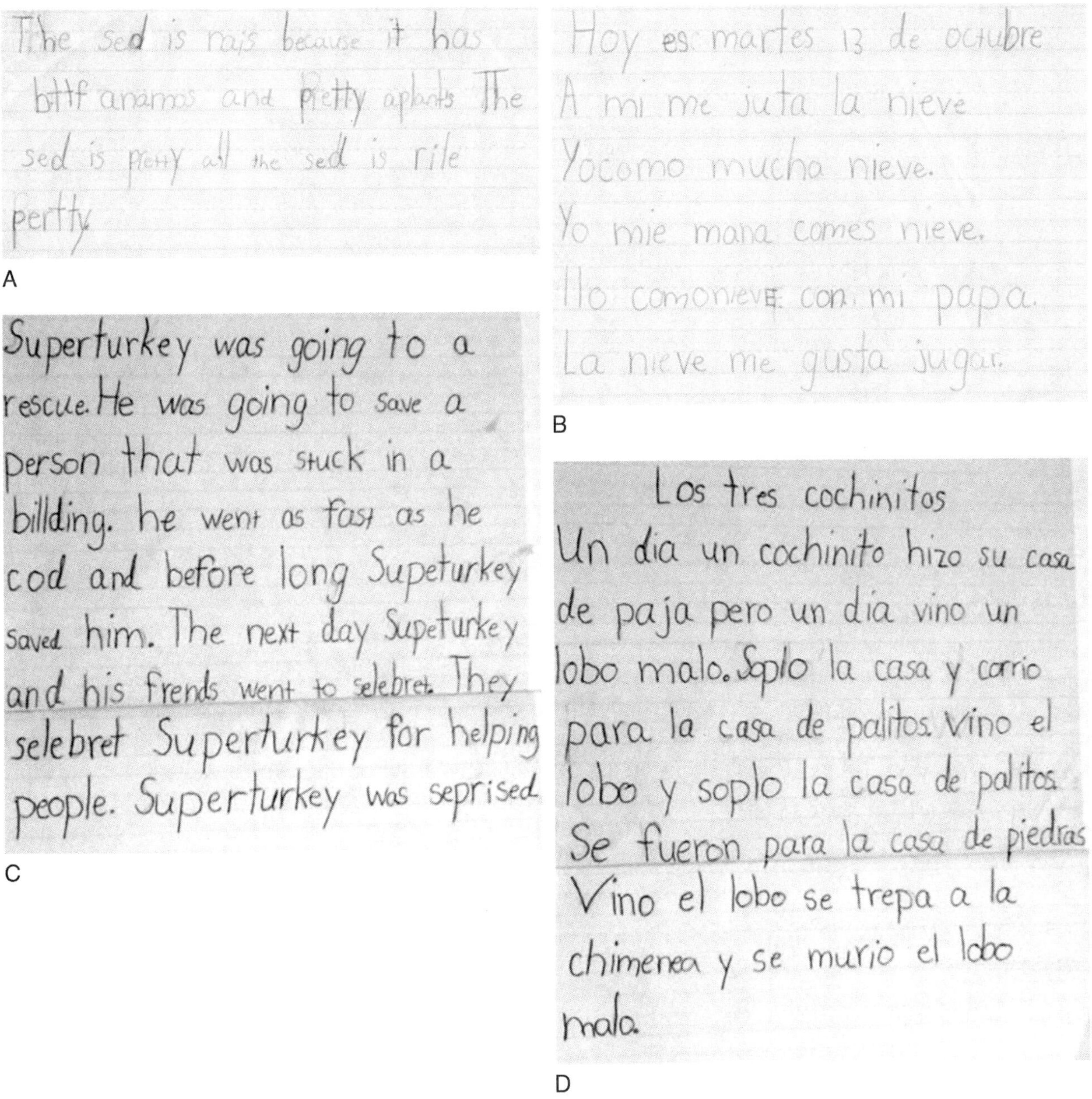

A

The sed is rais because it has
bttf anamos and pretty aplnts The
sed is pretty all the sed is rile
pertty

B

Hoy es martes 13 de octubre
A mi me juta la nieve
Yo como mucha nieve.
Yo mie mana comes nieve.
Ho comonieve con mi papa.
La nieve me gusta jugar.

C

Superturkey was going to a
rescue. He was going to save a
person that was stuck in a
billding. he went as fast as he
cod and before long Supeturkey
saved him. The next day Supeturkey
and his frends went to selebret. They
selebret Superturkey for helping
people. Superturkey was seprised

D

Los tres cochinitos
Un dia un cochinito hizo su casa
de paja pero un dia vino un
lobo malo. Soplo la casa y corrio
para la casa de palitos. Vino el
lobo y soplo la casa de palitos.
Se fueron para la casa de piedras
Vino el lobo se trepa a la
chimenea y se murio el lobo
malo.

Figure 4.1 Juan Carlos' beginning- and end-of-year writing samples in English and Spanish. **A,** Beginning of year (English). Translation: The zoo is nice because it has beautiful animals and pretty plants. The zoo is pretty all the zoo is really pretty. **B,** Beginning of year (Spanish). Translation: Today is Tuesday, October 13 I like snow. I eat a lot of snow. My sister eats snow. I eat snow with my Dad. I like to play in the snow. **C,** End of year (English). **D,** End of year (Spanish). Translation: The three pigs: One day a little pig made his house from straw but one day the bad wolf came. He blew the house down and ran to the house of sticks. The wolf came and blew the house of sticks down. They went to the house of stones. The wolf came down the chimney and the bad wolf died.

in the classroom. This should further support the students' oral development because they are already familiar with the text pattern.

Box 4.4 provides an overview of content and language objectives for the grades 1–2 emerging bilingual strand sample lessons that follow. These lessons focus on several days of literacy development in Spanish and 1.5 days of bridging to English. This format could be restructured to begin the week in English and then bridge to Spanish, depending on students' needs.

TABLE 4.2 Format for Grades 1–2 Emerging Spanish Bilingual Strand

	Day 1	Day 2	Day 3	Day 4	Day 5
Focus book	Oral: Concepts Vocabulary Self-assess	Echo/Choral read Discuss strategy	Echo/Choral read Discuss strategy	Independent read Bridge general ideas	Read Spanish/ English Self-assess
Word work	Spanish concepts *Dictado*	Spanish concepts *Dictado*	Spanish concepts *Dictado*	Cognates English	Cognates English
Rereads	Read in pairs	Retell in pairs	Retell in pairs	Independent	Spanish/English
Writing	Language experience approach	Sentence frames	Sentence frames	Modified *Así se dice*	English

Focus Book

Day 1 is dedicated to an oral introduction to the vocabulary and an overview of the text content. This is especially critical for these students to ensure that they build the necessary background to read, comprehend, and discuss the story. The LC teacher introduces the title of the bilingual text, *I Want My Bone!/¡Quiero mi hueso!,* pointing to the picture of a puppy and the bone on the cover of the text. Table 4.3 presents that text.

The LC teacher introduces new vocabulary by pointing to pictures in the book and guiding students to select TPR actions for each key vocabulary word. Articles are included

BOX 4.4 Content and Language Objectives for the Week

Tema	Podemos ayudar el uno al otro.	**Theme**	*We can help one another.*
OBJETIVOS NUEVOS/NEW OBJECTIVES			
Contenido	Yo podré emparejar el texto y las ilustraciones para recontar el cuento.	**Content**	*I will be able to match text and illustrations to retell the story.*
	Yo podré escribir oraciones sobre el libro.		*I will be able to write sentences about the book.*
Lenguaje	Yo podré usar palabras y oraciones del cuento.	**Language**	*I will be able to use the words and sentences from the story.*
REVISAMOS/REVIEWING			
	Yo podré formar y leer sílabas /ga/, /go/, /gu/.		*I will be able to make and read the syllables /ga/, /go/, /gu/.*
	Yo podré nombrar las partes de un libro (título, autor, ilustrador).		*I will be able to name the parts of a book (title, author, illustrator).*
	Yo podré usar letras mayúsculas y puntos.		*I will be able to use capital letters and periods.*

TABLE 4.3 *¡Quiero mi hueso! I Want My Bone!*	
¡Quiero mi hueso!	*I Want My Bone!*
La cachorra ha perdido su hueso. Está triste.	*Puppy has lost her bone.* *She's sad.*
--Toma un pez,-- dice el gato.	*"Have a fish,"* *says cat.*
--No, gracias,-- dice la cachorra. --Sólo quiero mi hueso.--	*"No, thanks," says puppy.* *"I only want my bone."*
--Toma una manzana,-- dice la vaca.	*"Have an apple,"* *says cow.*
--No, gracias,-- dice la cachorra. --Sólo quiero mi hueso.--	*"No, thanks," says puppy.* *"I only want my bone."*
--Toma un gusano,-- dice el pájaro.	*"Have a worm,"* *says bird.*
--No, gracias,-- dice la cachorra. --Sólo quiero mi hueso.--	*"No, thanks," says puppy.* *"I only want my bone."*
--Ven acá mi cachorra,-- dice Miranda. --Mira lo que encontré.--	*"Come here, my little puppy,"* *says Miranda.* *"Look what I found."*
La cachorra ve su hueso. Ahora está contenta.	*Puppy sees the bone.* *She is happy now.*

Innovation on text: *¡Quiero mi plátano!/I Want My Banana!* (Risk, 1996).

with each of the nouns to guide students in using them as scaffolds in reading and writing activities. Actual manipulatives or word–picture cards are helpful in reinforcing vocabulary. Several of the words may have been introduced orally or in print on previous occasions but are reviewed again to ensure that students have mastered them.

un pez	*a fish*
triste	*sad*
el gato	*the cat*
contenta	*happy*
un gusano	*a worm*
ha perdido	*has lost*
el pájaro	*the bird*
una manzana	*an apple*

Having students match picture and word cards or search the text for pictures representing the words given by the teacher helps reinforce vocabulary. This can be followed by having them also use the agreed on TPR action.

The LC teacher introduces the story and reinforces the vocabulary through an interactive picture walk. Use of pantomime, TPR, and illustrations supports student comprehension.

The teacher repeats student responses using complete sentences as a way to model language expectations to be added a bit later in the picture walk.

Scaffolding Comprehension of Plot

The importance of focusing on **language development** prior to reading with emergent bilinguals is highlighted in the following vignette. Students have greater comprehension of text if they participate in learning experiences such as these that scaffold both content and language. In this example, the use of an interactive picture walk and questioning strengthen receptive and expressive use of key vocabulary and concepts. This prepares students to explore the plot of this text, which is expanded to an exploration of the unit theme "We help one another."

Teacher	La cachorra está triste. [Enseña una cara triste.] Está triste porque no puede encontrar su _____.	*The puppy is sad. [He makes a sad face.] She is sad because she cannot find her _____.*
Students	hueso	*bone*
Teacher	Viene el gato. [Enseña la ilustración del gato.] Busquen las palabras --el gato--.	*Here comes the cat. [He shows the picture of the cat.] Look for the words "the cat."*
	¿Tiene un hueso para la cachorra?	*Does he have a bone for the puppy?*
Students	No.	*No.*
Teacher	¿Qué tiene?	*What does he have?*
Students	un pez	*a fish*
Teacher	Sí, el gato tiene un pez. Enseñenme el pez. Busquen las palabras --un pez--. ¿La cachorra quiere un pez?	*Yes, the cat has a fish. Show me the fish. Look for the words "a fish." Does the puppy want a fish?*
Students	No.	*No.*
Teacher	¿Qué quiere?	*What does she want?*
Students	su hueso	*her bone*
Teacher	Sí, la cachorra quiere su hueso. Ahora, ¿quién viene? [El maestro continúa así con la vaca y la manzana, el pájaro con el gusano, y la niña con el hueso.]	*Yes, the puppy wants her bone. Now who is coming? [The teacher continues in this manner with the cow and an apple, the bird with the worm, and the girl with the bone.]*
	Ahora, ¿está contenta la cachorra?	*Is the puppy happy now?*
Cyndy	Sí, la cachorra está contenta.	*Yes, the puppy is happy.*
Teacher	¿Por qué está contenta?	*Why is she happy?*
Jesse	Tiene su hueso.	*She has her bone.*
Teacher	¿Los animales trataron de ayudar a la cachorra? [Sí.]	*Did the animals try to help the puppy? [Yes.]*
Teacher	¿Como ayuda el gato (el pájaro, etc.) a la cachorra?	*How did the cat (the bird, etc.) help the puppy?*
Mildred	un pez	*a fish*

Review of vocabulary and plot was not the LC teacher's sole focus. He also related the theme of the unit to the particular story the students would be reading by asking the question, *¿Los animales trataron de ayudar a la cachorra?* (Did the animals try to help the puppy?)

This exemplifies the link between literacy and language objectives, that is, English language arts standards are replete with language development expectations and there is often overlap between language and literacy objectives for language learners. This redundancy provides excellent opportunities to expand students' language and higher-level thinking skills.

As in the other LC sessions, students complete a self-assessment at the beginning and end of the week. At each grade level students are guided to be more reflective in identifying how they used particular reading and writing strategies and how these strategies facilitated their learning. All three strands (advancing bilingual, emerging bilingual, and EAL) have the same types of self-assessments at each grade level that enable students to become more and more reflective and independent in their learning as the year progresses. Bilingual strands reflect progress toward goals in both languages and the EAL strand focuses on language and literacy development in English. Students can begin by dictating their responses to the LC teacher and begin writing them independently when they are able.

Matching Text and Illustrations

On day 2, the LC teacher and the students complete a choral reading of the story, stopping to point out picture clues and how they used what they already know, plus the first syllable, to figure out new words. The following vignette provides an example of this strategy development.

Teacher	*Miren la ilustración y la primera sílaba de esta palabra [contenta].*	*Look at the picture and the first syllable of this word [happy].*
	La cachorra está con _____.	*The puppy is _____.*
Andrew	contento	*happy*
Teacher	Sí, contenta. [El maestro proporciona la forma correcta de la palabra.] ¿Cómo sabemos?	*Yes, happy. [The teacher provides the correct form of the word.] How do we know?*
Mildred	La cachorra tiene una sonrisa.	*The puppy has a smile.*
Teacher	Sí, sabemos que si tiene una sonrisa, está contenta. Están usando lo que ya saben.	*Yes, we know that if she has a smile, she is happy. You are using what you know.*

As we see in the latter part of this interaction, the LC teacher guides the students to think more critically. He asks them not only to indicate whether or not the puppy is happy at the end of the story but to provide evidence from the text to support their response. Mildred states, "*La cachorra tiene una sonrisa.*" ("The puppy has a smile.") and the teacher points out that they are using what they know to formulate a response.

On day 3, a choral reading of the story is completed and then repeated to reinforce word recognition, comprehension, and fluency. The LC teacher continues to ask questions that review the plot about how the animals try to help the puppy, reinforce the strategy, and invite students to comment on the story with attention to the theme (How can we help one another?). The LC teacher uses the following sentence frames to assist students with discussing the story and then for use in a Readers' Theatre activity, where one student is the narrator and the other students read the lines of the various characters:

La cachorra está _____.	*The puppy is _____.*
La cachorra quiere un _____.	*The puppy wants a _____.*
--Toma _____, -- dice _____.	*"Take _____," says _____.*

--No _____, --dice _____.	"No _____," says _____.
--Sólo quiero _____.--	"I only want _____."

As the students progress in their language development, the scaffolding provided by the sentence frames is reduced, and eventually removed, and the students create their own Readers' Theatre texts.

Day 4 begins with independent reading of the story in Spanish and then moves to conducting an oral comparative analysis of the general ideas of the story from Spanish to English. Bridging activities in reading and writing guide students in applying what they know from one language to the other, making literacy development in both languages stronger. The following sentences are analyzed orally to provide a general summary of the story.

La cachorra ha perdido su hueso.	*The puppy has lost her bone.*
Está triste.	*She is sad.*
La cachorra ve su hueso.	*The puppy sees her bone.*
Ahora la cachorra está contenta.	*Now the puppy is happy.*

Picture cues are used as each sentence is analyzed to provide additional support. Students use their skills in both languages as resources to discuss how they think each sentence could be said in English, the LC teacher clarifies the result of the oral comparative analysis and has the students repeat it in English. In the writing portion of the session, the LC teacher and the students work together on a written comparative analysis of the sentences.

On day 5, the students read the story independently in Spanish, providing opportunities for the LC teacher to listen to individual students read and/or to conduct running records. An English reading of the translated sentences follows this portion of the lesson. Students open their Spanish texts to the appropriate page (to access use of visual cues) as they read each sentence. Cards with the translations may be clipped to each page.

Repeating the self-assessment they completed at the beginning of the week and comparing the results help students reflect on how much they have improved by the end of the week and identify areas that still need attention in one or both languages. Students use the TPR actions for key vocabulary as they complete the self-assessment.

Word Work

As students transition to the word work component of the session, they quickly review the vocabulary words on their word rings and move into work with the formation of syllables.

Forming and Reading Syllables

Word work for this book begins with a review of the syllables formed with the letter "*g suave*" (soft g, equivalent to hard g in English): /ga/, /go/, /gu/, as highlighted in the following vignette. Students write each syllable on their dry erase boards as the LC teacher reads them. Writing longer words containing these syllables provides additional practice in forming words in Spanish. Students are encouraged to consult with a partner if they are not sure of the spelling. They generally rely less and less on this support as the week goes on.

Teacher	La primera palabra tiene 2 sílabas. Vamos a escribir --gato--.	*The first word has 2 syllables. Let's write --gato-- [cat].*

(Students write --gato--.)

| Teacher | Ahora vamos a examinar las sílabas. ¿Cuantas sílabas tiene? Sí, tiene dos sílabas: --ga-to--. [El maestro continúa con este patrón con las siguientes palabras: goma, amigo, amiga, gusano.] | *Now we are going to take a look at the syllables. How many syllables does the word have? Yes, it has two syllables:*

 --ga to--. [The teacher continues this pattern with the remaining words: goma *(eraser),* amigo *(friend [boy]),* amiga *(friend [girl]),* gusano *(worm).]* |

Being able to form and segment words by syllables, as we've seen in this example, is an important literacy skill in Spanish that affects the fluency and accuracy of student reading. Therefore, it warrants emphasis in the word work portion of the LC sessions and can be expanded to include additional concepts as students gain facility with using syllables in reading and writing.

On days 1–3, students work on *dictados* (dictations) of three key sentences from the story. At the beginning of the year, fewer sentences may be used if students find the task especially challenging. The sentences for this example were chosen to focus on specific aspects of spelling (*quiero, ahora* [I want, now]), accents (*está* [is]), dialogue (*guiones* [quotation marks]), and antonyms (*triste/contento* [sad/happy]). Students repeat the same *dictados* each day of the week to internalize the language structures. One change from the text is made in the *dictado*. The original version of the text used English quotation marks in the Spanish translation, while the *dictado* uses *guiones* (*--Quiero mi plátano.--*) because these are more authentic to Spanish text. The LC teacher reads the entire sentence and allows the children time to write, repeating the sentences as needed.

La cachorra está triste.	*The puppy is sad.*
--Quiero mi hueso.--	*"I want my bone."*
Ahora la cachorra está contenta.	*Now the puppy is happy.*

The students write each sentence with a colored pencil and make corrections with a different colored pencil. They do not erase and rewrite; they write their corrections above the original, which enables them to analyze any errors and to note how much they improve each day. A discussion of the concepts under study (spelling, accents, dialogue, and antonyms) follows the correction of errors so students develop a stronger understanding of the structures with which they are working.

On days 4–5, students begin the bridging process by exploring Spanish/English cognates/ *cognados,* such as contenta/*content* in the preceding example. The students themselves generate these words as they note similarities in spelling and/or pronunciation. The LC teacher records the cognates as the students share them. Of course since not all texts include cognates, the teacher needs to determine in advance if there are any cognates before asking the students to search for them in the text.

In addition to cognates, elements of comparative analysis are included during this session to guide students in recognizing similarities and differences between the two languages and help them gain facility in applying their full range of bilingual language practices to this exploration. The difference in the ways that stated and implied subjects are used in English and Spanish is emphasized through several examples in this story:

Está triste.	*She is sad.*
Quiero mi hueso.	*I want my bone.*
Ahora está contenta.	*She is happy now.*

The comparisons are made briefly and orally as a way for students to examine how the subject is generally stated explicitly in English and implied in Spanish.

Rereads

Students reread books with a partner on day 1. On day 2, they retell stories they have read with a partner. The LC teacher models how to use the illustrations to retell the story. This activity provides opportunities for students to further develop their oral language skills. On days 3 and 4, students reread texts independently. If the LC teacher notes that students are not reading one or more of these texts with confidence and accuracy, they are returned to the focus book section of the session for additional work. Students may also practice rereading their English translations at least once per week.

Writing

Similarly to the pattern we saw with reading, writing is heavily scaffolded initially because students in this strand have not yet developed strong oracy in Spanish to use as a writing foundation. On day 1, the LC teacher takes a **language experience approach (LEA)** with students, prompting them to tell what happened in the story. The teacher records what the students say and then guides them to revise their sentences to provide a summary of part or all of the story. Here are examples of sentences generated by the students prior to editing:

El cachorra *wants a* hueso.	*The puppy wants a bone.*
Está triste.	*She is sad.*
La gato tiene *a fish.*	*The cat has a fish.*
La cachorra *finds his* hueso.	*The puppy finds her bone.*
El cachorra es *content.*	*The puppy is happy.*

On day 2, the LC teacher reviews the LEA and introduces sentence frames the students can use in pairs as they write about the story. On day 3, students review the LEA and then write independently in Spanish either using the sentence frames or writing on a self-selected topic. Note that the same language is repeated in several learning experiences to enable the emergent bilinguals in this group to internalize vocabulary and sentence structure.

Sentence Frames

La cachorra está _____.	*The puppy is _____.*
La cachorra quiere un _____.	*The puppy wants a _____.*
--Toma _____,-- dice _____.	*"Take _____," says _____.*

Day 4 focuses on having students work in pairs to complete the written portion of the comparative analysis activity using key sentences from the story, as described in the preceding focus book section. Learning experiences throughout the week prepare students for this activity. On day 5, students are given the opportunity to write independently in English and the teacher meets with individual students to ensure that the writing strategy for the week is being applied and to discuss their writing. Students in the emerging bilingual strand generally have well-developed oral language skills in English and this activity lets them explore writing in English.

ENGLISH AS AN ADDITIONAL LANGUAGE STRAND

In this strand we meet Benji, Orlando, Panhia, and Sophia. Vignettes featuring these students highlight how the LC teacher uses scaffolds to guide students in learning about the language

TABLE 4.4 Format for Grades 1–2 English as an Additional Language Strand					
	Day 1	**Day 2**	**Day 3**	**Day 4**	**Day 5**
Focus book	Introduction Discuss strategy Choral read Self-assess	Choral read Discuss strategy	Independent read Discuss strategy	Independent read Discuss strategy	Independent read Self-assess
Word work	Word work	Word work	Word work Dictation	Word work Dictation	Word work Dictation
Rereads	Pairs and discuss	Pairs and discuss	Independent	Independent	Independent
Writing	Self-selected	Self-selected	Self-selected	Self-selected	Share writing

of the text and in selecting a writing topic. Although similar learning experiences may take place in the classroom, the LC teacher provides additional repetition, scaffolding, and language practice to guide these language learners toward meeting grade-level literacy standards in their new language, English. Table 4.4 provides an overview of the LC components for grades 1–2 **English learners (ELs)** and how they might be organized for weekly sessions.

The students in this group are focusing specifically on development of speaking and listening skills for academic purposes as they listen to and talk about key vocabulary and concepts from their focus book. The LC and classroom teachers have noted that the students struggle with developing critical thinking skills in the content areas and will provide opportunities for students in both settings to work on elaborating their responses using content-area terminology and asking questions for clarification. The LC teacher does this by carefully scaffolding daily learning experiences with vocabulary activities and sentence frames that enable students to orally formulate expanded responses to prompts that build on each day's work. Writing activities then invite students to use these key terms and sentence frames to express what they have learned. Students and the LC teacher clearly observe how student writing on the topic expands each day.

Table 4.5 provides examples of content and language objectives used by both the LC and classroom teachers. In this example, the LC is organized around the Readers' and Writers' Workshop models. Schools/districts may elect to structure the LC around these models if they more closely match classroom instruction and enable students to more easily make connections between the two instructional settings.

When a Readers' Workshop format is used in the classroom in a **push-in** model, students are taught a mini-lesson. They then read self-selected texts at their levels while the teacher meets one on one with individual students. After these meetings, students work independently while the LC teacher meets with a group of students to read at their instructional level. Lastly, students have the opportunity to share and talk about what they have learned as readers, thus connecting their discussion back to the mini-lesson. In this example, anchor charts are used to display the content objectives to support student learning of "how to build conversations with our partners." Each day a new component is added to explicitly scaffold how to build on one another's conversations. Here are the objectives for each day:

Day 1: I will build on others' comments.

Day 2: I will ask questions to help me understand.

Days 3–4: I will build on others' comments.

Day 5: I will ask for more information to help me understand.

TABLE 4.5 Samples of Content and Language Objectives

	Day 1	Day 2	Day 3	Day 4	Day 5
	Language objective: Building on others' conversations				
Readers' Workshop	I will build on others' comments.	I will ask questions to help me understand.	I will build on others' comments.	I will build on others' comments.	I will ask for more information to help me understand.
	Content objective: Performance tasks using shared informative text				
Writers' Workshop	I will write and illustrate about a new fact I learned.	I will write and illustrate about an interesting fact.	I will write and illustrate about an unusual fact.	I will write and illustrate about a wondering as a conclusion.	I will share my informative text.

A Writers' Workshop model follows a similar approach. The teacher teaches a mini-lesson; students write individually while the LC teacher confers with individual students or groups of students. Finally, students have the opportunity to share and discuss their writing to connect their discussion back to the mini-lesson (Moses, 2015; Riddle Buly, 2011; Shagoury Hubbard & Shorey, 2003). The Readers' Workshop objectives are linked to the Writters' Workshop in that students use their text discussions as writing topics. Both workshops function in tandem to help students clarify and elaborate on language as they solidify what they can do at one level and progress to the next.

Focus Book

As teachers select new books, they need to take students' prior knowledge of the books' content into consideration. It is important, especially when working with language learners, that the students have some prior knowledge about the text content or that LC and classroom teachers formulate plans to build needed background knowledge. The students are going to read *Baby Owl Goes Away* (Rigby, 2001) and explore the theme of actions and consequences. To appropriately scaffold lessons, the language in the books should always be taken into consideration. The LC teacher builds on the language that the classroom teacher has taught previously, as well as the background experiences of the students. This is of critical importance in this strand because instruction takes place primarily in English with little or no home language support.

If the content objective is to create an understanding of certain strategies, the LC teacher selects a book that has appropriately leveled language to teach that particular strategy to the LC students. For example, the content objective for Monday is "I will build on others' comments." The language objective highlights the language needed for students to describe what they are expected to learn. When the LC teacher chooses a text it should lend itself to the development of the content and the language objectives.

When introducing a new book, the LC teacher starts by activating the students' prior knowledge. Making certain students understand the new vocabulary through discussions and picture walks is a must, especially when introducing nonfiction books. The teacher should display real-life objects for students to examine and manipulate as often as possible. If using real-life objects is impossible, pictures also serve as a means of conveying information. Teachers use TPR because this strategy helps ELs grasp new vocabulary words. TPR is especially important for ELs who are at more emergent proficiency levels in one or more languages because it allows them to demonstrate understanding and respond nonverbally to language prompts and use simple words and phrases at the most basic levels. With TPR, students make the connection from a movement to a word, that is, if the word cannot be recalled they can still perform the movement, which serves as their means of communication. It also allows the LC teacher to formatively assess the students' English language development.

The first time a student is exposed to a new text, the LC teacher should not expect the student to be able to read the book independently, even if the book is at the appropriate reading level. The introduction of the book should be more about the general theme. Once a student has been exposed to the book, has a general knowledge of the new vocabulary, and has been introduced to the strategy to be emphasized, the actual reading can take place. For students at emergent reading levels, the teacher can read each page, make comments, and invite students to share observations and then read the page chorally with the students. The teacher should observe if students are struggling and remind them of the strategies they can use to read new words or gain meaning from the text.

Teachers should be aware that some students can read (decode) the words but do not understand the concepts or plot. This is where teacher evaluation of comprehension is crucial. LC teachers pose questions or invite students to add comments and observations as the book is read to check for understanding and have students retell the text to verify comprehension.

On day 1 when the teacher introduces the book, the group starts by reading the title and the name of the author. The teacher also does a picture walk with the students. As the teacher completes the picture walk, the conversation is focused on the content objective, supported by the language from the language objective. The teacher might say, "Today we are going to start reading this book. The title of this book is _____. The author of this book is _____. This book is about a family who lives in Guatemala. Let's take a picture walk and see if we can build on each other's conversation of what the people do for work and play and how they get their food. Our content objective for today is "I will build on others' comments." I would like you to use the sentence frames I have posted on the board. I will read them to you." The teacher reads the sentence frames and guides the students' conversations in using language for academic purposes. As the students and teacher are doing the picture walk, the students activate prior knowledge on the content and the teacher guides them in building on one another's comments. When the discussion is finished, the students do a choral read of the book.

Reinforcing the Language of Text

As part of the discussion in this sample vignette, the LC teacher activates background knowledge students have about the use of quotation marks. She builds on comments by Benji, Sophia, and Panhia to define the term and extends the discussion with examples to clarify how use of quotation marks enhances the story and highlights the feelings of the characters.

Teacher	In class, we have been discussing actions and consequences, that every action has a consequence. In this book, *Baby Owl Goes Away*, it's dinner time and Baby Owl's mom tells him to stay with her. Instead of listening to her, he goes away. Let's do a picture walk to see what happens to Baby Owl.
	(after picture walk)
	In this book, you will notice these marks [teacher shows students quotation marks in the book]. These are called quotation marks. Have you seen these before?
Benji	Yes, in poem at last week.

Teacher	Yes, we did, Benji. You are correct. Does anyone remember why we have quotation marks?
Sophia	someone talking
Teacher	Exactly! When we see quotation marks, it means a character in the book is talking. And as readers, we have to make our voices match their voice when we read the text. For example, when Baby Owl's mom is telling him to stay with her do you think she's saying it like this? [Teacher gives an example matching character voice from the book.]
	Or do you think she's saying it like this? [Teacher gives a robotic example not matching the character voice from the book.]
Panhia	first one
Teacher	Yes, exactly! Do you think you can do this and make your voices match how the characters are speaking in the text?
Students	Yes

On day 2, the LC teacher reinforces the strategy introduced the previous day. For example, the teacher might say, "Yesterday, our content objective was to build on each other's conversation. Today as you reread and discuss the story in pairs, please use the sentence frames on the board to build on each other's conversations. I'll read them to you again." As students are reading in pairs, the teacher circulates and listens to their reading, and develops a brief conversation with each pair. The LC teacher takes anecdotal notes of each student's reading, as illustrated in Box 4.5. As the LC teacher takes anecdotal notes and shares positive observations with the students, good reading behaviors are reinforced and students are energized to continually improve their use of skills and strategies. For example, the teacher might say, "When I was listening to Benji read, I saw him reread a part of the

---

BOX 4.5 Examples of Student Anecdotal Notes

Student name: Benji   **Date:** 2-4

Book: *Monkey and Gorilla*

Strategies/Reading behaviors

- Fluent reading
- Self-correction
- Voice expression

Student name: Benji   **Date:** 2-11

Book: *A New Ice Cream Machine*

Rereading the book

Strategies/Reading behaviors

- *His*—substituted with *the*; reread and-self corrected
- *Flea market* (new vocabulary); reread and got mouth ready to say word (made connection to meaning)
- *Saw*—substituted with *was*; reread with mouth ready to say the beginning sound of *saw*
- *Money*—substituted with *cash*; reread looking at beginning sound

Student name: Benji   **Date:** 11-14

Book: *My Little Kitten*

Strategies/Reading behaviors

- Fluent reading
- *Lift*—used chunking (l—ift . . . lift)
- Used picture clues on page 2
- *Will*—used chunking (w—ill . . . will)

Student name: Benji   **Date:** 11-15

Strategies/Reading behaviors (during rereading)

- Benji noticed the rhyming words at the end of all the sentences.
- *Very*—did not pay attention to beginning sounds/ meaning; was asked to go back and reread

book because it didn't make sense to him when he read it the first time. When he reread it, he had a better understanding. And Benji, I also noticed that you read 'was' on page 5 and then reread the sentence and said 'saw'. Can you tell us what you did there?"

On days 3–5, students read the book independently. Prior to reading, the LC teacher models how to ask questions or request additional information to clarify meaning. Students need to know how to do this for academic purposes in all content areas. Sentence/question frames such as "Can you restate?" "What do you mean by _____?" and "Tell me more about that." are introduced. Students are encouraged to use these sentence frames with a partner when they need clarification of the text they are reading. As students independently read the book, the teacher listens to each student read and engages them in brief conversations that give them opportunities to use the sentence frames. The teacher carefully takes note of strategies the students are using confidently and those that they need to practice more.

Although Readers' and Writers' Workshop models may be commonly used in the classroom, additional repetition, focus on scaffolding comprehension, and oracy used in the LC make learning more comprehensible for language learners. This use of appropriate scaffolding, accompanied by immediate feedback, lets the LC teacher focus on the same goals as those being developed in the classroom.

During day 5 of the LC, students self-assess their reading behavior for the week. Students are asked to provide examples of how they used the language objectives at the end of the week. These may be completed orally or in writing depending on the students' writing level. For students who answer orally, the LC teacher should record their responses on the assessment form and use these to gauge student progress and inform instruction.

Word Work

As students transition to the word work component of the session, they quickly review the vocabulary words on their word rings. During word work, students expand their understanding of the more complex rules governing letter and sound relationships that help them read and write new words. Students have the opportunity to familiarize themselves with word patterns that they encounter in many of their books. In this part of the session, LC teachers use their judgment as to what is best for each individual group of students. The teacher can use words from the focus book or word rings to drive the word work section, or he or she can select words with patterns and/or other words that may not be from the focus book but are still important for the students' literacy development.

Expanding Word Analysis Skills

This example illustrates what a word work session might look like for an emergent reader when using the word "treat" with magnetic plastic letters and boards. Word patterns and pronunciation are emphasized throughout this activity.

(Teacher passes out the letters t, a, e, r, t to each student and instructs them to orient letters at the top of their individual magnetic boards. Teacher models organizing letters.)

Teacher   Find two letters and build the word "at." Now let's check it. [Teacher runs finger under the word while saying "'a' 't't spells the word 'at.'"] Now let's do this together.

Students   [Chorally say the word with the LC teacher while running their fingers under the word on their board.] "a" "t" spells "at." [The LC teacher continues with "rat," "ate," "rate," "eat," "ear," "tar," "art," "are," and "tear."]

Students are directed to manipulate the letters and sounds to form these new words. For example, after they form the word "ate," they could be directed to rearrange those same letters to make the word "eat." Students can also form the word "rat," and then add one letter to the word to make the word say "rate," demonstrating the role of the e-marker in changing a short vowel sound to a long vowel sound. Finally, they are directed to use all of the letters to form the mystery word, which in this is example is "treat." Making words activities are used in the classroom as well, and the LC and classroom teachers have aligned the types of word analysis concepts used across the two settings. However, they adjusted the level of words used in the LC to those the students have had experience with in their texts.

As students become more proficient at rearranging the letters in a word to form other words, they should be allowed to work with partners or independently to form the words on their own. They often delight in trying to determine the mystery word that uses all of the letters.

Beginning on day 3 and continuing through day 5, a dictation exercise is added. This can include 1–2 well-crafted sentences (depending on the readiness of the students) that highlight writing skills students need support with and that are related to the topic of the focus text. Students self-correct their sentences each day, using different colored pencils for writing and correcting. The LC teacher reviews the concepts under study with the students during each dictation session. Students note their progress in writing the dictation and explaining the concepts across the 3 days. If the writing concepts are not mastered at that point, the LC teacher incorporates them into the dictation for the next week. For example, the following two sentences might be used with a focus on differentiating "was" and "saw" because this confusion was noted in student reading and writing. Some students struggle with using word endings; hence the plural "apples" was used in one of the sentences. "She," referring to the girl, will be highlighted, as will the words "ate," "real," and "treat," which were included in word work patterns used earlier in the week. The meaning of "real treat" will also be discussed.

The little girl saw the apples.

She ate one and it was a real treat.

Rereads

Rereading helps to build student confidence and fluency. On days 1–2 they reread in pairs and have a discussion about their book to help build their oral skills. The topic or focus of discussion depends on the students' needs. For example, if the students need to work with main ideas, the teacher can guide their discussion around the main idea of the book. This discussion should be a quick mini-conversation between the paired students about the book, focusing on a specific skill. As students reread and have their discussions, the teacher circulates and may join in and guide the conversation as needed.

In the last part of the week, students reread independently to help build their confidence. Also, reading independently gives the teacher the opportunity to listen to each individual student for fluency and use of reading strategies. The teacher meets with individual students and takes anecdotal notes of strengths and weaknesses. This is also an opportunity for the teacher to evaluate each student by making a running record during the week.

Writing

To help students be successful in the writing component of the LC, teachers work with students to develop a list of possible writing ideas. Its purpose is to provide students with quick access to several ideas that optimizes the time spent actually writing. The list may include labeled pictures to help more emergent readers remember what they were thinking about when they generated the ideas. For some students at this stage of writing, pictures are their most efficient way of representing ideas. Once this list is created, it may be updated throughout the year and serve as a guide for several writing pieces. The LC teacher scaffolds prewriting activities by providing sentence frames, orally rehearsing what will be written, and encouraging students to illustrate their writing. These supports let EAL students write with greater understanding and confidence.

The LC teacher selects a writing strategy to develop over one or more weeks and organizes the sessions so the amount of scaffolding decreases and student independence increases as the week(s) goes on. In the sample Writers' Workshop lessons this week, students focus on selecting a topic as the strategy. The writing builds off the reading that students are doing during the week and is scaffolded to guide students in writing about texts and conversations with partners.

The LC teacher meets with individual students to guide application of the new strategy as well as strategies previously introduced and practiced. Emphasis is placed on creating meaningful and interesting writing and revising that day's writing. Each day, students verbalize the strategy, describe how they have used it, and reflect on how it improves their writing (metacognition). They also focus on revising and editing their work (skills that have been previously introduced and practiced) individually and with a partner. After the LC teacher has finished meeting with students, they complete a self-assessment of the quality of their writing piece, how they applied the strategy, and how the strategy supported their learning. They share each writing piece with a partner or with the whole group to practice reading their own writing and to gain confidence as writers. Listeners provide specific feedback (also previously taught) about content and the structure of writing.

Writing Informative Text

Benji and Orlando help clarify the expectations for the prewriting activity in the following vignette and the LC teacher provides a description of the part they are unsure of. (What does a "new fact" mean?) She carefully scaffolds the prewriting activity by having students first create a list of what they've learned and then use the list to select a writing topic.

Teacher	This week our writing strategy is selecting a topic. What do you think that means?
Benji	Pick something to write about.
Teacher	Yes. Our content objective for today is "I will write and illustrate about a new fact I learned." [Picture clues can be added to help clarify the content objective.] What does illustrate mean?
Orlando	draw
Teacher	Yes. What does a "new fact" mean? [Students aren't sure.]
	A new fact is a new idea you learned about in our focus book this week. The topic we are going to select or pick is going to be one of the new ideas you learned about in the book. Let's make a list of some new ideas you learned from the book. [Students make suggestions and the LC teacher writes them down.]
	This is the first step in selecting a topic. We think about or make a list of things we might write about. Which new fact do you want to write about? [Students select topic from list.]

The teacher indicates that the next step is to tell about a new idea or fact and models how to select a topic and what was learned about the topic. Individual students tell what they learned about the topic they selected and the LC teacher asks questions and invites other children to add details. Students orally share what they have selected, using the sentence frame "I learned that _____."

Students begin writing and drawing and the LC teacher supports their efforts in writing about their topics and illustrating them. Days 2–4 build on the first day of writing. The LC teacher briefly reviews the week's strategy, selecting a topic, at the beginning of each session; discusses the content objective for each day; and briefly models each. A sentence frame is presented each day and students orally share their ideas and then begin writing. Some students are only able to write a single sentence about the topic, but all are encouraged to write more if possible to describe their topics as fully as they can.

The content objectives and sentence frames for each day are outlined here:

Day 2: I will write and illustrate about an interesting fact.

"An interesting fact I learned is _____."

Day 3: I will write and illustrate about an unusual fact.

"An unusual fact I learned is _____."

Day 4: I will write and illustrate about a "wondering" as a conclusion.

"I wonder _____."

The LC teacher meets with students each day and guides them in applying the strategy, writing on the topic, and editing their work. Day 4 serves as a conclusion for the week's writing topic and students independently rehearse reading their writing for the week. On day 5, students share what they have written for the week with the group. Before the sharing session begins, the LC teacher guides the students in creating a title for their writing and adding the date. The sharing session encourages the use of the following oral language prompts from the language objective:

"My informative text is about _____."

"One new fact I learned is _____."

"An interesting fact I learned is _____."

"An unusual fact I learned is _____."

"My illustration shows _____."

This is a cumulative opportunity for students to develop and expand their oral language skills and use of language for academic purposes as they share their week's writing work.

CONCLUSION

Grades 1–2 are an ideal time to make the LC available for language learners who are struggling with literacy development in English and/or Spanish. At these grade levels they are often not significantly behind grade-level expectations in oracy, literacy, and metacognitive development, and the LC gives them the extra support they need to make significant progress toward these expectations. In grade 2 especially, students are able to build on the background they have acquired in kindergarten and grade 1 and with additional LC support are often able to make substantial progress in both literacy and language development. Many students at these grades levels have mastered bits and pieces of understanding about literacy development but have so far been unable to expand and integrate them into a cohesive whole that lets them effectively gain meaning from text or express ideas in writing.

Very often the LC plays a significant role in assisting students in developing the skills and strategies needed at this level to be successful in using language to communicate for a variety of purposes orally and in writing. As we have seen in the bilingual and English-medium strands with grade 1 and 2 language learners, LC teachers analyze the individual needs of students, target grade-level goals and standards, and provide scaffolded learning experiences within a supportive environment. The different pathways to literacy they make available enable language learners to make significant progress.

It is important for LC teachers to create a positive learning environment where students feel confident, are motivated to learn, and are willing to take risks with their language and literacy development. Sessions should be engaging, interactive, and manageable for language learners. As their literacy and language skills develop, students generally begin to demonstrate a genuine enthusiasm for reading and writing. Often this is accompanied by the emergence of a more positive attitude toward learning in general. Quite often, rapid linguistic and academic growth is a hallmark at this level and it is not unusual to see a student advance across several reading levels in a single academic year.

QUESTIONS FOR REFLECTION AND ACTION

- Analyze the role of bridging in the LC at grades 1–2. How might it be used to facilitate the development of biliteracy?
- How would you determine the needs of a group of students in your school/district in grades 1 or 2? Create a T-chart of oracy, literacy, and metacognition needs for a group of students at this level. How would you design an LC for these students that would address the same goals through different pathways?
- How would you develop a grade 1–2 framework for collaboration between LC and classroom teachers in your school/district?
- What factors (students, standards, EAL/bilingual program delivery models, human and material resources, staff development) need to be considered when designing an LC program to meet the needs of grade 1–2 students in your school/district? Brainstorm ways to deal with these factors to create an effective LC in your school/district.

5

Literacy Club with Language Learners in Grade 3

KEY CONCEPTS

- The focus in grade 3 is on more sophisticated development of higher-order thinking skills and the use of language for academic purposes in both bilingual and English-medium settings.
- Metacognitive development related to learning strategies, analysis of structure, and use of language are important components of a grade 3 instruction and intervention plan.
- Assessment measures at grade 3 focus on analysis of literacy and oracy skills related to the development of critical thinking and use of language for academic purposes.

Grade 3 **Literacy Club (LC)** students often have an uneven acquisition of prereading strategies (e.g., previewing a text or predicting with evidence) and have not yet developed the level of skills and strategies needed for advancing confidently toward grade-level expectations. For example, a student may rely almost exclusively on sounding out words letter by letter when encountering an unfamiliar word, rather than using syllables, word chunks, context clues, and prior knowledge—skills that are generally mastered in grade 1 or 2. Although students' development of literacy, language, and content may be uneven, the LC builds on what they can do and expands their critical thinking and metalinguistic skills.

This chapter begins with the advancing bilingual strand, continues with the emerging bilingual strand, and concludes with the English as an additional language (EAL) strand to illustrate how all strands lead to the same goals but take different pathways. Recall that the **advancing bilingual strand** targets students with strong Spanish oracy skills and uses two languages to reach **oracy**, **literacy**, and **metacognition** (**strategy development** and **metalinguistic awareness**) goals in both languages. The **emerging bilingual strand** is for students with strong oracy skills in English, and draws on these resources to reach the same goals of oracy and literacy in two languages, as well as strategy development and metalinguistic awareness. The **EAL strand** targets students from a wide range of backgrounds in English-medium classrooms or those in contexts where no **bilingual program** is available. This pathway has the same goals of oracy, literacy, and metacognition, and draws on home languages as important resources but does not have bilingualism or biliteracy as a goal or expected outcome.

LANGUAGE AND LITERACY DEMANDS

At the grade 3 level, the English language arts (ELA) standards move beyond grade 2 expectations by requiring students to use textual evidence, details, and illustrations more fully in speaking, reading, and writing. Greater attention is placed on analyzing how each section of text builds on earlier sections, distinguishing their own points of view from those in the text, and describing relationships among concepts and texts. In addition to introducing, developing, and concluding topics, students focus attention on using linking words/ phrases and dialogue in their writing.

These skills begin to prepare students for grade 4 standards that focus on summarizing one or more texts on a particular topic and interpreting visual, oral, and quantitative information to explain, describe, and draw inferences. They identify and compare similar themes and different points of view in a variety of genres. Students are expected to clearly introduce and develop well-organized writing topics that are supported by facts, details, and quotes and write conclusions related to the body of the text.

At grade 3 the four components of the LC (focus book, word work, rereads, and writing) may be addressed in any order in the sessions; however, it is important to emphasize both reading and writing every week, though not necessarily every day. At more emergent levels, it is easier to schedule both writing and reading in every LC session because the content is less complex and students complete each task relatively quickly. However, at grade 3, students begin to read and write more extended text and may need larger blocks of time to focus on these activities. Therefore, it may not be possible to schedule both reading and writing in every session. The LC teacher may arrange the schedule so that some days are dedicated more fully to reading-related activities and others to writing, as we see in Table 5.1.

TABLE 5.1 Sample Schedules

SAMPLE SCHEDULE 1

Monday through Thursday	Friday
■ Focus book ■ Word work ■ Rereads ■ Writing	■ Rereads ■ Writing ■ Share writing

SAMPLE SCHEDULE 2

Monday and Wednesday	Tuesday and Thursday	Friday
■ Rereads ■ Focus book ■ Word work ■ Writing	■ Writing ■ Rereads ■ Focus book ■ Word work	■ Rereads ■ Writing ■ Share writing

SAMPLE SCHEDULE 3

Monday and Tuesday	Wednesday and Thursday	Friday
■ Rereads ■ Focus book ■ Word work	■ Focus book ■ Word work ■ Writing	■ Rereads ■ Share writing

The work completed in the bridging activities for the two bilingual strands at the end of the week helps students expand the set of strategies available to them in becoming biliterate. Exploring cognates not only expands their vocabularies in two languages, it sharpens their ability to identify morphological and semantic cues that are known in one language and can be used to enhance meaning and understanding in their other language(s). This is especially applicable in the content areas, where many academic terms have cognates in English and Spanish. In the sample sessions that follow, LC students focus on identifying main ideas and inferences in **comparative analysis** activities. These types of experiences help students gain skill in applying literacy strategies across both languages and expand their repertoires of language practices.

TEACHER COLLABORATION

Grade 3 LC and classroom teachers work together to select strategies for both informational and narrative text throughout the year. However, because of the increasing emphasis on informational text and the fact that most teachers have already developed expertise in creating units of study using narrative text, a large number of examples developing themes using informational text are used in this book. The teachers collaborate on the selection of both content and language objectives and coordinate the types of learning experiences used in developing these objectives across the two settings to ensure that students have ample opportunities to develop them fully.

CONTINUOUS PROGRESS MONITORING

In addition to the usual **formative** and **summative assessments** used in the LC, highlighting the oracy development of our focal student, *Evelyn Gloria*, in the emerging bilingual strand enables us to focus more directly on how oracy is strategically developed and measured. Oral language samples provide us with one source of ongoing data about growth in the content and complexity of language use. Measurement in relation to specific language standards in both speaking and writing informs instruction for LC teachers in continually creating rich and supportive language environments, ensuring that students have a clear sense of language expectations, and providing opportunities for students to reflect on their own progress.

TEXT SELECTION

Because the complexity of informational texts steadily increases by grade level, it is important that LC students understand and use informational text features at grade 3. The LC teacher must determine which text features students have already mastered and which ones still need to be developed. Growth in oracy and literacy skills is crucial; therefore, texts must be selected that lend themselves to exploration of language for both social and academic purposes. Selection of linguistically and culturally responsive texts lets students see themselves reflected in print and enables them to build on their experiences in and understanding of the world.

Students at this level may be experiencing a great deal of frustration, especially with learning experiences involving informational text. The LC activities must be very student-centered to bolster the areas where students have an uneven profile of skills and strategies in learning. Selecting texts that reflect the culture, experiences, and interests of the students also heightens motivation for literacy-related learning experiences. Teachers must have the flexibility to focus on and strengthen areas of strategy development and critical thinking (metacognition), as well as areas of vocabulary, language structure, and discourse in linguistic development.

ADVANCING BILINGUAL STRAND

Our grade 3 students in the advancing bilingual strand, Esteban, Maricruz, Rolando, and Melanie, each have fairly well-developed oracy skills in conversational Spanish because Spanish is their home language. However, understanding and using language for academic purposes at grade 3 generally challenges them. LC participation lets them expand and solidify skills in this area, including using evidence from texts to support ideas or opinions, distinguishing between their own points of view and those of the author, or making connections among sentences and paragraphs in a text.

Table 5.2 provides a suggested format for LC sessions with advancing bilingual students. However, at this level, it may be necessary to make changes in the schedule to allow for longer periods of engagement in reading and/or writing to provide time for students to develop these skills. For example, if students have been working on supporting their opinions with textual evidence in their writing but they are struggling with this concept, learning would be more meaningful if they spend additional time mastering the concept rather than switching to other activities.

The LC and classroom teachers have collaborated in the example that follows to determine how best to work toward developing biliteracy for these students by integrating learning between the two settings. During planning time, the LC and classroom teachers plan collaboratively using assessments and work samples from each student to organize the most effective approach for teaching the students in both settings. In the classroom, as part of their science curriculum, the students are studying how some animals form groups to survive and they continue exploring this theme in the LC. In the LC, students are reading the text *Gansos migratorios* (*Migrating Geese*) by Veronica Angel, which focuses on the migrations of geese and how they work together to survive. Both teachers are focusing on the strategy of inference in reading and developing an informational piece in writing.

The LC and classroom teachers have noted, for example, that Esteban is struggling with applying background knowledge to make inferences. The LC teacher engages the students in scaffolded discussions that are especially helpful for Esteban in making these connections. Maricruz is given additional practice with irregular plurals and analyzing statements

TABLE 5.2 Format for Grade 3 Advancing Spanish Bilingual Strand					
	Day 1	**Day 2**	**Day 3**	**Day 4**	**Day 5**
Focus book	Introduction Choral read Self-assess	Read Discuss strategy	Read Discuss strategy	Read Bridge general ideas	Read Spanish/ English Self-assess
Word work	Spanish concepts *Dictado*	Spanish concepts *Dictado*	Spanish concepts *Dictado*	Cognates English	Cognates English
Rereads	Pairs	Pairs	Independent	Independent	Spanish/English
Writing	Spanish*	Spanish*	Spanish*	Modified *Así se dice*	English

*Self-selected topics.

BOX 5.1 Content and Language Objectives for the Week

Tema	Los animales forman grupos para sobrevivir.	Theme	*Animals form groups to survive.*

OBJETIVOS NUEVOS/NEW OBJECTIVES

Contenido	Yo podré hacer inferencias sobre los gansos basandome en el texto.	Content	*I will be able to make inferences about geese based on the text.*
	Yo podré formar opiniones sobre como los gansos sobreviven.		*I will be able to form opinions about how geese survive.*
Lenguaje	Yo podré escribir una opinión sobre como los gansos forman grupos para sobrevivir.	Language	*I will be able to write an opinion about how geese form groups to survive.*
	[usando un organizador gráfico + porque, por ejemplo, por esta razón]		*[using a graphic organizer + because, for example, for this reason]*

REVISAMOS/REVIEW OBJECTIVES

	Yo podré usar letras mayúsculas, puntuación, y deletreo correcto.		*I will be able to use capital letters, punctuation, and spelling correctly.*
	Yo podré identificar cognados entre palabras en inglés y español.		*I will be able to identify cognates between English and Spanish words.*

from Spanish to English. They collaboratively review the progress of all of the students in the group periodically using assessment data and work samples they have collected.

Content and language objectives for the sample advancing bilingual strand are outlined in Box 5.1. The content objectives are linked directly to the ELA standards being addressed in the classroom. The language objectives support learning language for academic purposes in the content areas and are differentiated according to students' levels of Spanish and English **language development**. Teacher data collection and student self-assessment measures are used that reflect both the literacy and the language objectives to provide teachers and students with the opportunity to gauge progress in each of these areas.

Focus Book

On day 1, the LC teacher begins by reviewing texts the students have already read on the theme of animal survival in the classroom, as a way to activate prior knowledge and link prior learning to the new text. Students discuss the animal groups they have already studied and how they work together to help one another. The teacher then introduces the new text by asking students to read the title and author. In the following activity, the emphasis is placed on identifying the main idea and supporting details. The teacher asks the students a series of questions to build background, practice vocabulary, and prepare them for writing later in the week involving making inferences.

Making Inferences

This example illustrates how the strategy of inference is introduced. Comprehension is enhanced as students are able to determine the main idea. Using context and prior knowledge to analyze the meaning of key vocabulary is part of this overview and the LC teacher works with Rolando a bit to figure out what *migratorios* might mean in this context. The LC teacher clearly **scaffolds** the strategy of inferencing by pointing out that the book never states why the geese migrate but that they can infer the reason by combining what the book says with what they already know about weather changes. This scaffolding assists the students in meaningfully exploring the concept of animals working together to survive and using academic language to explain what they have learned.

Teacher	¿Piensan que los gansos trabajan juntos para sobrevivir? Usen las ilustraciones para que se ayuden.	*Do you think the geese work together to survive? Use the illustration to help you.*
Esteban	Forman una --v-- cuando están volando.	*They form a "v" when they are flying.*
Teacher	Sí, ¿cómo le sirve al grupo si vuelan en forma de --v--?	*Yes. How does flying in a "v" formation help the group?*

(pause as students think)

Teacher	Vamos a leer para aprender si esta acción le ayuda al grupo o no. ¿Hay otros ejemplos de cómo los gansos se ayudan unos a otros? [La maestra acepta toda respuesta razonable.]	*Let's read to learn if this action helps the group or not. Are there other examples of how geese help one another? [Teacher accepts all reasonable responses.]*
	Muy bien. Cuando leemos este libro debemos determinar cómo los gansos se ayudan unos a otros para sobrevivir.	*Very good. As we read this book we will be deciding how geese help one another to survive.*

(pause as students begin to read)

Teacher	¿Qué significa la palabra --migratorios--? Si los gansos están migrando, ¿qué hacen?	*What does the word "migratory" mean? If the geese are migrating, what are they doing?*
Rolando	Están volando.	*They are flying.*
Teacher	Sí, Rolando están volando. Entonces, ¿que piensas que significa --migratorios--?	*Yes, Rolando, they are flying. Then what do you think "migrating" means?*
Rolando	Van a otro lugar.	*They are going to another place.*
Teacher	[La maestro continúa con el diálogo, enfocando en el cognado --inmigrante--.] Vamos a leer las primeras dos páginas juntos. [Después de leer] ¿Por qué los gansos deben salir y volar al sur? [La maestra acepta cada respuesta razonable. Respuestas pueden incluir --Porque hace frío.-- --Viene el invierno.--]	*[The teacher continues with the dialogue, focusing on the cognate "immigrant."] Let's read the first two pages together. [After reading] Why do the geese need to leave and fly south? [Teacher accepts all reasonable responses. Responses may include "Because it's cold." "Winter is coming."]*
	Sí, pero ¿por qué deben salir si hace frío o viene el invierno? [La maestra acepta toda respuesta razonable como, --No hay comida para ellos en el invierno.-- --No les gusta el frío.--]	*Yes, but why do they have to leave if it's cold or winter is coming? [Teacher accepts all reasonable responses such as, "There is no food for them in the winter." "They don't like the cold."]*

The LC teacher indicates that the book never tells us these things directly and yet we know them to be true. The students discuss why this might be, and the teacher clarifies that the strategy of inference means that we use clues the text and illustrations give us, as well as our prior knowledge. The LC teacher guides students to make connections to work done in the classroom on this topic and then provides more opportunities for students to locate inferences in the two pages they just read. Responses may include, *"Dice que es el otoño, y el invierno llegará pronto. La inferencia es que el invierno sigue el otoño."* ("It says that it is fall and that winter will come soon. The inference is that winter comes after fall.")

The LC teacher and students continue reading the text, stopping to discuss how the geese might be helping one another survive and if they can make additional inferences. At the end of the text, the teacher asks the students whether or not they think the geese work in groups to survive and indicates that they have just made an inference. She asks them to share statements from the text to support their inferences and tells them they will be writing to explain what they learned a bit later in the week. The teacher also recaps the use of inference in the text with a metacognitive activity by asking students to share inferences that they made while reading. A discussion follows about how making inferences helps them understand a text more fully. To end the first session with the focus text, students complete the reading/strategy portion of the self-assessment in Box 5.2. Note that in this self-assessment students are asked to first reflect on how using the inferencing strategy helped them learn, and then to set a goal for improvement. Both of these self-assessment activities strengthen students' metacognition. Students repeat the same self-assessment at the end of the week to reflect on their progress.

On days 2 and 3, the LC teacher rereads the text with the student, stopping to have them point out inferences they have made, clues they have used to make the inferences, and how

---

BOX 5.2 Beginning-/End-of-Week Student Self-Assessment

Nombre _____   Fecha _____

El libro es	This book is
Fácil Más o menos Difícil de leer.	*Easy Average Difficult to read.*
Estrategia de lectura: Hacer inferencias	*Reading strategy: Making inferences*
es Fácil Más o menos Difícil.	*is Easy Average Difficult.*
Ejemplo: Los gansos migran al sur en el invierno porque no hay comida.	*Example: The geese migrate south in winter because there is no food.*
Algo nuevo que aprendí usando la estrategia:	*Something new that I learned using this strategy:*
Estrategia de escritura: Formar opinions	*Writing strategy: Forming opinions*
es Fácil Más o menos Difícil.	*is Easy Average Difficult.*
Mi meta para mejorar:	*My goal to improve:*

making the inferences helped them understand the text more fully. They also work on using sentence frames to state their inferences: *Yo creo que _____ porque _____.* (I think _____ because _____.) The teacher provides practice with oracy skills by asking them to state what evidence they have for their inferences, which also serves as oral rehearsal for their writing on day 3.

On day 4, the students read the focus text in pairs or independently, reviewing the strategy and anything new they noticed in the text. Next the teacher works with the group to bridge the general ideas of the text from Spanish to English in an ***Así se dice*** (That's how you say it) activity (Escamilla et al, 2014). In this activity students underline 3–4 key sentences from the text they have been reading in Spanish that capture the main ideas of the text. They work together to determine how to express the same ideas in English, putting their work on a dry erase board. This is followed by a discussion of similarities and differences in vocabulary, sentence structure, and meaning across the two languages that enhances their metalinguistic awareness.

Analyzing Structures across Languages

The following vignette illustrates how students use Spanish and English to make meaning and analyze similarities and differences in structure across languages. They apply what they know of making plurals from one language to the other and then explore the concept of irregular plurals. They note "*se pone más frío*" is expressed as "it gets" rather than "it puts" in English, and they develop the cognitive flexibility to understand and manipulate meaning from one language to the other. The language component of this activity focuses on verbalizing structural differences across languages, which expands metacognitive skills.

Teacher	Miremos esta frase en la página 3: --Cuando el clima se pone más frío, los gansos vuelan al sur.-- ¿Cómo se dice esto en inglés?	*Look at the phrase on page 3:* --Cuando el clima se pone más frío, los gansos vuelan al sur.-- *How would we say that in English?*
Maricruz	when the temperature puts more cold	
Teacher	En inglés se dice, "when the temperature gets colder"	
Esteban	When the temperature gets colder, the gooses fly south.	
Teacher	Tenemos "one goose," pero tenemos "two _____."	We have "one goose," but we have "two _____."
Maricruz	gooses	
Teacher	Añadimos la --s-- para las palabras regulares en inglés pero la palabra "goose" en inglés es irregular.	We add the letter "s" to regular words in English but the word "goose" is irregular in English.
Maricruz	¡Yo sé! Es "geese." When the temperatures get colder, the geese fly south.	*I know! It's "geese." When the temperatures get colder, the geese fly south.*

An English translation of the text, *Migrating Geese,* is available, which allows the students to compare their translations from Spanish to English with an "official" translation of the text they had read in Spanish. The teacher underlines the sentences the students have analyzed in the Spanish text, and the students compare their translations to the English text and discuss how the structures differ from one language to the other. Students read these sentences in English, as well as the entire Spanish text, for their reading material on day 5.

Setting Appropriate Goals for Language and Literacy

On day 5 students repeat the self-assessment completed on day 1, review their progress, and set a goal for the following week, which assists them with determining how they are progressing in making inferences. The LC teacher helps the students set appropriate goals for continued progress in literacy by giving examples, asking students to reflect on what they need to improve, and how they might focus on a particular area. Through the creation of shared writing goals, students learn how to begin setting appropriate goals for themselves, as reflected in the following vignette.

Teacher	¿Quién tiene una meta para la próxima semana?	*Who has a goal for next week?*
Esteban	Quiero leer mejor.	*I want to read better.*
Teacher	Muy bien, pero esta es una meta muy grande. ¿Cómo quieres leer mejor?	*Very good, but this is a very large goal. What do you want to do to read better?*
Esteban	Quiero leer más rápido y no parar tanto entre las palabras.	*I want to read faster and not stop so much between words.*
Teacher	Esta se llama --leer con fluidez--. Tú puedes escribir --Quiero leer con fluidez--.	*This is called "reading with fluency." You could write "I want to read with fluency."*

The LC teacher continues the dialogue and supports students in writing their goals using ELA terminology where applicable. Responses may include "*Quiero practicar hacer inferencias.*" ("I want to practice making inferences.") Students generally need practice to understand how to set measurable goals and then how to use goal-setting to monitor their own progress. The interaction between the LC teacher and Esteban illustrates how students are guided to set appropriate goals that will be meaningful for them. Over time, most students are able to use goal-setting to become more independent in their learning. The individual goals that they set in these activities may include areas that other students in the general classroom have already mastered. Thus, they reflect the creation of different pathways for the students that bolster their skills and growth toward grade-level goals.

Word Work

At the beginning of the word work portion of the session, students quickly review vocabulary words on the word rings that they prepare for each new text. The LC teacher may wish to have students add sketches and/or notes on the backs of word cards where applicable as a scaffold to assist them in recalling pronunciation or definitions. On days 4–5, they add selected English words that have been introduced during the bridging portion as part of their comparative analysis activities for the week to the word cards. Spanish vocabulary words are written in red and English words in blue. Only a small, previously agreed on number of key words are selected from each text to be included on the word rings; this helps students increase the number of sight words at their disposal.

On days 1–3 students also begin work on identifying weak/closed (i, u) and strong/open (a, e, o) vowels and how diphthongs (*diptongos*) are pronounced and spelled.

Analyzing Formation and Syllabication of Diphthongs

The vignette that follows shows how students explore formation and syllabication of diphthongs, with attention to how they would apply an understanding of these patterns in word analysis. The LC teacher asks students to pronounce the vowels in Spanish and to notice how their mouths are more open when saying vowels than consonants, which provides a foundation for their work on diphthongs.

Teacher	Vamos a escribir la primera palabra. Tiene 6 letras, pués pongan 6 guiones en sus papeles. Escriban la palabra --cuidan--. --Los gansos cuidan a sus bebés.--	*Let's write the first word. It has 6 letters, so put 6 dashes on your papers. Write the word --cuidan--. "The geese take care of their babies."*
	(pause as students write)	
Teacher	Vamos a deletrear la palabra juntos: c-u-i-d-a-n, cuidan.	*Let's spell the word together: c-u-i-d-a-n, cuidan.*
	¿Cuántas sílabas hay?	*How many syllables are there?*
Melanie	dos, cui–dan	*two, cui–dan*
Teacher	Cuando una vocal débil combina con otra vocal débil o con una vocal fuerte, forman un diptongo.	*When a weak vowel combines with another weak vowel or with a strong vowel, they form a diphthong.*

The class continues with a discussion of how to divide the word into syllables and the LC teacher introduces the concept of diphthongs and how they are pronounced. The following words from the text are used as examples: *nieve* (snow), *hielo* (ice), *hierba* (grass), *vuelan* (fly), *paisaje* (landscape), *fueran* (were), *cuando* (when), *huevos* (eggs). In future lessons, these concepts are expanded.

Also on days 1–3, the students complete the following **dictado**, focusing on these grammar/spelling patterns: future tense, double vowels, and use of *ñ*. The *dictado* reinforces these concepts and provides opportunities for students to discuss what they notice about grammar, spelling, and language structure, which also expands their sense of **metalanguage**. Note that the first two sentences come from *Gansos migratorios* by Veronica Angel, which the students have already read.

1. Cuando el clima se pone más frío, los gansos vuelan al sur.

2. Es el otoño, y el invierno llegará pronto.

3. El paisaje estará cubierto de nieve y hielo.

1. *When the weather gets colder, the geese fly south.*

2. *It is fall, and winter will soon come.*

3. *The ground will be covered with snow and ice.*

Students use a different colored pencil to correct their work and do not erase their original writing. In this way they are able to note specific problem areas and how well they master these concepts during *dictado* exercises each day.

On days 4 and 5, students search for English cognates in the Spanish **focus book** as part of their bridging activities. Possible words for cognate study in this text include *abundante/abundant, aire/air, bebés/babies, distancias/distances, familia/family, formación/formation, frente/front, letra/letter, migran/migrate, migratorios/migratory, moverse/to move, norte/north, recupera/recuperate,* and *temperatura/temperature.* As the students find cognates, they create a T-chart to display in their study area, with the title of the focus book written across the top. The LC teacher verifies that the words are indeed cognates as the children find them and place them on the chart, actions that support kinesthetic learners. Once they are able to readily identify cognates, students may be paired and given a section of the text to search together to make the most efficient use of time. After the list has been created, students compare spelling, pronunciation, and meaning of words to expand their comparative analysis skills in examining the structure of words across the two languages.

Rereads

On days 1 and 2, students reread texts in pairs, and on days 3 and 4 they reread independently. During this time the LC teacher may choose to listen to individual students read; conduct **running records** to check for reading accuracy, strategy use, and fluency; and engage students in brief discussions about the text as a measure of comprehension. The LC teacher may share observations with the students about how they are applying skills and strategies while reading. On day 5, they reread a Spanish text along with the English equivalent.

Writing

On days 1–2, students self-select writing topics and orally share their ideas for writing with a partner as a rehearsal for writing, which enhances the development of oracy and better prepares them for writing. They can refer to their list of writing ideas if they are not readily able to select a topic. Day 3 writing features a shift in focus to the content topic for the week. The topic of how geese rely on being part of a group to survive has been read about and discussed throughout the week. Today students are asked to write an informational piece about how being part of a group is important for geese. They can use the form in Box 5.3 to organize their information and support their statements with textual evidence.

BOX 5.3 *Bosquejo para la escritura*/Writing Outline

ESCRITURA: FORMANDO UNA OPINION/WRITING: FORMING AN OPINION

Nombre _____   Fecha _____

Preparando para escribir/*Prewriting outline*:

Opinión/*Opinion*:

Pruebas/*Evidence*:

Conclusión/*Conclusion*:

Autoevaluación:*	Self-assessment:*
_____ Escribir una opinión	_____ *Write an opinion*
_____ Puntuación	_____ *Punctuation*
_____ Deletreo	_____ *Spelling*

*Marquen/*Score*: 1, fácil (*easy*); 2, más o menos (*average*); 3, difícil (*difficult*).

These learning experiences reflect the Next Generation Science Standard 3-LS2-1: Construct an argument that some animals form groups that help them survive.

Prewriting—Outlining Topic and Supporting Evidence

The following vignette is an example of scaffolding writing in science. Extending concepts into the writing portion of the LC provides additional opportunities for students to develop better understanding of the subject matter. The LC teacher has carefully scaffolded the writing activity because while students have been exposed to this type of writing in the classroom, they need additional practice to solidify these skills. In the LC they receive individualized support in refining skills introduced in the classroom.

Teacher	La primera cosa que vamos a hacer [como ustedes lo hacen en el salón de clase cuando están preparándose para escribir una explicación] es que debemos formar nuestra idea principal. Hablen con un amigo para expresar su tema.	*The first thing that we're going to do [just like you do in the classroom when you get ready to write an explanation] is that we need to form our main idea. Talk with a friend and tell how you will express your theme.*

(Students talk to their partners.)

Teacher	Escriban su tema en el papel que les di.	*Write your topic on the paper I gave you.*

(Each student writes topic on the paper.)

Teacher	Aprendimos que los gansos forman grupos para sobrevivir. Ahora debemos proveer pruebas o evidencia para describir cómo lo hacen. Podemos usar estas frases para ayudarnos:	*We learned that geese form groups to survive. Now we need to find proof or evidence to describe how they do that. We can use these sentence frames to help us:*
	Los gansos forman grupos para sobrevivir. Lo hacen por _____. También ellos _____ y _____. Por estas razónes, _____.	*Geese form groups to survive. They do this by _____. They also _____ and _____. For these reasons, _____.*
Maricruz	Se turnan cuando están volando gran distancias y un ganso se queda con otro que está herido.	*They take turns when they are flying long distances and one goose will help another that is wounded.*
Teacher	¿Hay otras pruebas? Hablen con un amigo.	*Do you have other evidence? Talk with a friend.*

(Students talk to their partners.)

Teacher	Para terminar la escritura debemos tener una conclusión. ¿Alguién tiene una idea acerca de cómo va a concluir su escritura?	*To finish our writing we need a conclusion. Does anyone have an idea about how to conclude your writing?*
Melanie	Los gansos son un buen ejemplo de cómo los animales forman grupos para sobrevivir porque ayudan el uno al otro.	*The geese are a good example of how animals form groups to survive because they help one another.*

Maricruz was able to read from the text to provide evidence of how geese work together and Melanie provided a very succinct conclusion for this writing activity that students can use as a model for writing their own conclusions.

On day 4, the students participate in a modified version of *Así se dice* (Escamilla et al, 2014), and complete a comparative analysis of the text from the *dictado* completed on days

1–3. Using the same text for both the word work and the *Así se dice* provides the repetition that is so necessary for LC students.

1. Cuando el clima se pone más frío, los gansos vuelan al sur.	**1.** *When the weather gets colder, the geese fly south.*
2. Es el otoño, y el invierno llegará pronto.	**2.** *It is fall, and winter will come soon.*
3. El paisaje estará cubierto de nieve y hielo.	**3.** *The ground will be covered with snow and ice.*

Discussions may revolve around the following phrase differences from Spanish to English—*el clima*/weather, *se pone*/gets, *al sur*/south, *el paisaje*/the ground—and how students use their language resources in Spanish and English to understand these differences.

On day 5, students write in English. They can write about the text they have been reading for the week or self-select a topic. Students are encouraged to work collaboratively if they need assistance because English is often the less well-developed language for this group. The LC teacher meets with students, has them orally state their ideas before writing, and guides them in completing their writing in English. Students use the writing self-assessment on day 5 to monitor their growth for the week and set a goal for the upcoming week. Oral rehearsal for writing and student collaboration serve as examples of how the LC can use the language skills of the group in Spanish and English oracy and literacy as resources for expanding the language skills of individual students.

EMERGING BILINGUAL STRAND

Students in the emerging bilingual strand generally have strong oracy skills in English and are at the early stages of Spanish oracy development. Some have no exposure to Spanish outside of the classroom (e.g., students from English-speaking homes in dual language programs), and others have varying degrees of oracy in Spanish that reflect their experiences using Spanish at home and throughout the community. Students in this strand may also have a broad range of literacy skills in Spanish and English. For example, students may be at grade level or beyond in English literacy and therefore ready to take on higher levels of Spanish literacy than their scores in Spanish would indicate. LC teachers can draw on their paired literacy approach to identify and use students' literacy strengths in English to accelerate literacy development in Spanish (see also Escamilla et al, 2014).

Here, Spanish reading ability is assessed with the ***Evaluación del desarrollo de la lectura 2* (EDL2)** test to measure accuracy, fluency, and comprehension using benchmark assessment books, which parallels the **Developmental Reading Assessment 2+ (DRA2+)** test in English. Although the grade 3 students in the following vignette scored at Level 3/emergent reader in Spanish on the EDL2, they are reading slightly above grade level in English. Therefore, the decision is made to have them move to a Level 8/early reader Spanish text because they have been in the bilingual program since kindergarten and have strong listening comprehension skills in Spanish. Additional support may be needed initially, but they should successfully navigate the challenges of the new level because they have already developed strong literacy skills in English. Table 5.3 provides an overview of the Spanish sessions in the emerging bilingual strand.

In the classroom, the students are studying the water cycle, a theme that the LC teacher also addresses. The text that the LC students are reading is a Reading A–Z, Level H/early reader text entitled, *El agua de la tierra/Earth's Water* by Katherine Scraper and translated by Lorena Di Bello. Although the classroom and LC teachers use different texts and learn-

TABLE 5.3 Format for Grade 3 Emerging Spanish Bilingual Strand

	Day 1	Day 2	Day 3	Day 4	Day 5
Focus book	Oral: concepts Vocabulary Self-assess	Choral read Discuss strategy	Read Discuss strategy	Read Orally bridge general ideas	Read Spanish/ English Self-assess
Word work	Spanish concepts *Dictado*	Spanish concepts *Dictado*	Spanish concepts *Dictado*	Cognates English	Cognates English
Rereads	Read in pairs	Retell in pairs	Independent	Independent	Spanish/English
Writing	Language experience approach— sentence frames	Paired—content	Paired—content	Paired—bridge	English

ing experiences, they both focus on the same goals, in this case text features (bolded words, pictures and captions, table of contents, glossary) as the strategy to be reinforced.

The students in the LC group need to strengthen background knowledge and use language for academic purposes as part of their study of the water cycle. The LC teacher uses a text that focuses on the different forms of water; in the classroom, students are also required to describe the water cycle, which serves as a review before beginning a unit on environmental changes and their impact on organisms. Their work in this unit of instruction is aligned with one of the Next Generation Science Standards that reads, "When the environment changes, the types of plants and animals that live there may change also." The LC text is supplemented with additional labeled graphics from the classroom to introduce and reinforce the terms and description of the water cycle as the week progresses. These concepts are reinforced through word work, discussion, and writing. Box 5.4 provides an overview of the content and language objectives for the sample lessons that follow.

The emerging bilingual strand includes Evelyn Gloria who we know is struggling with Spanish oracy and, to a lesser extent, writing in Spanish because her only exposure to Spanish is in the classroom. Her written and graphic responses to content indicate that she understands concepts quite well. However, despite the fact that she has been in a **dual language program** since 4K (kindergarten for 4 year olds), transcripts of her oral responses to prompts indicate that she understands concepts and questions in Spanish, but makes only minimal oral responses to them. The LC teacher, in collaboration with the classroom teacher, has chosen to address this area by providing more opportunities for Evelyn Gloria to develop her Spanish oracy. They scaffold this process by developing **total physical response (TPR)** actions for key vocabulary, using sentence frames and word banks to support oral responses, and guiding oral rehearsal for writing. Anecdotal records of oral responses and student self-assessments are used to assess Evelyn Gloria's progress using oral Spanish.

Focus Book

On day 1 the LC teacher orally introduces the concepts developed in the text and key vocabulary through the use of visuals and text features. She informs the students that they will talk about the water cycle and what might happen to organisms within an environment if the amount of water increases or decreases. A graphic of the water cycle to be used

BOX 5.4 Content and Language Objectives for the Week

Tema	El ciclo de agua	Theme	*Water cycle*

OBJETIVOS NUEVOS/NEW OBJECTIVES

Contenido	Yo podré describir el ciclo del agua usando un organizador gráfico— primero, después, entonces.	Content	*I will be able to describe the water cycle using a graphic organizer—first, next, then.*
Lenguaje	Yo podré hablar del agua de la Tierra, usando ilustraciones, palabras en negrita, tabla de contenidos, y glosario.	Language	*I will be able to talk about water on Earth, using illustrations, bolded words, the table of contents, and the glossary.*
	Yo podré hacer preguntas acerca del agua de la Tierra.		*I will be able to ask questions about water on Earth.*

REVISAMOS/REVIEWING

	Yo podré usar letras mayúsculas, puntuación, y deletreo correcto.		*I will be able to correctly use capital letters, punctuation, and spelling.*
	Yo podré identificar cognados entre palabras en inglés y español.		*I will be able to identify cognates between English and Spanish words.*

throughout this theme shows these concepts very simply. The group begins by reviewing the title, author, and translator of the text and then turns to the table of contents.

Using Text Features as a Reading Strategy

This vignette provides an example of how the LC teacher reinforces the use of text features that have been introduced in the classroom but that need additional review in the LC. The session begins with exercises in using the table of contents as a text feature. Evelyn Gloria and the other students in this group, Olivia, Carter, and Roberto, receive ongoing support in expressing their ideas in complete sentences and in expanding their Spanish vocabulary.

Teacher	¿Cómo nos ayuda la página tabla de contenidos cuando estamos leyendo?	*How does the table of contents help us when we are reading?*
Evelyn Gloria	"To know" dónde está "the information."	*To know where information is.*
Teacher	[a Evelyn Gloria] ¿Cómo decimos "to know" en español?	*[to Evelyn Gloria] How do we say "to know" in Spanish?*
Evelyn Gloria	saber	
Teacher	[a Evelyn Gloria] Sí, -- saber--. Ahora, repite usando una oración completa: --Nos ayuda a saber dónde podemos encontrar cierta información. --	*[to Evelyn Gloria] Yes, --saber--. Now say it again using a complete sentence: "It helps us know where to find certain information."*

(Evelyn Gloria repeats the sentence.)

Teacher	[a la clase] La página con la tabla de contenidos es parte de nuestra estrategia para la semana. [Escribe --	*[to the class] The page with the table of contents is part of our strategy for the week. [She writes "Characteristics of*

	Características de Texto Informativo-- en un gráfico y debajo escribe -- tabla de contenidos.]	*Informative Text" on a chart and writes "table of contents" under that.]*
	Otras cosas que nos ayudan en este libro son las fotos y las leyendas. [Enseña el primer ejemplo en el texto.]	*Other things that will help us in this book are the pictures and captions. [She shows the example in the text.]*
	Busquen las partes oscuras, ¿qué representan? Díganme en una oración completa.	*Look at the dark parts. What do they show? Tell me in a complete sentence.*
Carter	En las partes "dark" hay agua.	*There is water in the dark parts.*
Teacher	¿Hay mucha o poca agua en la Tierra?	*Is there a little or a lot of water on the Earth?*
Olivia	Hay mucha agua en la Tierra.	*There is a lot of water on Earth.*

The LC teacher continues briefly reviewing each photo and caption, asking questions, and pointing out key phrases. Students at earlier stages of Spanish oracy development, such as Evelyn Gloria and Carter, are encouraged to express their ideas as fully as possible in Spanish, but may use English terms and phrases when needed.

The teacher then discusses how the photos and captions contribute to the text, writing *fotos y leyendas*/photos and captions on the board. Finally, the teacher reviews bolded terms in the text to ensure that the students have an introduction to them. Students devise TPR actions for the key words: *el líquido* (liquid), *se congela* (freezes), *el sólido* (solid), *el gas* (gas), *invisible* (invisible), *se derrite* (melts) *y la evaporación* (evaporation). The classroom teacher uses the same TPR actions in the classroom, for example, students hugging themselves and shivering for *se congela* (freezes) and sinking slowly to the floor for *se derrite* (melts). The LC teacher guides a discussion about the importance of bolded terms and writes *palabras en negrita*/bolded words on the list. The teacher and the students do a choral reading of the text, stopping to clarify vocabulary and concepts. She also asks them to identify text features that they used to help them gain meaning from the text.

The students complete the reading/strategy portion of the self-assessment after the *libro nuevo*/focus book section and the writing portion after the *escritura*/writing on day 1. They complete the same self-assessment at the end of the week, which lets them evaluate how much they have improved. At the end of the week, they set a goal to focus on for the next week.

On day 2, the group begins with a choral reading of the text, using the TPR actions and stopping to discuss key concepts and vocabulary. The teacher asks questions to gauge comprehension and continues to reinforce the strategy of using text features from informational text to support comprehension.

Using Text Features to Locate Relevant Information

In the following vignette, the LC teacher helps students use the glossary of a text. These types of learning experiences assist students in using language for academic purposes to understand informational text more fully.

Teacher	Miren el glosario. ¿Cómo nos ayuda un glosario?	*Look at the glossary. How does a glossary help us?*
Roberto	Es "like" un diccionario.	*It is like a dictionary.*
Teacher	Sí, Roberto. Si no podemos recordar lo que significa una palabra, podemos buscarla en el glosario. También nos da	*Yes, Roberto. If we can't remember what a word means, we can search for it in the glossary. It also gives us the page number*

	la página donde podemos encontrar la palabra en el texto. Cada día vamos a añadir ilustraciones a dos de las palabras para ayudarnos a recordar lo que significan.	*where we can find the word in the text. Every day we are going to add illustrations to two of the words to help us remember what they mean.*

Students choose two words they wish to illustrate on their word cards. The definitions in the glossary are fairly complex for this group, so the teacher focuses more on having students identify the vocabulary, discuss what the terms mean, and draw illustrations on their word cards to help them remember the definitions.

On day 3, the students read the text with a partner or independently, depending on their level of comfort with the text. They are reminded to use TPR actions as they read. After reading, the teacher asks questions about the main concepts and key vocabulary.

Using Text Features to Support Meaning

Strategy development always includes a component about how we use the strategy and how it supports learning (metacognition), as highlighted in the following vignette. Even though these students have fairly emergent oracy skills in Spanish, the LC teacher still finds scaffolded ways of addressing complex concepts and taking advantage of their well-developed background and oracy skills in English. Using TPR, text characteristics, and key resources from the classroom, the students recognize that they have encountered these concepts previously and are able to activate their prior knowledge on the topic.

Teacher	¿Cuál es la estrategia que estamos usando esta semana?	*What strategy are we working on this week?*
Carter	las características de "information text"	*the characteristics of information text*
Teacher	Sí, las características de texto informativo. Y, ¿cómo usaron la estrategia?	*Yes, the text features of information text. And, how do we use this strategy?*
Evelyn Gloria	Las palabras en negrita mi ayuda porque puedo mirar las fotos.	*The bolded words help me because I can look at the photos.*

(Other students tell or demonstrate how they use the strategy to help them understand the text.)

Teacher	Un ciclo es un círculo que nunca termina. Vamos a leer la página 12 en el libro. ¿Qué le pasa al charco con el calor del sol?	*A cycle is a circle that never ends. Let's read page 12 in the book. What happens to the puddle from the heat of the sun?*
Roberto	Cambia a gas.	*It changes to gas.*
Teacher	Sí, el agua líquida se transforma en gas. Se llama --evaporación--. Repitan, --evaporación--. ¿Qué acción usamos para --evaporación--? Mira el gráfico. ¿Dónde está representada la evaporación?	*Yes, the liquid water is transformed into a gas. This is called "evaporation". Repeat, "evaporation." What TPR action are we using for "evaporation"? Look at the chart. Where is evaporation represented?*

The LC teacher has the students practice the sentence frames adding TPR actions to simulate the process. This is an oral review of the water cycle from the classroom but the students can use these sentence frames in their writing also. The sentence frames are especially useful for Evelyn Gloria because they provide the language she needs to express her understanding of the science concepts orally and in writing. This helps her gain confidence in explaining herself in Spanish.

On day 4, the teacher reviews "*evaporación*" and adds "*condensación*," referring to the captions and photos of clouds in the text. The following sentence frames, alongside the water cycle graphic from the classroom and TPR actions, are rehearsed:

1. En el aire, el gas _____ (se enfría), _____ (se levanta), y las gotitas de _____ (agua) forman _____ (nubes). Se llama _____ (condensación).

1. *In the air, gas _____ (cools off), _____ (rises), and droplets from the _____ (water) form _____ (clouds). This is called _____ (condensation).*

Bridging Main Ideas from Spanish to English

On day 4, after orally reviewing the first two stages of the water cycle, the teacher guides students through a bridging activity of the key ideas from the text. The following vignette demonstrates how the LC teacher supports students in using their linguistic resources in Spanish and English, as well as text features they have been studying, to analyze how to express the main idea and provide supporting details in Spanish.

Teacher	Vamos a analizar y traducir las ideas principales del texto del español al inglés. Vamos a usar los títulos de cada sección para ayudarnos. Miren el título en la página 4. Vamos a leerlo juntos.	*We are going to analyze and translate the main ideas from the text from Spanish to English. We are going to use the titles from each section to help us. Look at the title on page 4. Let's read it together.*
Students	El agua por todos lados.	*Water everywhere.*
Teacher	¿Cómo podemos decir esto en inglés usando una oración completa?	*How can we say that in English using a complete sentence?*
Evelyn Gloria	Water is everywhere. [La maestra escribe la oración en una tarjeta.]	*[The teacher writes the sentence on a card.]*
Teacher	Muy bien. Ahora lean esta sección con alguién.	*Very good. Now read that section with someone.*

(pairs read together)

Teacher	¿Cuales son unas oraciones que indican que "Water is everywhere"? [Los niños comparten 2 o 3 oraciones.]	*What are some sentences that indicate that water is everywhere? [The children share 2 or 3 sentences.]*
Teacher	Vamos a leer en voz alta el título para la segunda parte en la página 7.	*Let's read the title for the second section on page 7 together.*
Students	Los diferentes estados del agua	*The different states of water*
Teacher	¿Cuales son las 3 formas del agua que estudiamos? Usen los dibujos para ayudarles.	*What are the 3 states of water that we studied? Use the pictures to help you.*
Students	líquido, hielo, el Polo Norte, sólido, gas	*liquid, ice, the North Pole, solid, gas*
Teacher	Las 3 formas son líquido, sólido, y gas. ¿Cómo podemos traducir esta parte?	*The 3 states are liquid, solid, and gas. How could we translate that part?*
Students	Water can be a liquid, a solid, or a gas.	

The LC teacher concludes this discussion by having students locate sentences in their text that verify that water can be a liquid, a solid, or a gas. Asking students like Evelyn Gloria to formulate complete sentences in providing responses is another way to guide them in developing their oracy for academic purposes.

During the writing session on day 4, students work in pairs to write the translations in English, and sentence 3 (for *precipitación*) is added to sentence frames 1 and 2:

2. Cuando el agua cae de las _____ (nubes), se llama _____ (precipitación). El _____ (agua) cae como _____ (lluvia) o _____ (nieve).	**2.** *When water falls from the _____ (clouds), it is called _____ (precipitation). The _____ (water) falls as _____ (rain) or _____ (snow).*

On day 5, the students read the *libro nuevo*/focus book independently in Spanish and then read their translations to English to review the main ideas of the text. They place the translations on the appropriate page to access the picture cues as they are reading. Following the readings, the LC teacher draws a T-chart on the board. The top of one column says "*Más*" ("More") and the other "*Menos*" ("Less"). They have a brief discussion about what happens if the amount of rainfall increases or decreases and write notes in each column to summarize these facts. This helps prepare students for these types of academic conversations in the classroom by giving them prior exposure to the concepts and the vocabulary. Students repeat the self-assessment from the beginning of the week on day 5 and compare the results, focusing on where they have noted growth and setting a goal for the next week. LC teachers assist students with this task by asking them what they need to work on, and then guiding them to formulate appropriate goals.

Word Work

As students transition to the word work section of the session each day, they practice the vocabulary words on their word rings to enhance their sight word vocabularies. The LC teacher may wish to have students add sketches or notes on the backs of word cards where applicable as a scaffold to assist them in recalling vocabulary words and/or definitions. On days 4–5, they add selected English words that have been introduced during the bridging portion of the week. Spanish vocabulary words are written in red and English words in blue.

Forming Questions in Spanish

Students work on forming questions in Spanish for the *formando palabras*/word work section of the LC session. The teacher introduces the process on day 1, as highlighted in this vignette. Learning experiences, such as asking students to formulate questions from statements, provide them with meaningful opportunities to explore linguistic structures across the two languages.

Teacher	¿Cómo se llaman estos signos? [Pone los ¿? en la pizarra.]	*What do you call these symbols? [She puts the ¿? symbols on the board.]*
	(Students do not respond.)	
Teacher	Se llaman signos de interrogación. Repitan.	*They are called question marks. Repeat.*
Students	signos de interrogación	*question marks*
Teacher	Vamos a formar unas preguntas. Vamos a empezar con una oración y después vamos a cambiarla a una pregunta.	*We are going to form questions. Let's start with a sentence and then we'll turn it into a question.*
	El agua está en los charcos. [dibuja una imagen de un charco] Para formar una pregunta podemos decir, ¿Hay agua en los charcos? [Escribe la pregunta.]	*The water is in the puddles. [She draws a picture of a puddle.] To turn this into a question, we could say "Is there water in the puddles?" [She writes the question.]*

	Ahora, ayúdenme a formar otra pregunta. --El agua está en los lagos.-- ¿Quién puede formar una pregunta con esta oración?	*Now, help me form another question. "The water is in the lakes." Who can make a question from this sentence?*
Roberto	¿Hay agua en los lagos?	*Is there water in the lakes?*
Teacher	Sí. Ahora escriban esta pregunta en sus libritos.	*Yes. Now write this question in your booklets.*

The teacher continues the activity using sentences related to the water cycle theme. Students write the sentences as questions in their booklets, making sure to use question marks. The students continue practicing formation of questions on days 2 and 3.

On days 1–3, students practice a *dictado,* which focuses on main ideas from the text and key language features. Question formation, use of capitals (*la Tierra*), and accents (*líquido, enfría,cómo)* are the language features emphasized throughout the week. Note that the first two sentences come from the focus book, *El agua de la Tierra.*

1. La mayor parte del agua que vemos es líquido.

2. Cuando el agua se enfría mucho, se congela.

3. ¿Cómo se llama cuando el agua es invisible?

1. *Most of the water that we see is liquid. (p. 7)*

2. *When water gets cold, it freezes. (p. 8)*

3. *What do you call invisible water?*

Students use a different colored pencil to correct their work and do not erase their original writing. In this way they are able to note specific problem areas and how well they are progressing from day to day.

On days 4 and 5, students search for English cognates for Spanish vocabulary. There are many cognates that the students may suggest from this text (*aire*/air, *animales*/animals, *combatimos*/combat, *contaminada*/contaminated, *convierte*/convert, *cubierta*/covered, *diferentes*/different, *estados*/states, *evaporación*/evaporation, *forma*/form, *gas*/gas, *importante*/important, *invisible*/invisible, *lagos*/lakes, *líquido*/liquid, *océanos*/oceans, *parte*/part, *plantas*/plants, *Polo Norte*/North Pole, and *transforma*/transforms), so it may take two days to complete the list. As the students find them, they create a T-chart to display in their study area, with the title of the focus book written across the top. The teacher verifies that the words are indeed cognates as the students find them and place them on the chart. The students analyze the word pairs to note similarities and differences, as well as patterns in one language or the other. If time remains, students may sort the cognates into scientific and nonscientific terms.

Also on days 4 and 5, students are introduced to English language concepts. Since many of the cognates are the same or similar in spelling but have different pronunciations this may be the focus of part of this lesson. The following pairs might be selected and the students can examine differences in both spelling and pronunciation: *aire*/air, *animales*/animals, *evaporación*/evaporation, *gas*/gas, *importante*/important, *líquido*/liquid, *océanos*/oceans, and *plantas*/plants. Students analyze spelling patterns across the two languages, which contributes to their developing metalinguistic awareness.

Rereads

On day 1, students reread texts in pairs. On day 2 they retell a text to a partner, using illustrations and text features as scaffolds. This provides a good opportunity for additional oral language development, which is often a challenge for the emerging bilingual group. On days 3 and 4 they reread independently or they may choose again to reread in pairs. During this time the LC teacher may listen to individual students read or conduct running records to check for accuracy, strategy use, and fluency. Brief discussions or retellings of readings provide checks on comprehension. At the end of the session, the LC teacher regularly provides feedback to students indicating which strategies were observed, their level of fluency in reading, and a suggestion for improvement. This provides another opportunity for students to focus on implementing the skills and strategies being taught. On day 5, they re-read a Spanish text along with the English translation completed previously for that text.

Writing

On day 1, the LC teacher works with the students to complete a **language experience approach (LEA)** on the story. They have all shared the experience of reading the focus text and now contribute to writing about it. The LC teacher writes exactly what the students say and together they edit the writing to provide a summary of the text. She guides them in reviewing the photos and captions and using the headings to help them summarize the text. They use as much Spanish as they are able but supplement with English, which provides the teacher with a good overview of how well students comprehend the text and which Spanish language structures and vocabulary they are mastering.

The following is the resulting LEA chart:

There is mucha agua en *the Earth.*	*There is a lot of water on Earth.*
El líquido es agua.	*Liquid is water.*
El agua *frozen* se llama hielo.	*Frozen water is called ice.*
El agua invisible es un gas.	*Invisible water is a gas.*
El agua cambia.	*Water changes.*
El muñeco de nieve *melts* con el sol.	*The sun melts the snowman.*
El agua es importante.	*Water is important.*
Los bomberos usan el agua.	*Firefighters use water.*

After the key points of the text have been recorded and the the LEA chart edited, the LC teacher underlines the three states of water (*líquido, sólido, gas*) and reviews this concept with the students. They copy the revised summary in their notebooks and read it to a partner.

On days 2–3, students work in pairs to write their own text about the water cycle. They may use some sentences from the LEA chart but are encouraged to also write at least one or two original sentences based on the text. They may also use other sentence frames from the text and the water cycle graphic that were introduced during the week.

During the word work section of day 4, students do an oral comparative analysis of key ideas from the text in English, using headings and illustrations. During the writing portion of this session, students work in pairs to write those ideas in English. On day 5, students write in English. They may choose to work individually or with a partner to write about the content of the text or to self-select a writing topic, sharing ideas with a partner as a prewriting strategy. Since students in this group are often quite proficient in English, this session provides a good opportunity for them to practice their writing skills in English. This exemplifies using language as a resource in that students apply understanding about writing across the two languages.

Monitoring Evelyn Gloria's Progress

Evelyn Gloria's progress in Spanish oracy, as measured by anecdotal records (including transcriptions of responses) was notable. She progressed from very simple noun/verb responses to more elaborate responses that more accurately reflected her understanding from learning experiences. TPR, sentence frames, and word banks were most helpful and she found that these supports made her feel more confident in responding orally. She has begun to ask questions in Spanish, indicating a more sophisticated level of language use. It will be important to continue to provide a variety of opportunities for Evelyn Gloria to refine and expand her oracy skills.

A comparison of baseline and post-writing samples for Evelyn Gloria reflects strong progress in Spanish writing (Fig. 5.1). Content is clearly described and use of correct syntax is most notable. She has progressed in elaboration and use of detail. Vocabulary growth in speaking and writing is reflected by appropriate use of science terminology and the fact that fewer English words were inserted in the text when she did not know how to express words/ideas in Spanish. Spanish verb forms "*es*" and "*son*" are used as well. Additional emphasis on vocabulary development and verb tenses would be a useful continuing support for her. Evelyn Gloria has indicated that oral rehearsal before writing is very effective and it is important for her to be able to identify her progress and set goals for continued work.

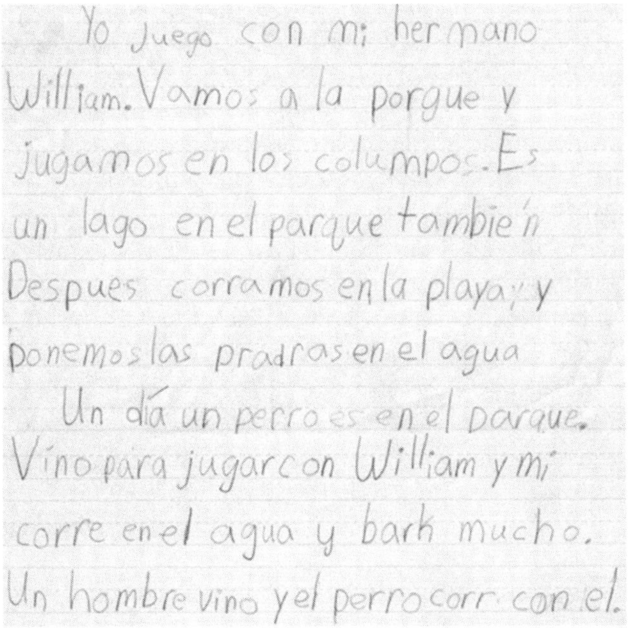
Yo Juego con mi hermano William. Vamos a la porgue y jugamos en los columpos. Es un lago en el parque tambie'n Despues corramos en la playa y ponemos las pradras en el agua
Un día un perro es en el parque. Vino para jugar con William y mi corre en el agua y bark mucho. Un hombre vino y el perro corr con el.

A

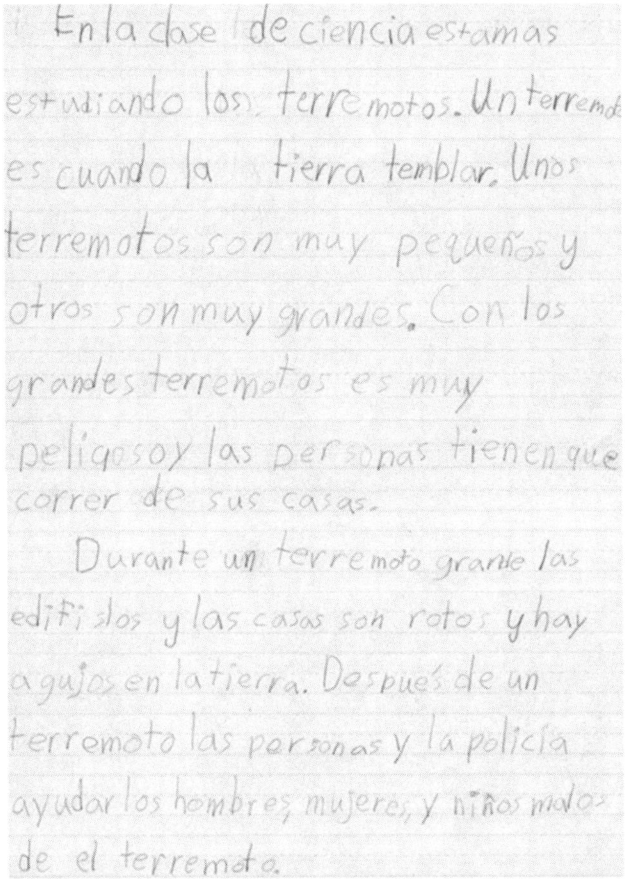
En la clase de ciencia estamas estudiando los terremotos. Un terremoto es cuando la tierra temblar. Unos terremotos son muy pequeños y otros son muy grandes. Con los grandes terremotos es muy peligosoy las personas tienen que correr de sus casas.
Durante un terremoto grande las edifislos y las casas son rotos y hay agujos en la tierra. Después de un terremoto las personas y la policía ayudar los hombres, mujeres, y niños malos de el terremoto.

B

Figure 5.1 Evelyn Gloria's beginning- and end-of-year Spanish writing samples. **A,** Translation: I play with my brother, William. We go to the park and play on the swings. There is a lake in the park also. After that we run on the beach and throw stones in the water.

One day a dog was in the park. He came to play with William and me, running in the water and barking a lot. A man came and the dog ran with him.

B, Translation: In science class we are studying earthquakes. An earthquake is when the earth shakes. Some earthquakes are very small and others are very big. With the big earthquakes, it is dangerous and the people have to run from their houses.

During an earthquake, large buildings and houses are destroyed and there are holes in the earth. After an earthquake, people and the police help men, women, and children injured in the earthquake.

ENGLISH AS AN ADDITIONAL LANGUAGE STRAND

The EAL strand of the LC is geared toward **English learners** in the English-medium classroom. They may represent several language groups, but all are struggling with literacy development in English. Some students, like twin sisters Sanda and Thura, are fairly recent arrivals to the United States; others, like Soua, were born in the United States. It is critical that all of these students receive meaningful **interventions** before they move on to higher grade levels where the content and the literacy expectations continue to increase at a rapid rate. The LC teacher tries to capitalize on academic and language resources the students already have and build on and extend background knowledge.

Table 5.4 gives an example of how the LC components might be developed across the week.

The classroom teacher plans to focus on an integrated literacy and science unit on how rising water temperatures are affecting organisms and possible solutions. This work develops the science inquiry goal of making a claim about the merit of a solution to a problem caused by environmental changes and their effect on the plants and animals that live there. The LC teacher collaborated with the classroom teacher to plan preteaching learning experiences to prepare the students for participation in this classroom unit. The LC teacher has carefully selected websites and grade-level newspaper articles on the topic to use in exploring the types of text they are using in the classroom for this unit. She has chosen texts that are within the instructional reading level of her students but cover the concepts in sufficient depth. The texts also lend themselves to the reinforcement of the strategy of cause and effect, which is aligned with ELA Reading for Information standards. At the end of the week they review the solutions they have read about and evaluate the one they feel is most likely to protect aquatic organisms and support their reasoning.

To address the content and language objectives outlined in Box 5.5, the LC teacher introduces the unit by asking students to preview the news magazine they are reading to help them recall what they know about global warming and how it affects organisms in various bodies of water. Prior to reading the text for the day the strategy of cause and effect is reviewed, with attention to how knowledge of this strategy supports learning from the text. The group creates a cause-and-effect chart and adds to it each day as they read about the impact of global warming on aquatic organisms. The students read independently or in pairs, pausing periodically to add information to the chart and discuss what they have learned, which enhances their use of language for academic purposes. During the second

TABLE 5.4 Format for Grade 3 English as an Additional Language Strand

	Day 1	Day 2	Day 3	Day 4	Day 5
Focus book	Introduction Discuss strategy Choral read Self-assess	Read Discuss strategy	Read Discuss strategy	Read Discuss strategy	Read Review strategy Self-assess
Word work	English concepts	English concepts	English concepts Dictation	English concepts Dictation	Dictation
Rereads	Read in pairs	Retell in pairs	Independent	Independent	Independent
Writing	Language experience approach— focus book	Content focus	Content focus	Self-selected topic	Self-selected topic

BOX 5.5 Language and Content Objectives for English as an Additional Language Literacy-Based Instruction	
Theme	Impact on the water cycle
Content	I will be able to make a claim about the merit of a solution to a problem caused when the water temperature rises and has an impact on aquatic organisms.
	I will be able to clarify meaning using text features.
Language	I will be able to describe impacts on the water cycle using cause-and-effect language orally and in writing.

half of the week, they read about possible solutions to the issue and add this information to the chart. They note the text features included in each section and how they used them to support understanding of text.

Focus Book

Comprehension of text is always the major emphasis in reading in the LC. At this level, students need opportunities to use previous strategies that they may not have completely mastered and internalize new strategies that are being introduced. Reading a new text provides an optimal opportunity for the teacher to help students become aware of the metacognitive processes they are employing in monitoring comprehension as they read new material. For example, when students self-correct the teacher may make note of their reading behavior and ask scaffolding questions to help them reflect and verbalize what they did to gain meaning from text.

Rereading as a Self-Correction Strategy

It is important that students are able to identify when meaning breaks down and describe how they use strategies to resolve miscues. Being able to name the strategies they are using reflects their growth in metacognition. In the following example, students are working with this sentence: Once in the air, water vapor circulates and can condense to form clouds and precipitation, which fall back to earth.[1]

Sanda	Once in the air, water vapor circulates and can contain to form clouds and percent, which fall back to earth.
	[Student rereads sentence.] Once in the air, water vapor circulates and can condense to form clouds and precipitation.
Teacher	Sanda, I noticed that at first you said "contain" and "percent" but then you went back and self-corrected. How did you know that you needed to reread?
Sanda	This not sound good. We learn about clouds and precipitation and I look at words more close. Then I read it better.

The LC teacher asks questions when necessary to help elicit a response that may include one of the following insights: "It did not make sense." "It did not sound right." "It did not look right." The teacher then asks how the student determined what the correct word was. Students can create a wall chart of the self-correction strategies that they learned and practiced

---

1. Sentence retrieved from climate.ncsu.edu

previously. They should be encouraged to consult them to reflect on their self-correction strategies:

- I thought about whether it made sense.
- I checked the picture and/or the word chunks.
- I thought about what I already know about this topic.
- I thought about what I read in the paragraphs before this.

Students need opportunities to assess their development of self-correction in preserving the meaning of text and developing metacognitive awareness. The teacher provides students with a self-assessment sheet at the beginning of each week and again at the end of the week to reflect on their learning.

Strategy development provides opportunities for students to develop higher-order thinking skills and to broaden their understanding and use of academic language across the curriculum. LC and classroom teachers collaborate on the sequence of strategies to be taught and practiced; however, LC students may occasionally need to focus on more basic strategies than those currently being studied in the classroom. It is critical for LC students to be able to use basic strategies confidently because many of the complex strategies assume facility with more basic skills. Table 5.5 outlines a sequence of strategy development that LC teachers have used for transitional-level students, that is, grade 3 students reading at DRA2+ levels 20–30, as a guide in the development and evaluation of strategies.

If the LC teacher chooses to focus on, for example, cause and effect as the strategy to be developed in the focus book segment, focus books that very clearly reflect cause-and-effect relationships are selected to introduce and practice the strategy. Students might think about how they have seen this strategy play out in their everyday lives or analyze use of cause and effect in previously read texts. Throughout the introduction and development of the focus text, students orally or in writing describe their ideas using the sentence frame "_____ happened because _____." They are guided to include phrases and/or vocabulary from the text in exploring cause and effect. Students become more adept at defining the strategy and describing how it supports their learning through self-assessments.

Also included in the focus book component of the LC is additional practice with the use of context clues and text features, such as bolded words and visuals, to identify the meaning of vocabulary and concepts in science-related text. LC students can have a vocabulary section in their writing notebooks where new words are added for each topic of study. While defining new words, students can describe, orally or in writing, the meaning of key words using the sentence frames "This means _____. A clue that helps me remember this word is _____." Students can include drawings or phrases/sentences from the text to enhance vocabulary development. Continuous practice in this area solidifies students' ability to use context clues and other resources to build academic vocabulary. Students periodically reflect on why it is important to record content-area vocabulary words and how they can use their entries as resources while reading and writing.

A reading log can be created to record each new book, and may include a column to indicate when focus books become rereads. A sample reading log can be seen in Box 5.6.

TABLE 5.5 Transitional-Level Reading Strategies		
Previous Strategies	**Expanding Strategies**	**New Strategies**
▪ Sequencing	▪ Summarizing	▪ Context clues
▪ Prior knowledge	▪ Main idea	▪ Supporting ideas
▪ Inferring	▪ Vocabulary (prefixes and suffixes)	▪ Cause and effect
▪ Text structure	▪ Compare and contrast	▪ Text features

BOX 5.6 Reading Log

Name _____

Page 1

These are the strategies I use to help me read and understand:

1. Look at the picture
2. Sound it out
3. Ask a question
4. Reread
5. Make a connection
6. Chunking
7. Word parts
8. Does it make sense?
9. Prior knowledge
10. Inference

11. Identify foreshadowing
12. Context clues
13. Text features
14. Scan
15. Skim
16. Cause and effect
17. Note taking
18. Have a clear purpose
19. Text structure

Page 2+

Start date	Title	Author	Reread date

On the back of the form, the teacher and student can regularly make note of the strategies that the student employs.

Word Work

On day 1, students practice the new vocabulary words on their word rings. The LC teacher may wish to have students add sketches or symbols on the backs of word cards where applicable as scaffolds to assist them in recalling vocabulary words and/or definitions. Word work continues to be an important part of the LC. Word work may be linked to specific focus books or to the students' reading levels.

Analyzing Word Endings

At this level, word work focuses on word parts, patterns, and meanings. Rather than specific words to form, students may be given certain criteria to use in producing a list of known words, such as creating a list of words with –ed (as seen in the vignette) or –ing endings and then sorting them into patterns and deducing spelling/pronunciation rules. Or students may be given multisyllabic words and asked to create a list of words they can form using the letters in the target word. Prefixes and suffixes are also formally introduced and practiced. Word meaning clues for a study of water-related terminology, such as *agua*, aquatic, and hydro, are emphasized and students share how they are using these clues to help them determine meanings of unfamiliar words.

Teacher	In class, Mrs. Smith tells me that you have been working on –ed endings in your shared reading. In our group today, we will continue our study on –ed endings. On my white board, I have some words. Can you help me read these words?
Students	look, visit, smell
Teacher	In English, the –ed ending can make these sounds at the end of words: /t/, /d/ or /id/.

On days 1 and 2, students focus on the preceding concepts. The same skills are reinforced across the first four days to ensure that students can internalize and apply these skills in subsequent literacy activities and students analyze spelling patterns and pronunciations with additional words. Beginning on day 3 and continuing through day 5, a dictation exercise is added. This may include 2–3 sentences that highlight the skills under study and reinforce previously studied writing skills, such as capitalization and punctuation. Students self-correct their sentences each day, using different colored pencils for writing and editing their work according to the model shared by the LC teacher. Students note their progress in completing the dictation each day and analyze what they are learning about grammar, spelling, and language structure. If the concepts are not mastered by the end of the week, the teacher incorporates them into sentences to be used the following week. Previously studied concepts are also revisited occasionally in subsequent dictations.

Rereads

Rereads are a daily component of the LC and are important in helping students practice fluency and develop confidence in reading. Additionally, they are another form of practice with sight words in context and a time to help students appreciate reasons for rereading, including enjoyment of the text, reading with fluency and expression, looking for details, and predicting or identifying foreshadowing clues. Students reread familiar text they have mastered in the focus book portion of the sessions. The LC teacher monitors students as they reread and may conduct running records during this time.

At this level, students will not necessarily reread an entire text because they are now engaged with longer reading materials. They are less frequently rereading with a partner (day 1) and more frequently reading independently (days 3–5). On day 2, students retell the text to a partner. This increases oral language development and provides opportunities to practice summarizing skills. The LC teacher listens to each pair and assesses how well they are able to summarize/retell texts and provides feedback to guide students in further refining this strategy.

Writing

Students should see themselves as writers. Growth toward this goal may be enhanced during the LC writing component by exploring an author's craft through carefully selected, brief mini-lessons. Following the mini-lessons, students write independently or in pairs, with support as needed. The LC teacher, in consultation with the classroom teacher, selects mini-lesson topics based on student needs and interests. Writing strategy mini-lessons include a focus on ELA and content standards that are being addressed in the classroom and in the writing process. Elements such as self-assessing, peer-editing, and sharing one's writing with the group may be included as mini-lessons for the week, but the primary goal is to guide students to write with greater skill and confidence. Mini-lesson topics related to prewriting, development of topics/genres, and editing/revising may be based on the needs of students in each group and/or the type of writing being emphasized in the classroom.

During the writing portion of each session, students respond to the text they have been reading. In this example, they use the chart they have created to explore cause and effect by using the sentence frame "_____ happened because _____" and phrases from the text to verify their statements. During the last two days of the week, they evaluate the solutions to changes in water temperature they have read about on the websites the LC teacher organized for them. They state each solution in their own words and then include a brief evaluation about how well they think this solution would protect aquatic organisms. Rather than sharing this final writing piece, students select the solution that they think has the most merit and defend it to the group. This serves as a good opportunity to enhance oracy and authentic use of language for academic purposes because the students present solutions and listen to the suggestions of other students in the group.

A suggestion for organizing the writing portion of the LC at this age level with students who require greater scaffolding might include the LC teacher conducting a shared writing or LEA activity on day 1. She introduces the strategy that will be the focus of the week and incorporates it into the activity. For example, using a text with a science theme, the group might focus on stating main ideas and adding details. The focus could also be organization of writing ideas, use of linking words, or creative introductions or conclusions. Previous work on capitalization and punctuation might be reinforced throughout the activity. The language resources that each student brings to this activity enhance the group's learning. Sanda, for example, uses science terminology correctly in oral responses, Soua is developing a fairly solid grasp of grammar and sentence structure, and Thura represents her understanding best in writing. The LC sessions are structured to enable them to learn from one another.

Links between reading and writing are continually reinforced. If the group is working on main ideas and details, for example, they might begin by discussing the first major idea presented in the text. The teacher asks for a volunteer to create a sentence describing the main idea and write it on a chart. A discussion of how to determine the main idea may ensue followed by selection of details related to the main ideas. Students propose sentences describing the details and the teacher writes them down. The LC teacher reviews the concept of main ideas and details and how they were used in their LEA. Finally, the LC group chorally reads the summary of the text and the teacher guides them in revising the text for accuracy and clarity. Since it was a shared writing activity, each student copies the text into their writing notebooks.

Rehearsing for Writing

The following vignette provides another example of using an LEA shared writing activity to prepare students for identifying main ideas and supporting details. The sentence frame serves as a good scaffold to ensure that students are not unduly challenged by having to think of both the content and language of the response at the same time.

Teacher   After reading a few books about how goods and services affect people in a community, let's put our thoughts in writing.

How do goods and services affect people in our community?

In your answer I would like you to use the sentence: Goods and services affect people because _____.

Thura   Goods and services affect people because with no goods like foods in community, we can't have eat.

Soua   Goods and services affect people because for example if we no have the service of people fixing cars, no have anyone to fix cars when break.

On days 2 and 3, the LC teacher reviews the strategy focus for the week (main ideas and details). Next the LC teacher chorally reads the LEA chart from day 1 with the students and encourages them to expand on the main ideas presented or to add new details. Students orally share their ideas for writing and then create a graphic organizer with phrases that summarize main ideas and details as a prewriting organizer. The daily repetition supports students in solidifying both language and concepts.

On days 4 and 5 students self-select a topic for writing, which helps them develop greater independence and confidence in their writing. They share ideas with a partner as an oral rehearsal before writing. As students write, the LC teacher meets with individual students. During these conferences, the LC teacher helps the student apply a writing strategy and/or revise or edit his or her writing. Students then share their writing with a partner, the LC teacher, or the whole group. The teacher provides feedback to the students by sharing anecdotal observations she made while meeting with each student. Students self-assess their writing at the end of the week and note their growth. Box 5.7 provides an example of a writing self-assessment specifically designed for the particular strategy and goals of the writing sessions. Note that this self-assessment is similar in structure to what we saw in an earlier grade but is more sophisticated in terms of writing focus and assessment of the writing process.

Copies of the writing sheets that focus on one specific writing strategy are created for the students, along with elements that characterize that strategy. Students continue to focus on a single trait or strategy until they have mastered it. This makes learning more manageable for students in that they have a specific area to focus on, practice, and self-assess. The LC teacher introduces the elements of the strategy and differentiates instruction according to what students can be expected to do with language given their current level of English language development. The LC teacher also provides opportunities for students to practice these strategies in their writing. A blank line is provided at the top of the page for the student to write the title of the piece. The blank area on the page can be used in connection with the mini-lesson, and as such, might include one of the following: prewriting, web of ideas, illustration, try-out words, or an outline. After writing, students self-assess their own writing pieces to verify that they selected a topic, worked on the writing strategy, and reviewed their own writing as outlined at the bottom of the sheet in the self-assessment. It is important that students date each piece of writing to allow them to review their work over time and verbalize their progress in writing development. This lets them take greater control over their own learning and expand their metacognitive skills.

When writing in response to text, students may find prompts helpful in selecting writing topics. Box 5.8 provides ideas for responding to narrative text, and Box 5.9 provides ideas for responding to informational text. Students may tape the prompt lists in their writing booklets to use as a reference while writing.

BOX 5.7 Writing and Assessment Sheet: Ideas

Name _____   Date _____

IDEAS

_____ *Pick an interesting topic*

_____ *Stay on topic*

_____ *Write on one main idea*

_____ *Include details*

_____

_____

_____

_____

_____

_____

_____

_____

_____

_____

_____

_____

_____

_____

I _____ *chose an interesting topic* _____ *worked on the target strategy* _____ *reviewed my writing*

This is how I rate my writing:

3 (very well)

2 (average)

1 (not very well)

BOX 5.8 Sample Prompts for Responding to Narrative Texts

1. This character reminds me of _____ because _____.

2. I predict that _____ because _____.

3. The most important event is _____ because _____.

4. If I were _____.

5. After reading, I wonder _____.

6. If I could change one thing about the story _____.

7. I feel (examples: surprised, sad, mad, happy, worried) _____ because _____.

8. If I could meet the character/author, I would say/do/ask _____ because _____.

9. I really do not understand _____ because _____.

10. I noticed _____.

11. I learned that _____.

12. I made a connection to _____.

13. Describe the major conflict in the story. What side are you on? _____.

14. This part is very realistic/unrealistic because _____.

15. Would you like to read more books by this author? Why? _____.

16. Do you agree or disagree with the character's view point? Why? _____.

17. Describe the setting, time, and place. Draw it.

18. How have your feelings changed as you read this story? Why? _____

19. What other ways could the problem or conflict have been solved? _____

20. How do the characters in the story feel about each other? _____

21. I like/do not like what (character and name, example: the main character's friend, John) did _____ in response to _____.

BOX 5.9 Writing Response to Informational Text

I learned _____.

I predict _____.

I wonder _____.

SUMMARIZE

1. To summarize, this book is about _____.

2. This chapter, _____, is about _____.

MAIN IDEA/DETAILS

1. The main idea of _____ is

_____.

2. The main idea is _____ and some

supporting details include _____

_____.

VISUALIZING

1. When reading _____ in my head I

pictured _____.

2. This is a picture I drew that shows what I thought

when I was reading:

QUESTIONING

1. A question I have is _____?

2. I found the answer to my question about _____

_____.

SEQUENCE

1. Put the events in order.

2. Make a timeline.

FACT VS. OPINION

1. One fact I found was _____.

2. One opinion I read was _____.

3. I agree/disagree with the opinion, _____,

because _____.

CONNECTION

Book title: _____.

I made this connection from the book: _____

_____.

COMPARE AND CONTRAST

1. _____ and _____ are similar because

_____.

2. _____ and _____ are different because

_____.

DRAW A CONCLUSION

Now I think _____ because

_____.

INFERENCE

Because I used the information from the book,

_____, and I know that _____,

I was able to infer that _____.

CONCLUSION

Emphasis is placed on oracy, literacy, and metacognitive development related to content-area concepts and themes in the grade 3 LC, as students progress toward grade-level goals along scaffolded and differentiated pathways. Very often, language learners have mastered some basic literacy skills in one or both languages but struggle with the complexity and pace of classroom instruction. In some cases, students may have strong literacy skills in one language and need additional support in transferring these skills to the other language. This was the case with Evelyn Gloria as an emerging bilingual. Although her literacy skills had become fairly strong in both languages, she needed greater opportunities to expand her speaking skills. Conversely, students in the advancing bilingual strand had strong oracy skills in Spanish but benefitted from the supports in literacy development and use of language for academic purposes in both languages. The students in the EAL strand worked in English and received supports in both literacy and language development. Although the students in these three strands all had similar goals, the pathways for helping them move toward content and language standards were customized for each group.

By focusing more fully on content-area oracy and literacy development, the LC teacher strengthens students' backgrounds to be more successful in reaching grade-level expectations. Collaboration with the classroom teacher is especially critical at this stage because students benefit from coordinated study of concepts, skills, and strategies between the two settings and have additional opportunities to develop oracy and literacy skills in meaningful contexts.

QUESTIONS FOR REFLECTION AND ACTION

- What are some additional ways to structure oracy development for students in the emerging bilingual strand?
- Develop assessment measures of critical thinking and use of language for academic purposes. How could they be adapted for use in the different pathways of the grade 3 strands represented in this chapter?
- What are the specific needs of language learners in your grade 3 bilingual program related to the development of literacy skills, especially in relation to use of informational text?
- What would an effective collaboration structure between the grade 3 mainstream classroom and LC teachers look like in your district?

6

Content-Based Literacy Club in Grades 4–5

KEY CONCEPTS

- Carefully scaffolded pathways at grades 4–5 enable students to develop critical thinking skills and the language needed for academic purposes in social studies and science.
- Learning strategies, literacy, oracy, and metalanguage are developed through content-based Literacy Club sessions at grades 4–5.
- Student assessment in grades 4–5 focuses on literacy development and use of language for academic purposes.

we probably wouldn't had b/c kids are already transitioned

The goals of the **Literacy Club (LC)** at grades 4 and 5 focus on oracy, content-area literacy, concept development, and metacognition. There is also a focus on the development of positive attitudes toward reading and writing because more positive attitudes generally accompany improvements in academic achievement. An attitude survey administered four times during the year in grades 3–5 monitors student changes in attitudes. The LC teachers also review district measures of reading progress, that is, the **Developmental Reading Assessment 2+ (DRA2+) test** in English and *Evaluación del desarrollo de la lectura 2 (EDL2) test* in Spanish. Work samples, teacher anecdotal records, and authentic assessments of application of language and content provide evidence of progress in understanding of content-area concepts. Reading and writing strategy development is measured through student performance in authentic application opportunities, as well as student self-assessment. Because all students at this grade level have developed relatively strong Spanish oracy, the **advancing** and **emerging bilingual strands** are combined into one bilingual strand. Writing ability can be monitored through use of the Literacy Squared rubric (Escamilla et al, 2014) in the bilingual strand and district writing rubrics for the **English as an additional language (EAL) strand**.

The LC format revolves around a content-based focus in grades 4 and 5. Content-area literacy in social studies and science becomes especially critical in classrooms at this stage; thus the LC structure changes to meet this need by focusing on literature, skills, and strategies related to social studies and science themes. Content-area themes, identified by the district for grades 4 and 5 in these two content areas, were selected for development in the LC.

Sergio, our grade 5 focal student, is featured in the bilingual strand, along with Brianna, William, and Alejandro. *Ai*, our grade 4 focal student, is reintroduced in the EAL strand, along with Cumar, Pua, and Emilio. Both Sergio and Ai have been in U.S. schools for several years, but have not flourished academically. Sergio's strong listening and speaking skills in Spanish are going to be used to strengthen literacy development in both languages and a number of **scaffolds** put in place to support language and content development in English for Ai. The chapter includes an overview of progress and next steps for Sergio and Ai.

LANGUAGE AND LITERACY DEMANDS

At the grade 4–5 level, the English language arts standards indicate that students are to summarize one or more texts on a particular topic and interpret visual, oral, and quantitative information to explain, describe, and draw inferences. Students identify and compare similar themes in texts and different points of view in a variety of genres. They are expected to clearly introduce and develop well-organized writing topics that are supported by facts, details, and quotes and write conclusions related to the body of the text.

These skills begin to prepare students for grade 5–6 standards that require them to summarize ideas, opinions, and points of view. Learning experiences that develop **critical thinking skills** in which students describe, analyze, explain, and draw inferences in a variety of contexts and for a variety of purposes are increasingly used. Use and interpretation of academic and figurative language are developed more fully and students are expected to apply information and understanding from a variety of sources.

Students in the bilingual strand participate in bridging activities to explore the structure of content-area vocabulary in science and social studies in both languages. These activities provide opportunities for students to identify theme and main ideas/details in English and Spanish reading material and to realize that these strategies are used in the same manner in the two languages. Discussions of meaning and structure across both languages extend students' understanding of what it means to be bilingual.

TEACHER COLLABORATION

Collaboration with grade-level teachers is critical in designing the content-based LC sessions. The content of LC themes is aligned with the themes students are studying in the general classroom, and LC teachers alternate between science and social studies themes to ensure that students make progress in both content areas. In some instances, LC teachers are able to preteach concepts, strategies, and vocabulary before the same concepts are introduced in the classroom, preparing students to participate more fully in classroom activities and discussions. At other times, the LC and classroom teachers simultaneously develop the same content concepts, providing students with additional opportunities to reinforce understanding and to contribute to learning experiences in the classroom with greater confidence. LC learning experiences reflect the specific needs of the students and are not merely an additional opportunity for students to complete assignments from the classroom. If students have struggled with the language and/or concepts of a particular unit, additional support in the LC may be warranted after the classroom unit has been completed. The teachers purposefully select content standards, materials, and learning experiences used in both settings.

The LC and classroom teachers collaborate to establish a schedule for teaching the various social studies and science themes throughout the academic year. They also collaboratively determine the content/language standards and learning strategies to be emphasized in each unit. This provides the LC teacher with valuable information in analyzing the standards that are associated with each of the themes to determine how to adapt the learning experiences to match the students' academic and linguistic levels. Once academic concepts have been selected, the LC teacher intentionally selects appropriate reading materials that will be accessible to the students, yet address the concepts for the unit. He or she takes care to include some weeks of study around narrative text, especially historical fiction related to social studies themes, to ensure that students have a well-rounded exposure to a variety of genres.

CONTINUOUS PROGRESS MONITORING

Student self-assessment is an especially important element in the grade 4–5 LC strand. Students in these strands are often struggling with language and content and they often doubt their own abilities to participate fully in learning experiences. Guiding students to understand what their needs are and to begin to measure progress toward their goals not only supports their academic progress but also enhances their attitudes toward learning. Therefore, attitude surveys are added to the formative and summative measures associated with assessment in the LC.

Traditional data from assessments of reading and writing progress are used, along with assessment of **oracy**, **strategy development**, and **metalanguage**—in two languages for Sergio and English only with Ai. These additional measures reflect the individual student needs being addressed and monitored and will support them in moving toward grade-level expectations.

SESSION FORMAT

The same components (focus book, word work, rereads and writing) are used at grades 4–5 as at previous grade levels, but the LC format is altered significantly to align students' needs with grade-level expectations. Word work focuses more fully on word patterns and meaning, and in reading students develop more in-depth skills and strategies related to informational text. Because they are reading more connected text by this point, they do not reread entire sections, but instead may reread selected passages for specific theme-related purposes. Writing is more focused than in the LC format at younger grade levels, where students are encouraged to select their own topics for writing. Instead, students expand understanding of social studies and science concepts through content-based writing topics, often developed collaboratively between the teacher and the student. Suggested journal prompts for both narrative and informational text were mentioned in relation to grade 3 and would be useful at this level also. Critical thinking skills are the focus in strategy development and graphic organizers are used extensively to guide students in organizing information with content-area concepts. A listing of skills and strategies developed for the content-based LC are featured in Table 6.1.

The order of the LC components may be altered to fit the needs of a specific group/theme. Because the reading and writing activities are more complex and extensive at this level, teachers often alternate days for reading and writing. However, the standard components of word work and rereads generally occur during most sessions. Box 6.1 provides an overview of the components that may be addressed in the content-based LC sessions in both the bilingual and EAL strands.

CONTENT-BASED BILINGUAL STRAND

At the grade 4–5 level, students from English-speaking homes enrolled in **dual language programs** have been in bilingual classrooms for several years. Although there is still a wide range of Spanish and English oracy, literacy, and metacognition skills among the students at this level, most have developed basic language skills. Therefore, the emerging

TABLE 6.1 Checklist of Reading Strategy Development		

Student Name _____ Grade _____

ELP Level _____ Independent DRA2+ Level _____

Skills and Strategies	Mini-Lesson Date	Notes on Student Use of Skill/Strategy
Sequencing		
Predicting		
Prior knowledge		
Inferring		
Summarizing		
Main idea		
Vocabulary		
Supporting ideas		
Compare and contrast		
Context clues		
Text features		
Skimming		
Scanning		
Evaluating		
Cause and effect		
Note taking		
Setting a clear purpose		
Making connections		

DRA2+, Developmental Reading Assessment 2+; ELP, English language proficiency.

and advancing bilingual groups are combined into a single heterogenous bilingual strand at this level, as stated previously. Some need additional Spanish language or literacy support, and learning experiences are organized so students with stronger skills in either oracy or literacy may support the learning of others in the group. The sessions are organized to focus on Spanish language content areas with bridging activities to English at the end of each week. Table 6.2 provides an overview of the grade 4–5 LC format for emerging/advancing bilinguals.

BOX 6.1 Overview of Content-Based Literacy Club Components

WORD WORK

- Emphasis on word meaning and meaningful analysis of word parts

FOCUS BOOK READING

- Development of more in-depth skills and strategies related to informational text
- Use of graphic organizers to guide student work with content-based concepts
- Development of critical thinking skills as focus in strategy development

REREADING

- Rereading of selected passages for specific comprehension-related purposes
- Rereading as preparation for writing/research

WRITING

- Develop collaborative writing topics between teacher and student
- Focus on social studies and science themes
- Integrate content-area language and concepts

Sergio, our focal student, is a fifth grader who arrived from Guatemala at the age of 7. He is officially designated as an **English learner** who has reached English language development (ELD) Level 3 in listening and speaking, and Level 2 in reading and writing, as measured by the **Assessing Comprehension and Communication in English State-to-State (ACCESS) test** for ELLs. Spanish is Sergio's home language, and he has reached Spanish language development (SLD) Level 6 in listening and speaking. However, Sergio struggles with reading and writing in both languages. According to *los descriptores podemos* (can-do descriptors), Sergio has reached SLD Level 3 in reading and Level 2 in writing. Furthermore, his reading level in Spanish, as measured by the EDL2, is significantly below grade level.

TABLE 6.2 Format for Grades 4–5 Emerging/Advancing Bilingual Strand

	Day 1	Day 2	Day 3	Day 4	Day 5
Focus book	Introduction Read Discuss strategy Self-assess	Read Discuss strategy	— — —	— — —	Read Spanish/ English Self-assess
Word work	Spanish concepts *Dictado*	Spanish concepts *Dictado*	— —	— —	Comparative analyses English/Spanish
Rereads	—	—	Specific purposes	Specific purposes	—
Writing	—	—	Spanish—content	Spanish—content	*Así se dice*

TABLE 6.3 Baseline Data: Sergio

Student	Sergio	
Grade	5	
Birthplace	Guatemala	
Home language	Spanish	
Age at arrival	7	
Program type	Dual language	
Entered program	Grade 2	
Language development	*English Level*	*Spanish Level*
Listening	3	6
Speaking	3	6
Reading	2	3
Writing	2	2
Observations	Comparable levels of reading and writing in English and Spanish	
Recommendations	Strengthen reading and writing in Spanish to support literacy development in both languages: ■ comprehension ■ strategy development ■ content and structure of writing	

The LC teacher knows that Sergio's ideas for writing are thoughtful and creative, and can serve as an important base for extending the skills he has developed thus far. Sergio's strong oracy skills in Spanish offer an important resource when bridging to English in the LC. Sergio can benefit from instruction in comprehension and strategy development linked to his fascination with science and social studies topics. He can also benefit from opportunities to analyze and interpret what he has read, which he finds particularly challenging with informational text. Table 6.3 summarizes these **baseline data**. The LC teacher, in collaboration with the classroom teacher, has chosen to address Sergio's needs by focusing on text features, developing comprehension strategies, and emphasizing the content and structure of academic writing. Strengthening his reading and writing skills in Spanish along with bridging activities in English supports literacy development in both languages.

Box 6.2 provides an overview of content and language objectives for the sample lessons that follow.

Focus Book

In this example, as part of a social studies theme in their classrooms, the students are studying how different groups of people adapt to their environments. The LC teacher is preteaching main concepts about desert survival in the LC sessions. Some students have lived in desert areas and can assist in activating background information for the group.

BOX 6.2 Content and Language Objectives for the Week			
Tema	El clima afecta a la gente de un lugar.	**Theme**	*Climate affects the people who live there.*

OBJETIVOS NUEVOS/NEW OBJECTIVES

Contenido	Yo podré identificar las ideas principales y detalles sobre la gente que vive en el desierto.	**Content**	*I will be able to identify main ideas and details about people who live in the desert.*
Lenguaje	Yo podré leer e interpretar información de mapas y tablas.	**Language**	*I will be able to read and interpret information from maps and tables.*
	Yo podré escribir una opinión sobre los pueblos del desierto usando pruebas de texto.		*I will be able to write an opinion about desert people using textual evidence.*

REVISANDO/REVIEW OBJECTIVES

	Yo podré usar pistas de contexto e ilustraciones para determinar el significado de palabras/frases.		*I will be able to use context clues and illustrations to determine the meaning of words and phrases.*
	Yo podré redactar y revisar la escritura. Yo podré usar la gramática, la puntuación, y la ortografía correcta en español.		*I will be able to edit and revise my writing. I will be able to use correct grammar, punctuation, and spelling in Spanish.*

The students are using a portion of the text, *Los pueblos del desierto/Desert People* (Meissner, nd) as their reading material.

On day 1, after reviewing the title and table of contents, the LC teacher reviews the headings, photos, and captions and asks students to use these resources, along with their own background knowledge, to share what they know about the desert. The students and the LC teacher create a word splash of key phrases as they share their ideas: *muy seco* (very dry), *el cactus* (cactus), *los coyotes* (coyotes), *muy frío por la noche* (very cold at night), *mucho calor* (very hot), *peligroso* (dangerous), *los camellos* (camels), *las culebras* (snakes), *el jaguar* (jaguar), *montañoso* (mountainous), *hay mucha arena* (there is a lot of sand), *arbustos* (bushes).

Activating Prior Knowledge

The following vignette demonstrates how the LC teacher activates and builds on students' prior knowledge in preparation for reading. First, students take the words from the word splash and form sentences describing the desert. Then the LC teacher invites students to pose questions they still have about the desert, first orally and then in writing, as a foundation for their exploration of the theme, "People adapt to the climate where they live."

Students	Es muy seco en el desierto. Hace frío por las noches y hay mucho calor durante el día. Hay animales en el desierto como camellos y jaguares. Es peligroso en el desierto porque hay culebras.	*It is very dry in the desert. It is very cold at night and very hot during the day. There are animals in the desert like camels and jaguars. It is dangerous in the desert because there are snakes.*

(Students continue with other sentences.)

Teacher	¿Tienen preguntas sobre el desierto antes de leer este texto? Por ejemplo, podrían preguntar ¿Es difícil vivir en un desierto?	*Do you have some questions about the desert before we read this text? For example, you could ask, Is it difficult to live in a desert?*

(Students share questions orally before writing them in their notebooks to give them more practice with forming questions, and also as an opportunity to hear the questions of their group mates.)

Teacher	Hay una palabra muy importante en este texto, --adaptarse--. Busquen la palabra en negrita en la página 5 y lean la oración que contiene la palabra. ¿Qué significa la palabra --adaptarse--?	*There is a very important word in this text, "adapt." Look for that bolded word on page 5 and read the sentence that has that word. What does the word "adapt" mean?*
Sergio	El desierto es muy seco.	*The desert is very dry.*
Teacher	[a Sergio] Vamos a leer las preguntas en la primera parte de esta página para ayudarnos.	*[to Sergio] Let's read the questions at the top of this page to help us.*
Sergio	[leyendo en voz alta] ¿Cómo sobrevive la gente en lugares tan calurosos y secos? ¿Dónde encuentran comida y agua?	*[reading out loud] How can people survive in such hot and dry places? Where do they find food and water?*
Teacher	Entonces, ¿qué significa la palabra --adaptarse--, Sergio?	*Then, what does the word "adapt" mean, Sergio?*
Sergio	Cómo sobrevive la gente en un lugar	*How people survive in a place*

The LC teacher reiterates that it is difficult to live in the desert because it is very dry and sometimes it is very hot or very cold, but the people change to survive there. They review the word "change" as a synonym for "adapt" (they must change to survive) and look for examples about how people change to survive in the desert as they continue reading.

Note how the LC teacher works with Sergio to guide him in using text resources to explore the meaning of the word "*adaptarse*" (to adapt). Sergio first makes a guess at what the word means, is then directed to read the opening questions to gain some additional insights, and finally is able to demonstrate a better understanding of the term. Very often the students in the LC at these grade levels have not yet developed these types of literacy strategies and need carefully structured opportunities to practice them.

The grades 4 and 5 teachers, along with the LC teacher, want to strengthen the map reading and interpretation of graphic information skills of their students. The LC teacher provides opportunities for the students to use a table in their **focus book** to determine what information about location, climate, and so forth of deserts around the world can be gleaned from the graphic. He also integrates this exercise with a language learning activity by having them formulate questions using information from the graphic. After the students gain some confidence in using the table, he asks them to summarize and analyze what they learned from the graphic.

Identifying Main Ideas and Details

Although the students state that identifying main ideas and details helps readers understand text more fully, their oral and written responses indicate that they are still struggling with this concept. The following vignette highlights the gradual release of responsibility to the students. The LC teacher first gives students a handout to scaffold their learning (Box 6.3). Then he uses a think-aloud to model how he locates the main idea and determines what supporting details he will search for. The students then form pairs to continue work in this area and the LC teacher stands by to support students as they work.

BOX 6.3　Main Ideas and Details Worksheet

LOS PUEBLOS DEL DESIERTO/DESERT PEOPLE

Tema	Como la gente se adapta al clima donde viven	**Theme**	*How people adapt to the climate they live in*

Antes de leer/*Before reading:*

Una pregunta que tengo _____　　　　　　*A question that I have* _____

Después de leer/*After reading:*

¿Encontré la respuesta a mi pregunta?　　　　　*Did I answer my question?*

Ideas principales y detalles/*Main ideas and details:*

Ejemplo: ¿Qué es un desierto?　　　　　　　　*Example: What is a desert?*

1. Idea principal: Hay diferentes tipos de desiertos.

1. *Main idea: There are different types of deserts.*

Detalle: Todos son secos.　　　　　　　　　　*Detail: All are dry.*

Detalle: Unos son fríos pero la mayoría son soleados y calurosos.

Detail: Some are cold but the majority are sunny and warm.

Los Tohono O'odham

2. Ideas principals:　　　　　　　　　　　　**2.** *Main ideas:*

Detalles:　　　　　　　　　　　　　　　　　　*Details:*

Los beduinos

3. Ideas principals:　　　　　　　　　　　　**3.** *Main ideas:*

Detalles:　　　　　　　　　　　　　　　　　　*Details:*

Teacher　Lean la primera página del texto y voy a indicar la idea principal y los detalles. Miran la hoja para hoy. El tema es --Cómo la gente adapta al clima de donde viven.-- Después de leer el título, --¿Qué es un desierto?-- y la primera oración encontré la idea principal, Hay diferentes tipos de desiertos. Si digo que hay diferentes tipos de desiertos, entonces para encontrar los detalles debo buscar cómo son iguales o diferentes. Escribí que todos son secos. Unos son fríos pero la mayoría son soleados y calurosos.

Read the first page of the text and I will point out the main idea and details. Look at the worksheet for today. The theme is "How people adapt to the climate where they live." After reading the title, "What Is a Desert?" and the first sentence I found out what the main idea was, "There are many types of deserts." If I say there are different types of deserts, then to find the details I'll need to search for ways that they are the same or different. I wrote that they are all dry. Some are cold, but most are sunny and hot.

The LC teacher continues with additional practice in identifying main ideas and details from the text. The students are able to indicate that headings and topic sentences generally provide the main idea of a passage. They also respond that the most important information about the main idea helps them identify the details. Modeling the process and then providing opportunities for students to practice and receive immediate feedback helps ensure that students gain more facility with this strategy. This is a solid example of how LC sessions are individualized for students. Identifying main ideas and details is an important strategy for any type of reading and research, and the LC teacher revises his plan and spends additional time teaching and practicing this concept when he notes that the students are not yet confident with it. The LC teacher listens to individual students read a portion of the focus book aloud and asks questions to check their comprehension while the other children continue reading in pairs or independently. The students stop reading when they reach the designated page in the text and discuss what they have read so far.

The LC teacher provides opportunities for the students to review the questions they wrote about the desert and to explain how they used text features and context clues to find answers to them. During this session the students completed the "main ideas and details" section of their handout. The teacher now asks two pairs of students to share what they entered as main ideas and details on their papers, making adjustments to their own responses as they listen to what the other students wrote and what evidence they offered. The LC teacher uses the completed work to have students summarize what they have learned about the Tohono O'odham people discussed in the book and how they adapt to living in the desert. Students complete the reading portion of the student self-assessment in Box 6.4 at the end of day 1 with the new focus book. They repeat the same assessment at the end of the week to note their progress and to set a goal for the next week.

On day 2, the LC teacher reviews the theme of the text, "how desert people adapt to their climates," by asking them to review the term "adapt" and to discuss how the Tohono O'odham adapt to living in the Sonoran desert using evidence from the text. They also discuss how finding the main ideas and details of a text helped them understand it better. The students discuss the process they used for identifying the main idea and finding sup-

---

BOX 6.4 Beginning-/End-of-Week Student Self-Assessment

Nombre _____   Fecha _____

Título: *Los pueblos del desierto*	*Title:* Villages of the Desert
Este libro es Facil Más o menos Dificil de leer.	*This book is Easy Average Difficult to read.*
Estrategia de lectura: Identificar ideas principales y detalles	*Reading strategy: Identify main ideas and details*
es Facil Más o menos Dificil.	*is Easy Average Difficult.*
Escribe un ejemplo de una idea principal y al menos dos detalles del texto:	*Write an example of a main idea and at least two details from the text:*
Esta estrategia me ayuda _____.	*This strategy helps me _____.*
Estrategia de escritura: Escribir una opinión	*Writing strategy: Write an opinion*
es Facil Más o menos Dificil.	*is Easy Average Difficult.*
Mi meta para la semana que viene: _____	*My goal for next week: _____*

porting details in the text (metacognition). They have indicated that it was difficult to decide which details were most important, so they focus on that skill when reading the second section of the text.

Today while the students are reading and working in groups, the LC teacher records anecdotal notes about each student. When the group completes the reading assignment, the LC teacher points out how individual students were observed using the following strategies: rereading; looking back at headings, pictures, and captions; asking a partner clarifying questions; and breaking unfamiliar words into parts or syllables. Sergio is making good progress in rereading when something does not make sense and he now regularly previews headings, pictures, and captions before reading. However, writing continues to be a challenge for him.

Reteaching a Concept

The students are becoming more adept at identifying the main idea of a text, but they continue to need additional practice in selecting important supporting details. In the following vignette, the LC teacher involves the students in a scaffolded lesson where they actively engage in listing all of the details and then determine which are the most important. This process provides the students with a strategy for identifying supporting details, which they will be able to practice in subsequent learning experiences.

Teacher	Ustedes indicaron que es difícil decidir cuales son los detalles más importantes. Vamos a revisar el primer título, --Los beduinos--. ¿Qué escribieron como la idea principal?	*You have indicated that it is difficult to decide on the most important details. Let's review the first heading, "The Bedouins." What did you write as the main idea?*
William	Los beduinos van de un lugar a otro en camellos buscando agua y comida.	*The Bedouins go from place to place on camel looking for water and food.*
Teacher	Muy bien. ¿Cuales son unos detalles sobre cómo se transportan y cómo buscan agua y comida?	Very good. What are some details about how they move about and look for water and food?

(Students offer some ideas and the teacher makes a list on the board. Together they determine which details are the most important and make changes on their worksheets.)

Teacher	¿Qué aprendieron acerca de cómo los beduinos se adaptan a vivir en el desierto?	*What did you learn about how the Bedouins adapt to living in the desert?*

(Students discuss what they have learned.)

Teacher	¿Para quién es más difícil vivir en el desierto: para los beduinos o para los Tohono O'odham?	*Who has a more difficult time living in the desert: the Bedouins or the Tohono O'odham?*

The LC teacher informs the students that they will be forming an opinion about this question and encourages them to begin thinking about this topic. The teacher speaks briefly with Sergio to help him formulate his opinion because he has been struggling with this concept. He recognizes that Sergio is uncertain what it means to formulate an opinion so he briefly reviews the concept with him now and continues to work with him as the week progresses. These examples are indicative of the types of supports that guide students in developing critical thinking skills in the content areas.

On day 5, the focus book section of the session takes place after the writing session; this lets students complete a **comparative analysis** from Spanish to English using the last paragraph of the text, which highlights the theme. This becomes the English reading material for the day. Students reread the last paragraph of the text in Spanish, as well as their English bridge of the text. They compare their ***Así se dice*** (That's how you say it) activity to the English version of the text, *Desert People*, point out what they noticed about the structure of the statements in each language, and discuss any differences in the translations they completed and those in the English version of the text. These activities further hone the students' sense of using all of their bilingual language practices to explore their two languages. After reviewing the current strategy of main ideas and details, the students repeat the self-assessment for the week, note progress, and set a goal for the following week.

Word Work

Students independently review new vocabulary words on their word rings in Spanish during the word work portion of the sessions on days 1–4 and in both English and Spanish on day 5. They may write definitions or draw pictures for words that are challenging in terms of definition and/or pronunciation. Spanish vocabulary words are written in red and any English equivalents introduced during the bridging section are written in blue.

At this grade level, students spend less time working on specific word formation and instead greater emphasis is placed on word meaning and usage. For example, word work for this text focuses on two areas, interpreting the sentence cues "*cuando*" (when) and "*pero*" (but) and understanding formation and use of imperfect tense verbs. Sentences used to study these cues also become the ***dictado*** for the week and emphasize use of commas (*comas*) with conjunctions.

Dictado	--La Tierra tiene diferentes tipos de desiertos, pero todos los desiertos son secos. Algunos desiertos son muy fríos, pero la mayoría son soleados y calurosos.-- (p. 4)	*"Earth has different kinds of deserts, but all deserts are dry. Some deserts are very cold, but the majority are sunny and hot." (p. 4)*

Using Conjunctions

The vignette that follows reflects the integration of language and content. Students become more critical readers, writers, and thinkers when they can participate in metalanguage activities that ask them to analyze how language is being structured and used. In this example, students focus on the use of the conjunction "but" to signal an exception. The LC teacher scaffolds his presentation of the concept as students analyze sentences from the text to determine how this conjunction is used. Students analyze the use of the conjunction "but" in their reading throughout the week.

Teacher	Vamos a leer las dos oraciones que tenemos aquí:	*Let's read the two sentences that we have here:*
	--La Tierra tiene diferentes tipos de desiertos, <u>pero</u> todos los desiertos son secos. Algunos desiertos son muy fríos, <u>pero</u> la mayoría son soleados y calurosos.-- (p. 4).	*"Earth has different kinds of deserts, <u>but</u> all deserts are dry. Some deserts are very cold, <u>but</u> the majority are sunny and hot." (p. 4)*
	Cada oración tiene dos partes. Una parte que es verdad para todos los desiertos y la otra parte es una excepción, o algo que no es verdad para todos. ¿Cuál es la parte que es verdad para todos los desiertos en la primera oración?	*Each sentence has two parts. One part is true for all deserts and the other part is an exception, or something that is not true for all. Which is the part that is true for all deserts in the first sentence?*
Alejandro	Todos los desiertos son secos.	*All deserts are dry.*

Teacher	Excelente. No importa si los desiertos tienen otras características, todos son secos. Entonces, ¿cuál es la excepción?	*Excellent. It's not important if deserts have other characteristics, all are dry. So then, what is the exception?*
Brianna	La Tierra tiene diferentes tipos de desiertos.	*Earth has different types of deserts.*
Teacher	Excelente. Hay diferentes tipos de desiertos, pero sabemos que todos son _____.	*Excellent. There are different types of deserts, but we know that all are _____.*
Sergio	secos	*dry*
Teacher	Usamos la palabra --pero-- para conectar la idea principal y la excepción. Se llama una --conjunción -- y ponemos una coma para separar las dos ideas.	*We use the word "but" to connect the main idea and the exception. This is called a "conjunction" and we put a comma to separate the two ideas.*

LC teachers must always be alert to the use of language in texts they select and take advantage of the opportunity to teach students how to read and interpret complex text. These are universal skills that can be applied to all areas of learning. Reinforcing these skills encourages students to read all text more critically and to notice cues that affect meaning. Aspects of grammar and language structure are embedded in word work sections of the LC across all grade levels. Explicit grammatical terms, such as "conjunction" in this case, are introduced in authentic and meaningful ways as they are encountered in the focus books.

On day 2 of word work, the students compile a list of imperfect tense verbs they have found in their text and write them on cards; they also write the infinitive of each verb (with assistance) on the card. They then sort the verbs according to patterns in the infinitives, which should lead them to sort the words into "ar," "er," and "ir" verbs. All of the imperfect verbs mentioned in the text have been used in the third person plural. The students work in pairs, selecting two verb cards from each pile, that is, two each of ar," "er," and "ir" verbs, and are then asked to conjugate their six verbs. The teacher works with individual pairs to see how well they are able to complete this exercise and to discuss when the imperfect tense is used. Student responses to this activity provide valuable feedback on how much additional work might be needed with verb conjugation and tenses.

On day 5, the LC teacher uses the bridge to lead the students through comparative analyses of language concepts in English and Spanish. The students begin by working together to create a list of English cognates for Spanish vocabulary in their readings. There are several cognates in this text and the LC teacher only joins in the activity when clarification is needed. For example, when the students translate "*serpientes*" as "serpents," they are asked to read the word in context from the text and quickly realize the term actually means "snakes." They are asked to read and translate a phrase from the text, "*Los Tohono O'odham cazaban serpientes cascabeles*" (p. 10). (The Tohono O'odham hunt rattlesnakes.) The students translate "*habitación*" as "habitat." The teacher again asks the students to read a phrase from the text, "*Había una habitación principal*" (p. 7), containing the vocabulary word and the students realize that the translation is "room." The same occurs with the term "*refugio*," which the students translate as "refuge;" they use the context of the sentence to learn that the word means "shelter" instead. These learning experiences assist students in appreciating the nuances of language structure and meaning across languages.

Rereads

Students use rereading of their current text for two specific purposes. First, on day 3, they use the reread opportunity to search for evidence for the opinion piece they are preparing to write. The students decide which of the two desert groups they have read about has the more difficult challenge of living in the desert. After they choose a group, they put an asterisk next to evidence in the text that supports their opinion, which they refer to when writing the opinion piece. They orally share their opinions about which group faces the greater challenges in living in the desert along with evidence to support their claims, which serves as good oral rehearsal for their writing. During the next reread activity, on day 4, they find additional sentences with the conjunction "*pero*" (but) and underline them in their texts. After they have found some samples they share them with the group and describe the main idea and exception in each sentence.

The LC teacher reminds students to use the skim and scan strategy they had learned in earlier lessons for each of the reread activities and reviews how to skim a page to find a particular piece of information. Observations are made to ensure that when skimming they are not reading the entire text and assistance is offered as needed in applying this strategy.

Writing

During the writing portion of the sessions on days 3 and 4, the students write an opinion piece about which group of people they think has the greater challenge living in the desert. The students prepare for writing using an outline, as shown in Box 6.5.

Preparing to Write an Opinion Piece

The next vignette further demonstrates the integration of language and content. The students have read and interpreted the text, focused on informational literature skills and strategies, and now will write with an emphasis on the content-area objective of how groups of people adapt to their environments. After sharing orally they begin by writing an opinion statement about which group has the greater challenge surviving in the desert. They may use the sentence frame provided in Box 6.5 or write their own statements.

Sergio's Writing	[on document camera] En mi opinion es más difícil para los beduinos vivir en el desierto.	*In my opinion it is more difficult for the Bedouins to live in the desert.*
Teacher	Ahora tenemos que presentar nuestras razones para demostrar por qué es tan dificil vivir en el desierto para el grupo que hemos elegido. Pueden usar el texto con las razones que marcaron para demostrar su opinión. Leanlas y después cierren los libros y escriban sus razones.	*Now you have to present your reasons to demonstrate why it is more difficult for your group to survive in the desert. You can use your text to find the reasons that you marked to demonstrate your opinion. Read them over and then close your book and write them in your own words.*
Sergio's Writing	[on document camera] Los beduinos mudan muchas beses. Viben en tendas de campana. Coman frutas y vegetal. Es dificil encontar agua.	*The Bedouins move many times. They live in tents. They eat fruits and vegetables. It is difficult to find water.*

(The teacher reads Sergio's writing with him and they revise some sentences to demonstrate how it is difficult for the Bedouins to survive in the desert.)

Although Sergio's writing includes a few spelling mistakes, the LC teacher is concerned with content at this point in the writing process and does not address spelling now. The LC teacher indicates that they will write a conclusion, "as a summary of what we have written to make certain that our readers understand our opinion and our evidence. Read the sentence at the bottom of the paper. You may use this example or you may write your own conclusion." The LC teacher has noted that Sergio is progressing in his ability to form an opinion and provide supporting evidence. He allows Sergio to complete as much of the

BOX 6.5 Opinion Writing Worksheet

Mi opinion/*My opinion:*

Introducción/*Introduction:*

En mi opinión, es más difícil para los _____ vivir en el desierto.

In my opinion it was more difficult for the _____ to live in the desert.

Información sobre/*Information about:*

Donde viven

Como es el clima

Como es el terreno

Where they live

What the climate is like

What the terrain is like

Cuerpo de la escritura/*Body of the writing:*

Pruebas que apoyan mi opinion

Evidence that supports my opinion:

Una cosa muy difícil para los _____ es que _____.

One very difficult thing for the _____ was _____.

Otra cosa muy dificil para los _____ es que _____.

Another difficulty for the _____ was _____.

Los _____ deben _____.

The _____ had to _____.

Conclusión/*Conclusion:*

Resumen de la escritura/*Summary of my writing:*

En mi opinión es muy difícil para los _____ sobrevivir en el _____ desierto, porque deben _____.

In my opinion it was more difficult for the _____ to survive in the _____ desert because they had to _____.

work as he can independently, but he reviews his responses with him and helps him clarify and expand his writing.

The students conclude their writing and share it with a classmate or the LC teacher. During the remaining time of the writing session, the students edit and revise their writing independently and then with another group member. The LC teacher emphasizes the format of an opinion piece, and stresses a focus on correct grammar, punctuation, and spelling.

During day 5 of the writing session, students participate in a modified *Así se dice* or bridging activity, where they complete and review a comparative analysis of a portion of the text from Spanish to English. Students work in pairs to complete a comparative analysis of the paragraph and are encouraged to discuss differences of opinion they may have in regard to meaning and structure from one language to the other. Students are generally paired so that one student is stronger in one language and the other is stronger in the second language. Such grouping lets the pair bring greater linguistic expertise to the activity and enables each student to take advantage of his or her language strengths.

Whole group discussion takes place when pairs are unable to negotiate the translation. Once the analysis is completed, students review the English version of the text and analyze how it compares with their own translations. In the case of differences in translation, students must decide if both are equivalent or whether they have made errors and how they made those errors. Students also discuss different dialects of Spanish and how they affect structure and meaning, which contributes to their developing metalinguistic awareness.

Monitoring Sergio's Progress

The following writing activity demonstrates that Sergio needs assistance in supporting his opinions and using **language for academic purposes**. The activity requires students to supply appropriate information in the sentence frames. Sergio's sample shows that he needs additional practice in selecting evidence to support his opinion and writing a conclusion. His subsequent writing samples will be used to monitor his progress in this area. The LC teacher provides support for spelling and grammar in all writing activities.

Sergio's Writing Sample

En mi opinion es más dificil para los beduinos vivir en el desierto. Una cosa muy difícil para los beduinos es que es mu kaleenta. Los beduinos deben trabajar.

In my opinion it is more difficult for the Bedouins to live in the desert. One very difficult thing for the Bedouins is that it is very hot. The Bedouins have to work.

However, one month later, while working on a unit about the Maya, Inca, and Aztec civilizations, Sergio's prewriting sample for a compare-and-contrast writing piece demonstrated progress in his ability to organize information for writing in a particular genre. The LC teacher engaged Sergio in an oral discussion to determine what position he wished to take in comparing the Aztec and Maya civilizations, that is, were they more alike or different from one another. He was able to clearly articulate his position in Spanish that the two civilizations had much in common and writing his opinion would become the topic of the LC writing segment. Next Sergio created the following T-chart to help him add more in-depth information from his reading. Although he created parallel topics (*Maya* and *Azteca*), he listed only food items that were different, rather than contrasting several characteristics of the two civilizations.

Maya	Azteca
los mayas tuberon palomtas [the Mayans had popcorn]	los aztecas tuberon chocolate [the Aztecs had chocolate]
los mayas comeron mais, fruta, animals, malon insetos perros, chiles, y calbasos [the Mayans ate corn, fruit, animals, melon, insects, dogs, chiles, and squash]	los aztecas comeron mais chocolate [the Aztecs ate corn, chocolate]

Again, although Sergio has a few spelling mistakes, they do not get in the way of comprehension and so the teacher does not address them during this activity. The teacher asked the students to share the information they'd compiled, and revise their own T-charts. Sergio was able to expand his focus on similarities and differences in foods to add that the Mayans made contributions in mathematics, the Aztecs had *chinampas* (floating gardens), and both had pyramids.

The focus for Sergio has been on analyzing/interpreting text and writing in the content areas. He has improved in both areas, moving from a Level 3 to a Level 4, based on the ELD2 assessments that measure accuracy, fluency, and comprehension of reading, and from a level 2 to a beginning Level 3 on the Literacy Squared writing rubric.

The LC may not be available to Sergio during the next academic year because the model is only designed through grade 5, and it is uncertain whether an adapted model of the program will be designed for the middle school level. He has made a great deal of progress in solidifying basic skills and strategies, but further support would enable him to expand his oracy, literacy, and metacognition skills. His district is in the process of exploring how the LC might be adapted for older students.

CONTENT-BASED ENGLISH AS AN ADDITIONAL LANGUAGE STRAND

As we see in Table 6.4, the content-based EAL literacy strand is organized in the same way as the bilingual strand for students in grades 4 and 5, with a reading emphasis on some days and content-area writing on other days. Rereads also take place for specific purposes, such as to clarify, provide evidence, or share interesting information.

In the example we highlight here, the LC teacher has developed a unit on immigration with her students, which she preteaches before this unit of study is explored in the classroom. Because many of her students have immigrated to the United States themselves or their parents and relatives have done so, the teacher recognizes that the students bring personal interest and enthusiasm to this topic. There are valuable opportunities for students to activate prior knowledge and heighten comprehension of this topic, making it a very good choice for this group. Box 6.6 provides an overview of the grade 4–5 content and language objectives for the sample lessons that follow.

Our focus student in the EAL strand is Ai, a grade 4 student from Thailand who has been in the United States since grade 1. As we can see in Table 6.5, Hmong is Ai's home language, which she speaks and comprehends very well. Although Ai is currently enrolled in a Hmong heritage language class at school where she has some exposure to Hmong script, she has not had the opportunity to learn to read and write in Hmong. Ai's ELD levels in listening and speaking are also quite advanced (Level 5). However, Ai struggles with literacy. She has only reached ELD Level 2 in reading and writing, and her DRA2+ score indicates that she struggles with identifying main ideas and using details appropriately.

TABLE 6.4 Content-Based Literacy Instruction for English as an Additional Language Strand

	Day 1	Day 2	Day 3	Day 4	Day 5
Focus book	Introduction Read Discuss strategy Self-assess	Read Discuss strategy	— — —	— —	Read Review strategy Self-assess
Word work	English concepts Dictation	English concepts Dictation	— —	— —	— —
Rereads	—	—	Specific purposes	Specific purposes	—
Writing	—	—	Content topic	Content topic	Edit Share writing

BOX 6.6 Content and Language Objectives for the Week

Theme   Immigration past and present

NEW OBJECTIVES

Content   I will be able to identify main ideas and details in texts about immigration.

Language   I will be able to do research to compare and contrast information about immigration.

I will be able to read and interpret maps and timelines.

REVIEW OBJECTIVES

I will be able to use context clues and text features.

I will be able to edit and revise my writing.

I will be able to use English grammar, punctuation, and spelling correctly.

TABLE 6.5 Baseline Data: Ai

Student	Ai	
Grade	4	
Birthplace	Thailand	
Age at arrival	6	
Program type	Pull-out ESL	
Entered program	Grade 1	
Language development	*English Level*	*Hmong Level*
Listening	5	6
Speaking	4	6
Reading	2	—
Writing	2	—
Observations	Stronger in listening and speaking in English than in reading and writing	
Recommendations	Needs support with ■ reading and comprehension ■ academic language ■ oracy ■ content and structure of writing	

Ai's difficulty with using language for academic purposes in reading and writing makes it challenging for her to respond appropriately to content-area prompts and she would benefit from opportunities to expand and practice use of content-area language. The LC and classroom teachers focus on strategy development, summarizing, and rereading for a purpose as scaffolds to support Ai in strengthening her language and literacy skills. These supports help in dealing with grade-level, content-area concepts through pathways designed specifically for her and the other students in her group.

Writing is very challenging for Ai and it takes her a long time to put her ideas on paper. Oral rehearsal for writing, along with use of word banks and sentence frames, make Ai feel more comfortable and confident with her writing. However, it is clear from the baseline writing sample that follows that Ai brings a great deal of understanding about immigration to the task and that she is able to compare the experiences of Mexican and Chinese immigrants quite accurately.

The china and Mesico cam US for same.

Bote to got pees and life.

China far, but Mesico not far.

Bote work har.

Ai can make her ideas understood. The writing sample also suggests several aspects of writing (elaboration of ideas, spelling, prepositions, etc.) that might become the focus of writing instruction with Ai.

Focus Book

In this example, the focus book component of the LC is addressed on days 1, 2, and 5. The main reading focus provides an opportunity to review what has been read and link the theme to writing experiences.

On day 1, the teacher begins with a review of the reading students have done so far about immigration in previous LC sessions. She has selected a series of books about immigration that are organized in the same format. This gives the students additional practice in familiarizing themselves with text features.

The students begin with a review of the three main concepts about Mexican immigration in the focus book, which are the same as those for the previous book they'd read about Chinese immigration:

1. People choose to immigrate for many reasons.
2. People who immigrate face many challenges.
3. People who immigrate contribute to the life and culture of the society they join.

They also review what they've learned about why people leave their home and immigrate to a new land. The LC teacher invites students to share their own backgrounds in relation to immigration to activate prior knowledge.

Students read the first several pages and complete a chart about main ideas and details as they read. They are reminded to use headings and topic sentences for main ideas and to skim the text for supporting details. They complete the first main idea together and then work individually or with a partner to complete the rest of the chart in Box 6.7.

Utilizing Graphic Information to Enhance Text Comprehension

On day 2, the LC teacher begins by reviewing what the students learned about immigration from the previous day's reading and draws their attention to additional text features before reading the selection for the day. The following vignette highlights how the LC teacher uses text features to prepare students for reading. Asking students to summarize

BOX 6.7 Immigration Worksheet: Main Ideas and Details

Theme   Immigration

Focus   Main ideas and details

Key concept 1 _____

Main idea

　　Detail

　　Detail

　　Detail

Key concept 2 _____

Main idea

　　Detail

　　Detail

　　Detail

Key concept 3 _____

Main idea

　　Detail

　　Detail

　　Detail

Vocabulary I learned when reading about Antonia Hernández:

what information they will learn about the featured famous person helps them form the habit of reading and interpreting graphic information included in text as valuable sources to clarify and expand meaning.

Teacher	Let's take a look at some features that we have in this text. Turn to the map on page 7. What does this map show us?
Ai	Is map of United States and Mexico.
Teacher	Look at the map key. What does it tell us?

Pua	It shows the part of the United States that belonged to Mexico before 1848.
Teacher	That is the yellow part.
	(Students are amazed at how much larger Mexico used to be.)
Teacher	What happened in 1848 that caused Mexico to lose so much land?
Cumar	There was Mexican War and they lost.
Teacher	Today we'll read about key concept 3 [asks students to identify the concept and reviews key vocabulary definitions located in margins and how to identify main ideas and details].
	Look at the table of contents to review key concept 3 and what famous Mexican person we will read about. What pages should we turn to and who is the famous person?
Students	Antonia Hernández, page 21.
Teacher	On pages 22–23 we have a timeline of her life. Take a look at the timeline and work with a partner to figure out important events in the life of Antonia Hernández. Then we'll read the biography of Antonia Hernández on pages 21–26 to find out why she is an important Mexican immigrant and what contributions she made to U.S. society.

After reading, the students discuss if they think these were important contributions and provide evidence from the text to support their points. This practice gives students additional opportunities to develop critical thinking skills and language for academic purposes. In subsequent lessons, the students continue to review the use of text features in informational text and the development of questions to guide reading. In their journals, they paste maps where they have drawn routes used by various groups to enter the United States. Particular attention is given to the history of Ellis Island during this time period.

Because students are reading and writing longer selections, they may not read and write each day. Some days may be devoted almost entirely to reading and others to writing, depending on the particular literacy activities. For example, for an earlier writing activity during the immigration unit, students used most of one session to write simulated letters as Jewish immigrants. They read additional text selections on Jewish immigration before writing their letters and then spent time outlining and, finally, writing their letters. Ai struggled with reading some of the texts, reread some sections more than once, and discussed the passages with her LC teacher. However, Ai was anxious to outline her ideas and write her letter, which reflects her level of motivation for learning. Her writing needed a great deal of editing and revision but her ideas were clear and creative.

Students have a folder of materials that they use as resources in their LC sessions. Each folder includes a goal sheet, where students record their personal goals for literacy development. They also have a list of each text they've read while participating in the LC, which lets them track how much they are reading and how they are progressing across reading levels. In a section of their LC booklets of key concepts, skills, and strategies, they record notes on what they've learned about each of the topics under study. A small packet of word cards for each area of study is also included. On each word card, the students have recorded the word, a picture, the definition, and a sentence from the text using the term. Classroom and LC teachers generally collaborate to compile a list of the most important vocabulary terms they want students to understand and be able to use in a particular unit and these are included in LC lessons. The LC teacher may identify additional key vocabulary words that students have not yet mastered. Writing pieces are also kept in the folder. In Ai's folder she has her latest text, writing pieces that she has completed and arranged by date, a booklet of word work activities, reading/writing strategy information, and a list of each of the texts that she has mastered in the LC.

In social studies, the LC and classrooms teachers determined that students needed to strengthen map skills. Therefore, creation and interpretation of maps has become an integral part of all social studies units. For example, in a previous unit the LC teacher provided students with a U.S. map during their study of regions. Students completed information sheets for each region and participated in a number of activities using the large maps that the LC teacher had hung in the learning space. Interesting and informative books on each region of the United States were used as reading material. For example, in studying the southwest region, a colorful book about San Antonio was selected that highlighted the key concepts of geography, economy, and so forth that the teacher addressed with each region. Students used their word/picture vocabulary cards and webbing activities that highlighted the topographical characteristics of each region to further enhance their map skills. Interpretation of timelines was another skill that was woven into many sessions. Ai was very fascinated by map work activities. The visual information was very clear to her and she was able to make connections and draw conclusions.

In science, the LC teacher focuses on the human body and planets because these are two important themes for grades 4 and 5. LC instruction is closely interwoven with grade-level classroom instruction for these themes. Future plans for the grade 4 and 5 students include developing units on light, energy, and electricity in science, and more on the study of their state for grade 4 social studies. The teacher also plans to do an historical fiction unit during the semester, to closely link this genre with content-area instruction in social studies.

Word Work

As students begin their LC session, they quickly review the key vocabulary words on their word rings for this text, which include content-area and function words. Word work sessions are scheduled for days 1 and 2 in this example. Additional sessions may be added if needed, especially at the beginning of work with a particular group. The teacher bases word work on the students' needs.

Strengthening Word Analysis Skills

Even though it is a very basic skill for this level, today the LC group is working on long /i/ words having the –igh pattern because the teacher has noted that the students are struggling with this particular pattern in their reading and writing. The following vignette illustrates how the LC teacher developed a lesson to address this gap:

Teacher   Here are a few examples of –igh words. Write as many additional examples as you can think of on your dry erase boards

(Students share the words they wrote [high, thigh, light, bright, might, right, tight, fight, fighter, fighting] and the teacher adds them to the master list.)

Teacher   Note all of the words that you made that have "fight" as the root word. Can you name them?

Ai   fight, fights, fighter, fighting

Teacher   "Fight" is the root word and we can add endings or suffixes to make more words, like "fighter" and "fighting."

Do you remember the e-marker rule? [another area the students struggle with] Can you write some long /i/ words that have an e-marker?

(Students write a number of other long /i/ words that use the "e-marker" rule [nice, ice, strike, spike, site, bite, like, ride, slide]. The students read each word and determine whether or not it fits the e-marker rule.)

Although the students readily grasped the –igh pattern after practice, if left unaddressed it would have continued to be an area of uncertainty. With careful observation, the LC teacher can continually strengthen their word analysis skills, as well as their **metacognitive awareness** of how language is structured.

As we can see, LC teachers can do so much with simple word analysis activities. In addition to teaching the –igh pattern, the LC teacher takes advantage of the words the student generate to review word formation rules (e.g., root words, suffixes, parts of speech) and pronunciation rules (e.g., long /i/ words that use the e-marker rule). The students repeat the review of long /i/ words on day 2. They also review the various forms of other content vocabulary including the root word "migra" (meaning to wander, moving from place to place) and compile a list of words using this root (immigrate, immigration, immigrant, immigrating). They then determine the part of speech for each word and its meaning, which is a metalanguage activity that lets students explore language structure patterns.

As noted in the bilingual strand, students at this level can often experience difficulty in interpreting complex sentences, and word work can really help them. For example, two or three sentences may be selected during word work sessions for students to explore for meaning and structure:

Teacher   1.   "<u>Next</u>, the braceros were <u>sent across the border</u> to a <u>center in the United States</u>." (Pile, 2005b, p.11)

If this is what they did "next," what did they do before that step?
Hint: You will find the information in the sentences before this one.

Also two ideas are contained in this sentence.
"The braceros were sent across the border."
"They went to a center in the United States."

2.   "<u>This</u> meant . . . ." (Pile, p. 11)

What does "This" refer to?
Hint: You will find it in the sentences before this one.

With these types of activities, students gain experience in unpacking sentences and learning how to interpret clues to meaning. In the preceding examples, they explore referents (next, this) that signal that the reader must make connections to other parts of the text.

Dictation is a component of the word work session as well and, in this example, is linked to the theme of immigration and morphological patterns being studied. The following selection focuses on capitalization (United States, Mexican), formation of –tion words (destination, immigration), and spelling of vocabulary words (immigrants, challenges). The students will repeat the dictation on days 1 and 2, using a different colored pencil to correct their work and to note their progress across the two days.

Dictation

The United States is a popular destination for many Mexican immigrants.

Immigration to a new country often includes many challenges.

If students are still insecure with the dictation and understanding of the underlying concepts, it may be repeated on other days.

Rereads

Unlike LC sessions at earlier levels, students reading at these grade levels do not reread previously read texts. Instead they reread their current texts for specific purposes, similar to the work of the bilingual strand.

Skimming as a Reading Strategy

Often students need to skim and scan to find information, which provides an authentic opportunity for students to practice these strategies, as illustrated in this vignette.

Teacher	Today we are going to focus on challenges Mexican immigrants faced years ago and discuss whether you think those problems still exist today. Look at what you wrote for key concept 2: "People who immigrate face many challenges" (p. 10). Find the words on pages 10–11 that support what you listed as a challenge.

(Students read passages to support the challenges they listed and then discuss whether each is still a challenge for immigrants today.)

Ai	Mexican immigrant to work hard learn English.
Emilio	They still have to work long hours and do hard work in the fields. I think Cesar Chavez made things a little better.

(Teacher asks two students to demonstrate how they used skimming to find their evidence.)

(Students review how skimming is a helpful strategy.)

Although Emilio is able to express his ideas much more fully in English, it is evident that both Ai and Emilio have understood the text and are able to make connections to the challenges that immigrants face today. Ongoing support in developing these critical thinking skills allows them to transfer these types of skills to other learning experiences.

Writing

For writing, the students work on comparing and contrasting the experiences of Chinese and Mexican immigrants. Previously they read the text *Chinese Immigration: Immigration to the United States* (Pile, 2005a) and are currently reading the text *Mexican Immigration: Immigration to the United States* (Pile, 2005b). For both texts they have completed a worksheet outlining the three key concepts:

1. People choose to immigrate for many different reasons.
2. People who immigrate face many challenges.
3. People who immigrate contribute to the life and culture of the society they join (p. 4).

Preparing to Write Compare-and-Contrast Essays

The following vignette provides another example of guiding students in the development of analytical thinking skills. The lesson is scaffolded in a way that takes advantage of previous experiences and provides them with resources, such as previous worksheets, a Venn diagram, and compare/contrast sentence frames (Box 6.8) to make the preparation for writing more manageable.

Teacher	In our writing this week, we are going to work on writing a piece to compare and contrast the experiences of Chinese and Mexican immigrants in the United States. What does it mean to compare two topics?
Ai	We tell how same.
Teacher	Then what does it mean to contrast two topics?
Cumar	We write about how they different.
Teacher	We will take a look at what we wrote for each of the key concepts [teacher reviews first key concept] for Chinese and Mexican immigration and then look at how their

experiences were the same or different. [reviews words that can be used to contrast ideas and gives some examples]

Did the Chinese and Mexican immigrant groups come for some of the same reasons? [creates a Venn diagram with students as a graphic organizer for this information]

(Students review notes and discuss reasons for immigrating that are the same for each of the key concepts and highlight these ideas with the same colored highlighter.)

Teacher   [indicating Box 6.8, discusses words to use in making comparisons and gives some examples]

Were there some reasons that were different for each group?

(Students discuss that there was a Civil War in China and a Revolution in Mexico. The teacher leads the group in a discussion about how these are different, but both involved conflict.)

Teacher   In your first paragraph, you will tell how the reasons that Mexicans and Chinese immigrants came to the United States were the same (compare) and then how they were different (contrast). Make your writing interesting by making sure that your sentences don't all start the same. Use your worksheets for the two books to decide what you want to say. Tell a partner what you plan to write, and then write your first paragraph.

After students complete their first paragraph, they review it independently and then with a partner or the LC teacher. After edits and revisions to the first paragraph are made, students repeat the same process for the other two key concepts. This group of students enjoys sharing their work with one another and they have improved their own preparation for writing through this process.

BOX 6.8 Sentence Frames for Writing Compare-and-Contrast Statements

Compare (e.g., *both, same, also, similar, alike*):

_____ and _____ both _____.

Both _____ and _____ are _____.

_____ and _____ are the same because _____.

_____ is similar to _____ because _____.

_____ and _____ are alike because _____.

Contrast (e.g., *different, but, however, on the other hand*):

_____ is different from _____ because _____.

_____ is _____, but _____ is _____.

_____ is _____, however, _____ is _____.

_____ is _____. On the other hand, _____ is _____.

Writing a Conclusion for Explanatory Writing

The following vignette concludes the work begun in the previous activity, and students review what they have written and learned on the topic to draw a conclusion. The students all have strong opinions about their conclusions, in part because the topic was of interest to them and they had some personal insights about the lives and challenges of immigrant groups. The LC teacher takes the three ideas presented by Pua, Emilio, and Ai and has the class work together to write a conclusion, which provides yet another scaffold in learning to write for academic purposes.

Teacher	Now that you have finished comparing and contrasting Chinese and Mexican immigrant groups, do you think they are more alike or different?

(Students discuss their opinions.)

Teacher	We need to write a conclusion to finish our piece. As you compared and contrasted the two groups what did you notice?
Pua	It hard for both group.
Emilio	They all work hard.
Ai	Are many Chinese and Mexican thing in our country.
Teacher	Let's take these three ideas and write a summary together. [Students dictate and teacher writes the conclusion on the board.]
	You may use this conclusion, because we all wrote it together. If you have some different ideas about what you want to say at the end, you may add them to what we wrote or write your own conclusion.

After the students complete their writing and edit it for content and grammar, they share it with a partner, the LC teacher, or the entire group. The writing reflection in Box 6.9 is pasted in their notebooks and they analyze their written use of comparison and contrast.

BOX 6.9 Writing Reflection: Compare and Contrast

Name _____ Date _____

COMPARE

These are some words I used to compare: _____

CONTRAST

These are some words I used to contrast: _____

SENTENCE VARIETY

Name two things you did well in writing a compare-and-contrast piece.
1.
2.

Name one thing you want to improve in writing a compare-and-contrast piece.
1.

Monitoring Ai's Progress

After two months, **running records** indicate that Ai has begun to improve in comprehension, as evidenced by the nature of self-corrections she makes while reading and more accurate retelling of text. Anecdotal records reflect that she has begun to use text and prior knowledge in predicting with evidence but struggles with making inferences and drawing conclusions. She has found sentence frames and word banks very useful in building vocabulary and providing her with the supports she needs in responding to oral prompts.

Ai is becoming more confident with her writing, as shown in the following opinion writing draft:

> I come from Thailand. Many Hmong family here wen we come. I think har for firs family get here. Dey not no uder family and no English. Dey lrn how do evertin. Wen we come dey help us more eez for us. We than dem for help us.

The LC teacher reviews Ai's writing with a focus on content and genre. The teacher notes that Ai readily outlines what she wishes to express in her writing and makes good use of writing resources available to her. Her use of more in-depth text evidence and creativity is apparent in her writing samples. She finds oral rehearsal helpful, but often feels less shy sharing ideas with a partner than the LC teacher. Continued opportunities of this nature support Ai's ongoing progress in writing for a variety of purposes.

The LC teacher continues to focus on strengthening structural elements and use of academic language for writing in the content areas and will introduce narrative writing as well. Ai will benefit from instruction in each of these areas, but it is clear that she also needs ongoing individual support to continually refine spelling and grammar. She reserves a section of her notebook to enter spelling words she frequently needs to reference. She also includes a section for samples of original and corrected sentences (metalanguage) that she and her teacher or classmates have worked on. For example:

- Many Hmong family here wen we come.
  Many Hmong families were already here when we came.
- I think har for firs family get here.
  I think it was hard for the first families who got here.
- Dey not no uder family and no English.
  They did not know other families and they did not know English.

Ai will continue in the LC for the upcoming academic year. It is evident that this instruction and intervention model serves her well and she has improved a great deal in all language domains. She was anxious and relieved to hear that she would remain in the LC for at least another semester because she recognizes that she still relies heavily on the supports it offers.

CONCLUSION

Classroom teachers have informally reported that students who participate in the LC are more excited about learning in science and social studies when they have had the opportunity to preview concepts with the LC teacher. In addition, they engage more fully in classroom activities and discussions because they already have some background about the topic and have had opportunities to practice the language surrounding the topic. Being able to respond to questions and prompts, sometimes before other students in the classroom, boosts their confidence and self-esteem as contributing members of the classroom learning community. Conversely, the LC teacher has noted that students share additional information about concepts they have learned in the classroom when they come to the LC. This results in greater opportunities for language learners to study concepts more fully and to solidify their understanding as they move between the two settings. Students clearly focus on the same goals as their classmates, but the additional language, literacy, and content-area supports reflect use of different pathways to help ensure student success.

In addition to collaboration and focusing attention on the same concepts in the two settings, the content-area focus at grades 4 and 5 provides opportunities for the LC teacher to carefully examine which linguistic and/or content skills and strategies the students need to develop and practice. Once these areas are identified, the LC teacher scaffolds instruction so that students have a nonthreatening environment in which to gain expertise and confidence with these concepts. Oracy, literacy, and metacognition goals are interwoven throughout all of the components of the LC sessions to provide students with the redundancy needed to master and transfer them to learning in the general classroom. An emphasis on the use of language for academic purposes permeates LC work at grades 4–5.

QUESTIONS FOR REFLECTION AND ACTION

- What are some effective oracy, literacy, and metacognition practices that might be used in content-area literacy sessions in the LC that would reflect a focus on the same goals using different pathways?
- What are some additional learning strategies that would let grade 4–5 language learners develop critical thinking skills and use of language for academic purposes?
- What are the most pressing oracy, literacy, and metacognition (strategy development and metalanguage) needs of grade 4–5 students in your school/district who might be candidates for LC participation?
- What are some additional ideas for creating an assessment plan in grades 4–5 based on the integration of literacy with social studies and science?
- What considerations would have to be taken into account in your school/district to create an integrated literacy and content-area plan for use in the grade 4–5 LC?

7

Creating a Literacy Club

KEY CONCEPTS

- The planning stage for creating a Literacy Club includes an analysis of sociocultural foundations and goals, selection of language learner strands, and outline of Literacy Club sessions.
- Ongoing and meaningful professional development in the areas of teaching, learning, and assessment is an integral component of a successful Literacy Club.

The **Literacy Club (LC)** is a comprehensive delivery model focused on the specific language and literacy needs of language learners in diverse sociocultural contexts. It reflects the design of a **Response to Instruction and Intervention (RtI²)** plan in that individual student needs are determined, targeted instruction in language and literacy is provided, and student progress is continually monitored. Instruction is regularly adjusted as students' needs change. The major purpose of the LC is to facilitate growth for language learners, in bilingual or English-medium programs, who are struggling with areas of **oracy**, **literacy**, and/or **metacognition** in one or more languages, and to support them in moving toward grade-level expectations as fully as possible.

Throughout this book, we have seen the clear and consistent application of this model with a range of language learners in the **advancing bilingual**, **emerging bilingual**, and **English as an additional language (EAL) strands**. The theme of "same goals by different pathways," based on the LC framework, has played out in many ways throughout this book. For example, language and literacy development are tightly interwoven at every grade level and across every language strand, highlighting the importance of developing them in tandem. Collaboration between LC and classroom teachers has helped maintain a focus on grade-level literacy standards and language goals. The close alignment between the two venues has helped solidify learning for students because they have two opportunities each day to be immersed in the same language and concepts. **Continuous progress monitoring** has ensured that students' ever-changing academic and linguistic needs were evaluated and instruction has been designed to match those needs. **Scaffolding** and **differentiation** of instruction in the different strands have provided the specific pathways for working toward grade-level standards.

APPLYING THE LITERACY CLUB FRAMEWORK

The fidelity of this particular RtI² instruction and intervention model is best preserved by carefully applying the sociocultural foundations and goals within language learner strands and LC sessions. The following sections provide an overview of each of these areas that teachers and administrators can use to adapt, implement, monitor, and evaluate the LC framework at the local level. The LC protocol in Table 7.1 can be used to determine the degree to which each component of the foundational plan has been incorporated into an LC design for your school/district. Later, this same plan might be used in relation to program evaluation at various points in the planning and implementation stages.

Sociocultural Foundations

The sociocultural foundations of the LC framework include linguistically and culturally responsive pedagogy, student-centered instruction, scaffolded and differentiated learning opportunities, teacher collaboration, and continuous progress monitoring. These five areas of practice make up the foundation for designing an LC plan that can meet the needs of the language learners to be served in any context:

- *Linguistically and culturally responsive pedagogy* is reflected by incorporating the culture and experiences of the students in learning activities and materials.
- All instruction and intervention plans are *student-centered* and focused on each student's specific learning needs.
- LC teachers *scaffold and differentiate content, literacy, and language learning activities* to provide maximum opportunity for student growth and success.
- Meaningful *collaboration* with the classroom teacher(s) takes place on an ongoing basis to ensure that language learners reach the same goals along different pathways.
- A rigorous plan of authentic and *continuous progress monitoring* ensures a balance of challenge and support that enables students to work toward grade-level language and literacy expectations.

Goals

The goals of the LC framework—oracy, literacy, and metacognition—drive the actual content of the LC sessions. Providing an **intervention** for students in literacy alone has been the traditional solution for students who struggle with reading and writing, and often these types of interventions focus heavily on phonics with only secondary emphasis on reading for meaning. In contrast, the LC approach gears teaching, learning, and assessment specifically toward language learners, and as such fully integrates both language and literacy. For students in bilingual strands who struggle with language and/or literacy development in one or both languages, instruction takes place in both languages to take advantage of what they know and can do in each language. In addition, the metacognition goal focuses on the development of **critical thinking skills** through an emphasis on **metalanguage** and **strategy development**. Care should be taken that these three goals (oracy, literacy, and metacognition) are clearly evident throughout any adaptation of the LC for use in a school/district.

Session Strands and Components

Selection of language strands (advancing bilingual, emerging bilingual, and EAL) should be based on the students' needs and the district's resources. Students in the advancing bilingual strand include students whose home language is Spanish and who are enrolled in any type of **bilingual program**. These students generally have adequate oracy skills in Spanish but need literacy support. Students in the emerging bilingual strand include students whose home language is English, as well as **simultaneous bilinguals** whose English is stronger than their Spanish and who are enrolled in dual-language bilingual programs. These students generally need support with oracy in Spanish and may also need literacy support. The EAL strand is designed for students from any language background who are not in bilingual classrooms; these students generally need additional support with English literacy and language. Each of these strands should be evaluated to ensure that oracy, literacy, and metacognition components are embedded in the design of the strands and sessions. In actuality, the strands reflect one of the ways that linguistically and culturally responsive pedagogy is applied concretely in practice.

Each LC session should involve a focus book section that emphasizes reading for comprehension, strategy development, oral discussion, and fluency. The word work component gives students an opportunity to manipulate word structure and meaning. Dictation activities expand this learning to let students explore semantics, syntax, and language structure in the context of sentences related to the theme of the week. Rereads reinforce sight word vocabulary and text structure, while also strengthening reading fluency. Daily writing and writing strategy instruction allows students to organize, practice, and refine writing as a method of communication. Teacher evaluation and student self-assessment are important components of the LC sessions that enable LC teachers to continually challenge and support students in moving as fully as possible toward grade-level expectations in oracy, literacy, and metacognition.

PLANNING, IMPLEMENTATION, AND REFINEMENT

Intervention endeavors that have a positive and lasting impact on children's academic and emotional growth are carefully planned, implemented, and continuously refined. The LC is no different in this regard and it is more complex than many plans because of the language/oracy component that must be developed as well. The opportunity for language learners to receive effective linguistic and academic supports that enable them to be more successful in school is certainly worth the effort.

Behind every successful intervention program is a dedicated and knowledgeable principal/administrator. The LC is no different in this sense either. Even though student mobility or attendance, scarcity of resources for materials and professional development (PD), and lack of fidelity to training might pose challenges in getting the LC up and running smoothly, committed administrators make it happen. When positive results from student participation begin to appear, appreciation for the LC soon develops (Hartl & Grogan, 2011).

Strengthen Tier 1 Structures for Language Learners in the Classroom

Prior to considering the design and implementation of the LC, it is beneficial for schools/districts to review and enhance Tier 1 classroom practices for emerging bilinguals, such as the development of oral language and the use of **total physical response**, visuals, sentence frames, and other sheltered instruction strategies (Echevarria, Vogt, & Short, 2012). This focus may improve instruction for all students in the classroom and may further support growth in oracy, literacy, and metalanguage for language learners. Using the following

TABLE 7.1 Literacy Club Planning and Evaluation Protocol

Assess the level to which the elements of the LC framework are fully embedded in your LC Plan and/or program evaluation (1, not at all–5, fully embedded). Provide evidence to support your assessment, and identify one or two recommendations for action that your team could take to improve implementation.

	1	2	3	4	5	Evidence
Sociocultural Foundations						
Linguistically and culturally responsive pedagogy						
Student-centered instruction						
Scaffolded and differentiated learning activities						
Teacher collaboration						
Continuous progress monitoring						
Recommendations for Action						
Literacy Club Goals						
Oracy						
Literacy						
Metacognition						
Strategy development						
Metalinguistic awareness						
Recommendations for Action						

Strands

Advancing bilingual					
Emerging bilingual					
English as an additional language					
Recommendations for Action					

Session Components

Focus book				
Word work				
Rereads				
Writing				
Recommendations for Action				

methods, Tier 1 practices might be reviewed to determine if students' language levels in both languages are taken into consideration when planning instruction:

- Differentiation of teaching, learning, and assessment that reflects the students' language levels
- Implementation of vocabulary, language structure, and discourse levels of language learning
- Creation of learning experiences in the classroom to actively involve all students in meaningful reading, writing, listening, and speaking activities in one or both languages
- Use of effective scaffolds, such as audio/visual supports, opportunities for interaction, and flexible grouping, to support language development

Strong classroom teaching enhances the LC's impact because the LC is not a substitute for effective classroom instruction but serves as a support that builds on the work of the classroom. A plan to continually refine both the Tier 1 structures for language learners in the classroom and ongoing improvements in the design of the LC is an important component for program evaluation and improvement. Having this review process in place helps ensure that the educational experience for all students is as dynamic and meaningful as possible and that the evolving needs of individual students are more fully met.

Following are suggested guidelines that may prove useful for planning, implementation, and assessment in the LC. The flexible nature of the LC itself enables schools/districts to adapt the plan to meet their circumstances. However, maintaining rigorous levels of language/oracy, literacy, and metacognitive development is essential, as is the ongoing use of assessment to monitor student growth and inform instruction. The most successful implementation of the LC occurs when there is a genuine and purposeful collaboration between classroom and LC teachers, with a focus on strategy development, oracy, and literacy.

Create a Leadership Team

It is important to establish a leadership team for planning and organizing the implementation and ongoing refinement of the LC. The membership of the team depends on whether the LC's creation is occurring at the individual school or district level; in either case, however, it is good to have a wide representation of constituents. Members should include the building principal(s), the English as a second language (ESL)/bilingual coordinator, and ESL/bilingual teachers who have been invited to teach in the LC. Literacy experts or curriculum directors may also be invited to join but care must be taken to maintain the focus on best practices with language learners. The initial charge of this team is to determine the level of need for this type of intervention in the school/district, define the LC's purpose and goals, design the assessment plan, and determine the language strands to be developed.

Design the Literacy Club Format

A tentative format for organizing the LC could be determined at this point to facilitate planning. This phase includes the determination of language strands to be developed, along with a decision about the delivery plan to be used (push-in vs. pull-out). After the number of students who might benefit from participation in the LC in each school and the number of LC teachers the school/district could support has been determined, the LC design is ready to move forward.

Strand Selection

Three grouping options are outlined in the book: two bilingual strands (advancing and emerging) and one English-medium strand (EAL). Depending on the number of potential students eligible for the bilingual strands, these two strands could be combined. It is not recommended, however, that multi-age groups spanning several grade levels be formed to work together in the LC because this negatively affects the self-esteem of older students and makes it more difficult to focus on grade-level standards for specific students.

It is important that students in bilingual programs who are eligible to participate in the LC be placed in one of the bilingual strands. This premise reflects a holistic understanding of bilingualism and biliteracy, and assumes that **bilingual learners** draw on all of the languages in their linguistic repertoires to develop oracy, literacy, and metacognition. When teachers analyze bilingual students' language and literacy strengths side by side, they can leverage students' stronger languages in ways that accelerate literacy development and content learning.

Delivery Plan to Be Used

The plan for offering English language supports for **English learners (ELs)** is generally made at the school or district level and the LC teacher is required, at least initially, to follow the plan in place. Many experts in the field, however, indicate that students tend to have stronger achievement patterns when engaged in push-in intervention plans (e.g., see Allington & Cunningham, 2006; Gibbons, 2015; Routman, 2012). Of course, care must be taken to clearly define the teachers' roles and responsibilities in any delivery plan.

If a **pull-out plan** is used and the LC teachers are to work with students from several classrooms in a separate location, it is easier to form homogenous grade-level groups. The administrator may wish to specify that groups may not be scheduled during their guided reading or group literacy instruction time; however, the LC sessions may be considered part of the independent work time of the literacy block. A drawback to the pull-out plan is that students must leave the classroom, and they find it challenging to be separated from their classmates and estranged from their classroom work. It also places a heavier burden on the collaboration process between LC teachers and classroom teachers. If grade-level teachers are already working very collaboratively and teaching at basically the same pace, this may not be as challenging.

If a **push-in plan** is used, the LC teacher works with the students within the classroom. LC and classroom teachers work together to create a plan that best integrates classroom goals and objectives with the work done in the LC. This plan would be effective at every grade level and content area. Groups are likely to be heterogeneous, but the work of the students can be more easily tied to the expectations of the classroom because the LC teacher is more intimately aware of the goals and learning experiences used in the classroom. Collaboration between the LC and classroom teachers is likely to be stronger as they are working in the same setting. It is, however, more challenging to design LC sessions within the structure of the classroom to ensure that language learners get the support they need. The challenges of this plan include differentiating instruction for diverse groups of learners and managing materials needed for use in a number of classrooms.

Scheduling of Literacy Club Sessions

The LC is most effective when LC teachers and their students meet 4–5 times per week for the allotted times (30 minutes per day for younger students and 45 minutes per day for older students). Shortening the meeting times or including more than four students in sessions lessens the LC's effectiveness for the language learners for whom it was created. Administrators can make the LC sessions a non-negotiable part of the school day. Scheduling is affected by the number of teachers available to teach in the model.

Establish a Plan for Professional Development and Collaboration

As with the implementation of any new educational program, it is necessary to ensure that all educators have a strong background in the purpose, design, and expectations of the LC.

The language and metacognition foci are unique to the LC and teachers need a strong understanding of these principles and how they are developed to successfully implement LC groups in their schools/districts.

Professional Development

An intensive PD plan is a critical component of any successful project. An RtI² model that promotes the integration of oracy and literacy with a focus on continually aligning literacy instruction with language learning requires specialized PD (Gottlieb, 2013). Therefore, it is essential to determine who is providing the initial and ongoing PD for the staff who is administering or teaching in the LC. At times, especially during the initial implementation of the LC, outside experts might be required to assist schools/districts in planning and implementing this intervention. As the program becomes better established, LC teachers whose students have been particularly successful might be called on to share their expertise as part of the PD experience.

PD for the LC must encompass an understanding of the format of the sessions; the development of goals surrounding literacy, oracy, and metacognition (strategy development and metalanguage); the role of assessment; the selection of materials to match language/literacy standards; and the process for collaborating with classroom teachers. In bilingual strands, PD would also address the development of bilingualism/biliteracy and the use of bridging and **translanguaging**. We have found that a strong PD plan that includes ESL and literacy specialists and incorporates suggestions from LC teachers working with the students positively affects student achievement.

In the examples in this book, PD was organized for LC teachers during the school year to continually review student progress, strengthen sociocultural foundations of the LC, and refine the teaching/learning/assessment process. Other PD sessions might be used to model successful approaches, study relevant research, and collaborate in the design of needed materials to better meet students' needs. Summer PD sessions of approximately one week were reserved for making more major refinements to the operation of the LC and to create additional resources for LC teachers. (English and Spanish writing templates are examples of student materials prepared during one summer work session.) Input regarding potential improvements in content and format offered by those teaching in the LC helps ensure that the PD is relevant to the students being served and enhances the skills of the LC teachers. Each group of LC teachers has different needs and these can be identified and addressed by the LC leadership team. Veteran LC teachers often play a vital role in assisting with PD for newer LC teachers. For example, LC teachers highlighted in this book brought ideas and materials forward that frequently became formal materials or practices within the LC. This was of particular importance because these innovations were designed specifically for the students with whom they were working.

Teacher Collaboration

Students in the LC tend to make the most academic and linguistic progress when there is meaningful and ongoing collaboration with their classroom teachers. This was especially evident in the grades 4–5 content-based sessions when both LC and classroom teachers noted how the students shared their understanding and use of **language for academic purposes** across the two settings and engaged more fully in classroom learning experiences. Administrators can enhance the successful nature of this collaboration by building meeting time into the teachers' schedules. If possible, LC teachers work with a limited number of grade levels so that they form closer professional working relationships and can plan more fully across a narrower range of language and content standards. If it is necessary for the LC teacher to meet with a broad range of grade levels, arrangements could perhaps be built into the schedule for him or her to meet with one grade level group each day of the week.

The ESL and/or bilingual coordinator might facilitate the meetings initially to clarify the role of each teacher and how they might be expected to work together. In these sessions they might discuss the ways to select common language and learning goals, differentiate and scaffold the same goals through different pathways, create compatible but differentiated assessments of the same goals, and maximize student learning across the two settings. The LC and classroom teachers review the profiles of students who are to be included in sessions and note their linguistic and academic strengths and challenges in each language. They discuss the genres, learning strategies, vocabulary, themes, and language foci being developed in the classroom and determine how these might be incorporated into the work of the LC. At times the LC teacher may preteach concepts that are likely to be challenging for LC students in the classroom. At other times, he or she teaches the same concepts simultaneously or continues working with the concepts after they are completed in the classroom, if students in the LC found them particularly challenging. The pacing between the two venues is kept as close as possible but at times the LC teacher needs to spend more time building background, teaching preliminary skills, and so forth to ensure that the instruction is differentiated to meet the students' needs in each group.

A second element of the collaboration is to monitor student progress. Assessment measures used in each setting are shared and progress in both language and literacy are closely monitored. The student self-assessments used in the LC provide good evidence of how the students are viewing themselves as learners and can provide insights into student learning. Often students demonstrate greater progress in the LC setting than in the general classroom because it is a smaller, more secure setting for them. Changes in attitude toward learning are also shared because students often become more confident and willing to participate in classroom learning experiences as their language and literacy skills improve. They also often become more positive about engaging in literacy-based learning experiences. Once students reach grade-level expectations in the classroom and stay at this level for a time, the teachers and the ESL/bilingual coordinator determine when students are ready to exit the LC.

As mentioned earlier, another component of the collaboration is to establish a process for continual refinement of the instruction and student response to the intervention. This provides another opportunity for LC and classroom teachers to consider meaningful ways to integrate the cultural background of the students into the learning experiences. Adjustments in instruction, materials, learning activities, and/or assessments in one or both of the languages should be considered when students are not making progress in one setting or the other. On the other hand, if students begin to make rapid progress, options for accelerating instructions should be considered because the purpose is to move students along as quickly and fully as possible toward grade-level expectations.

Assessment/Continuous Progress Monitoring Plan

Assessment is an integral part of the LC. A number of the components described in the following sections (many of which may already be available through district testing) can be used to authentically monitor student progress and the effectiveness of the LC. Therefore, it is important to determine what data are needed and the most expedient way to gather and interpret that information to continually measure student progress in oracy, literacy, and metacognition to inform instruction. In this way, unnecessary duplication of testing can be avoided.

Baseline Data

Schools/districts need to determine if sufficient district and classroom-level data are available to create a meaningful profile of students who would be candidates for the LC. Information on language and literacy development would need to be collected, including time in the United States; language(s) used at home; reading, writing, listening, and speaking levels for each language; areas of strength and need in each language; and attitude toward learning. See Table 7.2 for a suggested student profile sheet.

Classroom teachers generally collect the initial data and review them with the ESL/bilingual coordinator and LC teachers; then students are selected for the LC. Some are selected because they have been in language programs for some time but are progressing slowly in oracy and/or literacy development. For example, *Ai*, a grade 4 student in the EAL strand, struggled with both English **language development** and literacy. ***Evelyn Gloria***, a grade 3 student in a **dual language program**, needed opportunities to develop her Spanish oracy skills. ***Sergio***, a grade 5 student in the bilingual strand, has been in the United States for a longer period of time but has not reached grade-level literacy expectations and needs intensive support to accelerate his literacy development. Grade-level groups of four or fewer can be organized once the data have been reviewed and students are selected.

TABLE 7.2 Baseline Data Profile Sheet

Name		
Grade		
Birthplace		
Age at arrival		
Language(s) spoken at home		
Program type		
Program entry date		
Language development	*English Level*	*Spanish Level**
Listening		
Speaking		
Reading		
Writing		
Observations[†]		
Recommendations		

*If a language other than Spanish is used in the bilingual program, or if student's home language is other than Spanish, include here.

[†] Note strengths and challenges in each language and across languages.

Summative Assessment Plan

Four times per year, interim testing provides valuable information about how students are progressing in the LC. These **summative assessments** might include the **Developmental Reading Assessment 2+ (DRA2+) test** for reading in English and the comparable *Evaluación del desarrollo de la lectura 2* **(EDL2) test** for reading in Spanish (for students in bilingual strands), running records, district writing evaluations, and so forth. Other district level measures may be substituted if they provide insights into how the students are progressing toward language and content standards in one or both languages. At a minimum, these assessments should provide insights into students' progress in reading comprehension, strategy use, and writing in the target language(s) at specific points during the academic year as part of the LC assessment plan.

These quarterly data are analyzed by the LC and classroom teachers. The ESL/bilingual coordinator and other district administrators charged with monitoring student progress also review the data. Regular reports are prepared by the ESL/bilingual coordinator to document the program's effectiveness. The data may be used as one component of a regular review process for the design and function of the LC and may highlight refinements that can be made to continually improve the effectiveness of the intervention, such as expanding the plans for the development of oracy at each grade level. Student progress on quarterly assessment measures is shared with the students as well, so they might gauge their own growth, which often proves to be very motivational.

Formative Assessment Plan

Organizers need to determine how a **formative assessment** plan is implemented during LC sessions. Teachers may conduct regular **running records** to monitor student accuracy, fluency, and strategy use. Anecdotal records of retelling and discussing text can be used to provide information about comprehension and oracy and LC teachers can also keep checklists or additional anecdotal records of student progress. These data are analyzed to monitor ongoing individual student progress toward language and content goals and instruction evolves as the student's needs change.

Student self-assessment is an integral part of the LC. Determining how students will have regular, ongoing, and substantive opportunities to evaluate their progress and set goals for their own learning should be a part of the assessment plan. The self-assessments should reflect the language and content standards that the students are working toward. They review their work and set goals for themselves in terms of content, language, and strategy use. Plans may also be established to have students collect their self-assessments in a binder or a booklet and analyze them regularly. This metacognitive reflection is designed to guide students in becoming more independent in their learning.

Selecting Literacy Club Teachers

In an optimal situation, teachers who already hold ESL and/or bilingual teaching licenses are selected to teach in the LC. With this background, LC teachers have a stronger understanding of the linguistic, cultural, and academic needs of language learners. In one particular district, several of the ESL teachers' groups were transformed into LC groups, with very positive results. In other instances, bilingual and ESL teachers moved from classroom positions to become LC teachers. This also worked well for some teachers who wished to move from full- to half-time positions. In some instances the LC teachers conduct LC sessions for a portion of their time and serve as bilingual or ESL teachers for the remainder. Other licensed teachers may be selected to work as LC teachers, but they would need intensive training in language acquisition/standards, effective instruction with language learners, and integration of language and content.

It is essential that LC teachers have very well-developed language and literacy skills in the language(s) of the LC sessions they are teaching and have a proven record of success with language learners. LC teachers teaching in the bilingual strands, for example, must have very well-developed oracy and literacy skills in both languages of instruction and should also be very familiar with the cultures represented in these strands. In the EAL strand, the LC teachers must have a very good understanding of how to work with students from several language backgrounds at one time and be able to capitalize on the linguistic and academic resources they bring to the LC sessions.

PD sessions for LC teachers begin with an overview of the philosophy, sociocultural foundations, goals, and design of the LC, as mentioned earlier. Demonstration lessons are provided on an ongoing basis or as needed to ensure that LC teachers are familiar with the session formats and understand how the LC sessions differ from traditional classroom instruction. As part of the PD sessions, they also design their first sets of lessons, prepare materials, and set up the learning environment(s) where they teach. LC teachers generally appreciate being mentored during their first several weeks and feedback sessions provide opportunities for them to make refinements.

Selecting Students to Participate in the Literacy Club

Selection of students to participate in the LC can occur in a variety of ways. Generally classroom teachers identify their students who are struggling the most in terms of oracy and literacy, and compile available data to document student performance. At the same time, the ESL/bilingual coordinator may review assessment data and determine which students seem to be in the greatest need of additional support. As mentioned earlier, implementation of effective Tier 1 measures in the classroom should also be enhanced to support linguistic and academic growth for all language learners. Before the student selection process begins, the school/district should decide whether students identified with learning needs are eligible for inclusion in the LC. Some schools have reviewed the number of services these students are receiving and the amount of time they are engaged with these services and opted to not include their special needs students in the LC. In other settings, they have been included.

Often a small committee of teachers and administrators with expertise in literacy and language learning makes recommendations for the students to be included in the LC. The number of students that can be selected depends, of course, on the number of available LC teachers. Schools/districts may consider launching the LC with a limited number of teachers/students and then increase the number as the data show positive results and/or resources are allocated for expansion. The ESL/bilingual coordinator generally establishes the schedule for the LC teachers at each grade level, with groups of four or fewer students.

Materials Criteria and Selection

Materials used in the LC should be thoughtfully selected to support student learning of content and language objectives. The types and genres of literacy materials that are used in the LC throughout the year need to be determined, especially if content areas and literacy are integrated. The identification of particular units, concepts, and strategies that are the focus of LC instruction necessitate selection of corresponding materials. The materials should be aligned to a developmental progression of both language and content standards across the academic year and reflect the students' culture and experiences wherever possible. The materials must also align with classroom objectives and be used to preteach, parallel teach, or review the concepts being developed in the classroom.

All of the EAL strand materials are in English, though the LC teacher may include home language supplementary materials where appropriate. The English–Spanish (languages other than Spanish may be incorporated, depending on the student population) bilingual strands need quality English and Spanish materials for beginning-of-week instruction and end-of-week bridging. Several texts written originally in Spanish should be used, as opposed to all texts that are translations of the original English, to ensure that students have adequate opportunities to engage with authentic Spanish language and cultural representations. Cultural relevance should be a major criterion in selecting all materials for use in the LC.

Generally, separate materials are set aside for use in the LC to make them readily accessible for LC sessions. Students are often significantly below grade-level expectations and the materials used in the classroom are often at the frustration level for these students. Therefore, LC teachers search for age-appropriate materials at the students' instructional level that still deal with grade-level concepts with sufficient depth—all of which highlights the complexity of this task.

Materials available to match the language and content standards should be organized for use with the various LC groups. If more than one teacher per grade level is using the LC materials, additional sets of materials need to be made available. The purchase of additional instructional materials is often necessary. Schools and districts without the funds to purchase all the materials needed may wish create a plan to make them available over time.

If a push-in plan is used, LC teachers need a dedicated space within each classroom to work with students and/or to store materials. LC teachers involved in a pull-out plan need a dedicated professional working space within the building that is conducive to small group literacy and language instruction.

Session Planning Framework

Creating a framework for lesson planning simplifies the process and helps ensure that oracy, literacy, and metacognition (strategy development and metalinguistic awareness) goals are reflected in all plans. Those involved in the administration and implementation of the LC might refine the kindergarten template in Table 7.3 or the grade 3 sample plan in Table 7.4 to meet the needs of their particular situation.

LITERACY CLUB WITH OLDER STUDENTS

Questions have been raised about the possibility of extending the LC to support language and literacy development with older students. While the answer to this question is beyond the scope of the LC as it is proposed here, there is little doubt that this format might be appealing for use with older students, especially those who have experienced interrupted schooling or are not progressing rapidly enough to ever approach grade-level expectations. It would be essential to begin by creating language and academic profiles that document how long students have been in the United States, their language environments, skills in each language, and successes and challenges in academic settings.

Many of the same considerations in terms of LC design—selection of students and teachers, focus on language and content standards, regular and ongoing assessment of progress—would seem to be applicable, especially in newcomer programs or sheltered classes. The grade 4–5 design in Chapter 6 might provide the best model as a starting point for designing LC sessions with older students. Organization of students into small groups of 3–4 at this level would also be essential to meet the wide range of academic and linguistic needs of each student.

Students might meet for one class period per day at the middle and high school levels, in lieu of an ESL or resource class period. A push-in or pull-out plan might be used, depending on the philosophy of the school/district. Collaboration between content and LC

TABLE 7.3 Literacy Club Planning Template for Kindergarten

LEVELS 1–3: ENGLISH LEARNER LITERACY CLUB LESSON PLANS

Elements	Monday	Tuesday	Wednesday	Thursday	Friday
Theme ■ Content standard ■ Content objective ■ Language objective ■ Strategy					
Focus book ■ Picture clues ■ Echo/choral reading ■ Left to right ■ Concepts of print: 1st letter ■ 1-1 matching/pointing					
Word work ■ Word rings ■ Letter work w/unknown letters ■ Build words ■ Dictation					
Rereads (Retell) ■ Partner ■ Independently					
Writing ■ Brainstorm ideas ■ Capital letters ■ Punctuation					
Assessment ■ Language ■ Content ■ Student self-assessment					

Student names _____

teachers would be critically important at this level, especially with classes where labs and demonstrations are regularly used.

Two important considerations would need to be made with older students. Because students are older and are likely to have wider gaps in their knowledge base for particular subjects, the LC teacher may need to do more preteaching to build prior knowledge, enhance study skills, and develop critical thinking skills. Selection of materials may also be more challenging at this level because grade-level texts are often challenging, even for students who meet grade-level expectations. Materials must be selected that represent grade-level standards, but are manageable in terms of reading/comprehension level and, wherever possible, reflect the students' culture and experiences. Age-appropriate content and format are crucial considerations to respect the age, interest level, and background of

TABLE 7.4 Weekly Plan Sample

Theme: Animals form groups to survive
Content objective: Students will be able to write an opinion essay
Language objective: Students will be able to organize their writing using a prewriting outline of opinion and supporting evidence
Strategy: Students will be able to make inferences

Focus book: *Gansos migratorios**

	Monday	Tuesday	Wednesday	Thursday	Friday
	Intro Inferencing Self-assess	Rereads Inferencing	Rereads Inferencing	Pairs/independent Inferencing	Read: Contrastive analysis Self-assess
Rereads	Pairs	Pairs	Independent	Independent	Spanish text + English translation
Word work	Word rings Weak/strong vowels	Word rings Weak/strong vowels	Word rings Weak/strong vowels	Word rings Cognates	Comparative analysis
Writing	Self-select	Self-select	Content topic	*Así se dice*	English writing "Opinion" Content topic

*Retrieved from www.readinga-z.com

the students. One initial solution might be to have students use their own edited writing entries on particular topics as reading material for the group, which would ensure that instructional texts were within the linguistic and academic background of the students. The LC may prove to be a very effective venue for supporting older emerging bilinguals in making greater progress toward grade-level expectations.

CONCLUSION

When implemented appropriately and thoroughly, the LC proves to be an effective model of intervention. A preliminary informal study of student progress has shown positive results (Hartl & Grogan, 2011). All of the grade 1–3 students in this study were at emergent and beginning English language levels, yet demonstrated progress in listening, speaking, reading, and writing after participating in the LC for one year. Accelerated progress was noted in the development of speaking ability at all levels and this was attributed to the emphasis on the development of oracy and metacognition in each of the LC sessions.

The various LC components provide language learners with the tools to accelerate development of oracy, literacy, and metacognition. Students have the opportunity to engage in activities related to all of the language domains in the LC as they strengthen both language and literacy skills. Well-developed sessions allow the LC teacher to structure authentic and meaningful content, language, and metacognitive learning experiences that positively affect student success in both the classroom and the LC.

QUESTIONS FOR REFLECTION AND ACTION

- Assemble a leadership team and agenda for the design of the LC in your school/district. How will you include EL teachers and the ESL/bilingual coordinator, as well as administrators and specialists who are involved with the education of ELs?
- Which language strands (advancing bilingual, emerging bilingual, EAL) would best match the needs and resources of your school/district?
- Who would be most qualified to teach in the LC? Do they have the literacy and language expertise to effectively support students in moving toward grade-level expectations?
- Outline a PD plan for LC teachers. What are the plan's short- and long-range goals?

Glossary

advancing bilingual strand: A recommended strand of the Literacy Club that is focused on students who have well-developed oral communication skills in Spanish but who struggle with literacy development.

Así se dice **(That's how you say it):** A learning activity designed by Literacy Squared where students work in pairs to translate and interpret short passages from one language to another. Students learn about complexities and subtleties across two languages.

Assessing Comprehension and Communication in English State-to-State (ACCESS) test: A large-scale language assessment designed by WIDA for use with K–12 English learners/emerging bilinguals.

baseline data: Initial collection of data regarding student academic and linguistic knowledge. Subsequent data collection measures student progress from this point.

bilingual learner(s) (BLs): BLs are students learning in two languages, though a broad range of language skills may be represented in each language.

bilingual program(s): Teaching academic content in two languages, generally in a native and secondary language (though some students may enter as bilinguals) with varying amounts of each language used in accordance with the program model.

> **one-way:** The majority of students speak a language other than English as they are learning English. Students receive instruction in both languages.

> **transitional:** Students receive instruction in their non-English language while they are learning English. English eventually replaces the students' first language.

> **two-way bilingual/dual language:** There is a mix of students who speak two languages. Students receive instruction in both languages.

comparative analysis: The systematic study of a language pair to identify its structural, syntactical, and semantic differences and similarities.

concepts of print: Emergent literacy skills for young children that reflect basic knowledge about how print functions in text.

continuous progress monitoring: A scientific process to assess students' academic performance, quantify rate of improvement or responsiveness to instruction, and evaluate the effectiveness of instruction.

critical thinking skills: The ability to make reasoned judgments that are logical and well thought out.

Developmental Reading Assessment 2+ (DRA2+) test: An individually administered measure of a student's reading level, accuracy, fluency, and comprehension.

***dictado*:** An approach designed by Literacy Squared that consists of weekly dictation and language analyses to strengthen spelling, grammar, syntax, and semantics in Spanish or English and foster cross-language connections.

differentiation: The process whereby a teacher changes the material that is being taught (content), the way the content is taught (delivery), and/or the means of assessing what has been learned (product) to better meet the students' needs.

dual language program(s): A program that teaches students literacy and content in two languages. One half of the students speak one language and one half of the students speak the second language; in this way the students learn from one another.

emerging bilingual strand: A recommended strand of the Literacy Club that is composed of students who struggle with literacy development and who lack well-developed oral communication skills in Spanish.

English as an additional language (EAL) strand: A recommended strand of the Literacy Club that is English-medium based. Students complete reading and writing assessments in English and teachers use student performance data in English to guide instruction and monitor progress.

English as a second language (ESL): Refers to a rigorous program for teaching emerging bilinguals to understand, speak, read, and write in English through links to content and language standards.

English learner(s) (ELs): ELs speak one or more languages and are in the process of learning English.

***Evaluación del desarrollo de la lectura 2* (EDL2) test:** A measure that assesses reading accuracy, fluency, and comprehension in Spanish.

focus book: The text selected each week to serve as the main focus for Literacy Club instruction.

formative assessment: Measures to monitor student progress and provide feedback to both teachers and students during a lesson or unit that enhance teaching and learning.

intervention(s): Learning scaffolds made available to students who need additional academic or linguistic support.

language development: The process by which language is learned.

language experience approach (LEA): Students and teachers participate in a shared writing activity based on a common experience of the participants. Listening, speaking, reading, and writing activities may be connected to the LEA to support the development of oracy and literacy.

language for academic purposes: The language needed by students to do school work. It is the language used in textbooks, in classrooms, and on tests; it includes specific structure and vocabulary that differs from that of everyday social interactions.

literacy: The ability to use reading and writing in a variety of contexts for a variety of purposes to interact with and understand the world.

Literacy Club (LC): A systematic response to instruction and intervention program that provides support for students in dual language/bilingual and ESL settings who are facing academic and linguistic challenges in achieving grade-level proficiency.

metacognition/metacognitive awareness/understanding: Consciousness of one's own thought processes.

metalanguage/metalinguistic awareness: Awareness and understanding of how one uses languages. For bi/multilinguals, it involves the relationships between and within languages.

oracy: The oral language skills and structures necessary for a child to become literate. Students have opportunities to learn, apply, and practice this language.

pull-out plan: This ESL program model removes students from the classroom for intensive instruction in English language and academic content.

push-in plan: In this program model, ESL teachers work with English learners/emerging bilinguals in the classroom in co-teaching or support roles

Response to Instruction and Intervention (RtI²): This is a Tier 2 targeted or supplemental intervention. It consists of small groups of students (usually 3–5) who do not respond sufficiently to the most effective Tier 1 instruction and criteria (Gottlieb, 2013).

Response to Intervention (RtI): This is a multi-tier approach for the early identification and support of students with learning and behavior needs. The RtI process begins with high-quality instruction and universal screening of all children in the general education classroom.

running records: Informal literacy assessments to measure fluency, accuracy, and use of strategies to support reading. Miscues (reading errors) provide insights into how children make meaning of text.

scaffolds/scaffolding: Supports (e.g., use of first language, total physical response, working with a partner or small group) that help move students to ever deeper levels of thinking and independence in learning and using language.

sequential bilingual: Someone who becomes bilingual by learning one language at birth and learning another at a later point in time, often at the beginning of formal education.

simultaneous bilingual: Someone who learns two or more languages at the same time.

strategy/strategy development: A learning process that supports understanding and critical thinking.

summative assessment: Measures to record student performance on standardized tests or at the conclusion of a unit of study. Results of these measures are often used in grading and/or program evaluations.

total physical response (TPR): A language teaching method developed by Asher (1969) that links language and conceptual development with physical movement to support learning.

translanguaging: The rule-governed integration of two languages to communicate thoughts, feelings, and ideas. Translanguaging also refers to the study of the similarities and differences between two languages through comparison and translation activities.

References

Allington, R., & Cunningham, P. (2006). *Schools that work: Where all children read and write* (3rd Ed.). Boston: Allyn & Bacon.

Angel, V. *Gansos migratorios/Migrating geese.* [Strong, S., Trans.] Retrieved from www.readinga-z .com

Asher, J. (1969). The total physical response approach to second language learning. *Modern Language Journal, 53*(1), 3–17.

August, D., & Shanahan, T. (Eds.). (2006). Executive summary: *Developing literacy in second-language learners: Report of the National Literacy Panel on language-minority children and youth.* Mahwah, NJ: Erlbaum.

Badía, A. (2011). *Los brazos son para abrazar.* Vero Beach, FL: Rourke Classroom.

Beeman, K., & Urow, C. (2013). *Teaching for biliteracy: Strengthening bridges between languages.* Philadelphia: Caslon.

Clay, M. M. (1985). *The early detection of reading difficulties.* Auckland, NZ: Heinemann.

Clay, M. M. (2000). *Running records for classroom teachers.* Portsmouth, NH: Heinemann.

Clay, M. M. (2005). *Literacy lessons designed for individuals. Part one: Why? When? and How?* Portsmouth, NH: Heinemann.

Clay, M. M. (2013). *Literacy lessons designed for individuals. Part two: Teaching procedures.* Portsmouth, NH: Heinemann.

Echevarria, J., Vogt, M., & Short, D. (2012). *Making content comprehensible for elementary learners: The SIOP model* (4th Ed.). Boston: Allyn & Bacon.

Escamilla, K., & Hopewell, S. (2010). Transitions to biliteracy: Creating positive academic trajectories for emerging bilinguals in the United States. In J. Petrovic (Ed.), *International perspectives on bilingual education: Policy, practice, and controversy.* Charlotte, NC: Information Age.

Escamilla, K., Hopewell, S., Butvilofsky, S., Sparrow, W., Soltero-González, L., Ruiz-Figueroa, O., & Escamilla, M. (2014). *Biliteracy from the start: Literacy Squared in Action.* Philadelphia: Caslon.

Feldman, J., & Karpetkova, H. (2010). *Arms are for hugging.* Vero Beach, FL: Rourke Classroom.

Fountas, I., & Pinnell, G. (2008). *When readers struggle: Teaching that works.* Portsmouth, NH: Heinemann.

Fountas, I., & Pinnell, G. (2010). *The continuum of literacy learning, Grades PreK–8* (2nd Ed.). Portsmouth, NH: Heinemann.

Freeman, Y., & Freeman, D. (2008). *Academic language for English language learners and struggling readers: How to help students succeed across content areas.* Portsmouth, NH: Heinemann.

Freeman, Y., & Freeman, D. (2011). *Between worlds: Access to 2nd language acquisition* (2nd Ed.). Portsmouth, NH: Heinemann.

García, O., Ibarra Johnson, S., & Seltzer, K. (2017). *The translanguaging classroom: Leveraging student bilingualism for learning.* Philadelphia: Caslon.

García, O., & Li Wei. (2014). *Translanguaging: Language, bilingualism and education.* New York: Palgrave Macmillan.

Gibbons, P. (2015). *Scaffolding language, scaffolding learning: Teaching second language learners in the mainstream classroom* (2nd Ed.). Portsmouth, NH: Heinemann.

Gottlieb, M. (2007). *Assessing ELLs, bridges from language proficiency to academic achievement.* Thousand Oaks, CA: Corwin.

Gottlieb, M. (2013). *RtI²: Developing a culturally and linguistically responsive approach to response to instruction and intervention (RtI²) for English language learners: Connecting to WIDA standards, assessments, and other resources.* Madison, WI: Board of Regents of the University of Wisconsin System, on behalf of the WIDA Consortium.

Gottlieb, M., & Nguyen, D. (2007). *Assessment & accountability in language education programs: A guide for teachers and administrators.* Philadelphia: Caslon.

Harste, J. (2003). What do we mean by literacy now? *Voices from the Middle, 10*(3), 8–12.

Hartl, J., & Grogran, G. (2011, April). Presentation of findings. Pat Bricker Memorial Award Research Grant. *Wisconsin State Reading Association.*

Henn-Reinke, K. (2004). *The reading club: A guide to a literacy intervention program for reluctant readers in Spanish and English.* Lanham, MD: Scarecrow Education.

Himmele, P., & Himmele, W. (2009). *The language-rich classroom: A research-based framework for teaching English language learners.* Alexandria, VA: ASCD.

Honigsfeld, A., & Dove, M. (2010). *Collaboration and co-teaching: Strategies for English learners.* Thousand Oaks, CA: Corwin.

Krashen, S. (2004). *The power of reading: Insights from the Research* (2nd Ed.). Cambridge, MA: Cambridge University Press.

Meissner, D. (n.d.). *Los pueblos del desierto/Desert people.* [DiBello, L., Trans.] Retrieved from www.readinga-z.com

Moses, L. (2015). *Supporting English learners in the reading workshop.* Portsmouth, NH: Heinemann.

Pile, M. (2005a). *Chinese immigration: Immigration to the United States.* Margate, FL: National Geographic School.

Pile, M. (2005b). *Mexican immigration: Immigration to the United States.* Margate, FL: National Geographic School.

Pinnell, G. S., & Fountas, I. C. (2010). *The continuum of literacy learning, grades K–2: A guide to teaching.* Portsmouth, NH: Heinemann.

Response to Intervention Action Network. Retrieved from http://www.rtinetwork.org/

Riddle Buly, M. (2011). English language learners in literacy workshops. Urbana, IL: National Council of Teachers of English.

Rigby. (2001). *Baby owl goes away.* Boston: Houghton, Mifflin, Harcourt.

Risk, M. (1996). *I want my banana! ¡Quiero mi plátano!* [de Wolf, A., Illus.] [Martin, R., Trans.] Hong Kong: Barron's Educational Series.

Routman, R. (2012). Mapping a pathway to schoolwide highly effective teaching. *Phi Delta Kappan, 93*(5), 56–61.

Scraper, K. *El agua de la tierra/Earth's water.* [DiBello, L., Trans.] Retrieved from www.readinga-z.com

Shagoury Hubbard, R., & Shorey, V. (2003). Worlds beneath the words: Writing workshop with second language learners, *Language Arts, 81*(1), 52–61.

Thomas, W., & Collier, V. (2009). *A national study of school effectiveness for language minority students' long term academic achievement.* Honolulu: University of Hawaii at Manoa, Center for Research on Education, Diversity, and Excellence.

Thomas, W., & Collier, V. (2012). *Dual language education for a transformed world.* Albuquerque, NM: Dual Language Education of New Mexico–Fuente Press.

Vygotsky, L. S. (1987). Thinking and speech. In R. W. Rieber & A. S. Carton (Eds.), *The collected works of L. S. Vygotsky: Problems of general psychology* (Vol. 1, pp. 39–285). New York: Plenum.

Vygotsky, L. S. (1962/2012). *Thought and language.* Cambridge, MA: MIT Press.

Index

Note: Page numbers followed by b, f, or t refer to boxes, figures, or tables, respectively.